Thomas Aquinas on God and Evil

Thomas Aquinas on God and Evil

BRIAN DAVIES

OXFORD
UNIVERSITY PRESS

OXFORD
UNIVERSITY PRESS

Oxford University Press, Inc., publishes works that further
Oxford University's objective of excellence
in research, scholarship, and education.

Oxford   New York
Auckland   Cape Town   Dar es Salaam   Hong Kong   Karachi
Kuala Lumpur   Madrid   Melbourne   Mexico City   Nairobi
New Delhi   Shanghai   Taipei   Toronto

With offices in
Argentina   Austria   Brazil   Chile   Czech Republic   France   Greece
Guatemala   Hungary   Italy   Japan   Poland   Portugal   Singapore
South Korea   Switzerland   Thailand   Turkey   Ukraine   Vietnam

Published by Oxford University Press, Inc.
198 Madison Avenue, New York, New York 10016

www.oup.com

Oxford is a registered trademark of Oxford University Press

Library of Congress Cataloging-in-Publication Data
Davies, Brian, 1951—
Thomas Aquinas on God and evil / Brian Davies.
p.   cm.
Includes bibliographical references and index.
ISBN 978-0-19-979089-0; 978-0-19-979090-6 (pbk.); 978-0-19-979098-2 (ebook)
1. Thomas, Aquinas, Saint, 1225?–1274.   2. God (Christianity)   3. Good and evil–Religious
aspects–Christianity.   I. Title.
B765.T54D349 2011
231'.8092—dc22   2010032479

Printed in the United States of America
on acid-free paper

For Sara and Robert Pennella with thanks, and for Tommy Tong, also with thanks

Contents

Preface, ix
Abbreviations, xiii

1. The Problem of Evil, 1
2. Aquinas, Philosophy, and Theology, 9
3. What There Is, 19
4. Goodness and Badness, 29
5. God the Creator, 39
6. God's Perfection and Goodness, 51
7. The Creator and Evil, 65
8. Providence and Grace, 79
9. The Trinity and Christ, 97
10. Aquinas, God, and Evil, 113

Notes, 133
Bibliography, 159
Index, 165

Preface

Thomas Aquinas (c. 1224–74) is one of the most historically important of Christian philosophers and theologians. Canonized in 1323, his writings have been extremely influential over many centuries. Scholars today, whether they agree with him or not, would generally regard him both as a giant among medieval thinkers and as a touchstone of Christian orthodoxy. Recommended to Roman Catholics by popes such as Leo XIII, whose encyclical *Aeterni Patris* (1879) led to a renaissance of Thomistic studies in twentieth-century ecclesiastical contexts, Aquinas is also now much studied in secular ones. In recent years numerous essays and books on his philosophy have appeared, written by people of various religious persuasions or none. In short, Aquinas is a figure with whom to reckon if one has any interest at all in philosophy or theology.

In this book I offer an account of Aquinas's teachings on the topic of God and evil while trying to place him in the context of contemporary discussions. What follows is not a philosophical or theological evaluation of Aquinas on this topic. Rather, it is an attempt to explain what his thinking on God and evil amounts to when taken as a whole, while sometimes noting how it compares and contrasts with what others have said. Philosophical and theological discussions of God and evil often refer to Aquinas but hardly ever try to present an overview of what he has to say on the topic, one that requires reference to things that Aquinas observes when not explicitly talking of God and evil. In this volume my aim is to present such an overview.

I aim to do so because I am not aware of a book-length treatment of Aquinas on God and evil that provides such a thing, and also because Aquinas, when read as a whole and not just in snippets, offers what I regard as a challenging alternative (or at least an alternative) to many contemporary discussions of God and evil.[1] Philosophers and theologians often refer to "the problem of evil," and they spend much effort and time trying to comment on it. Some argue that the problem shows belief in God to be unreasonable. Others hold that it can be dealt with so as to leave belief in God intact. An interesting aspect of Aquinas's thinking is that he takes the problem of evil as commonly construed to be no problem at all. His approach to God, goodness, and evil makes virtually no mention of it. Yet he has a lot to say about God, goodness, and evil. What follows is intended to explain what this amounts to.

As I have said, this book is not an evaluation of Aquinas on God and evil. A critical discussion of all that I am about to report Aquinas as saying would make for a book in itself (or, perhaps, several books). When expounding Aquinas, however, I try to do so sympathetically so that readers might be able to hear him speaking for himself. And I venture some aids to reflection in my final chapter, ones clearly intended as favorable to Aquinas, and ones that I hope to be able to develop in a later work. For the most part, though, my primary concern is to help readers to get a sense of what Aquinas has to say on God and evil in the light of many things that he writes while speaking as both a philosopher and a theologian. That goal, perhaps, is enough for one volume. I should add that the present one is aimed at students of philosophy and theology as well as general readers interested in Aquinas or the notion of God and evil. I hope that teachers of philosophy and theology, and people professionally concerned with Aquinas's thinking, shall find something of interest in what I write. But they are not my target audience. Hence, what follows presumes no previous knowledge of philosophy, theology, or Aquinas on the part of the reader.

When quoting from Aquinas I have tried to cite available English translations, though I have sometimes modified them (while noting when I have done so). Unless otherwise stated, quotations from the Bible come from the New Revised Standard Version. Notes to my chapters sometimes elaborate on points I make in my main text and appear in note form only to prevent this text from seeming cluttered. I would, however, suggest that readers pay attention to the notes so as to appreciate what I am saying in the main text and so as to appreciate how I think that this might sometimes be qualified or supplemented. I should add that in composing my bibliography I have not slavishly tried to include every text mentioned in my notes, and that I include some texts not mentioned in my notes since I think that they might help readers to think more about what this book is about.

For advice and help on earlier versions of the present text I am much indebted to Christopher Arroyo, Victor Austin, James Claffey, Peter Groves, Jon McGinnis, Turner Nevitt, and Christopher Upham.

Abbreviations

CT   Compendium Theologiae (Compendium of Theology)
QDM Quaestiones Disputatae de Malo (Disputed Questions on Evil)
SCG Summa Contra Gentiles
ST   Summa Theologiae

Thomas Aquinas on
God and Evil

I

The Problem of Evil

Psalm 19 declares that the heavens proclaim the glory of God. And millions of people believe in God and worship him daily. Yet, when it comes to God's existence, many other people would call themselves atheists or agnostics. Why so? Those who identify themselves as atheists or agnostics have usually given some serious thought to the question of God's existence. They have, on *reflection*, arrived at a *conclusion*. And, for some of them, the conclusion is that there are no good reasons to believe in God (or that those that have been offered are all bad ones). Yet, so I suspect, most atheists or agnostics are what they are not because of their views on purported reasons for believing in God but because of what is commonly referred to as "the problem of evil." They just cannot see how belief in God can be reconciled with the evil to be found in the world. For them, the psalmist's "glory of God" lies behind an impenetrable cloud of pain, suffering, disease, poverty, destitution, horrors, and human wrongdoing, a cloud that leaves them quite unable to endorse belief in God given that God is traditionally supposed to be all powerful, all knowing, and good.[1]

God and Evil: Detractors of Theism

A classical example of someone for whom this is the case is David Hume (1711–76). In his famous *Dialogues concerning Natural Religion,* he writes: "Epicurus's old questions are yet unanswered. Is he [God] willing to prevent evil, but not able? Then is he impotent. Is he able, but not willing? Then is he malevolent. Is he both able and willing? Whence then is evil?"[2] Hume clearly thought these questions to be ones that, when properly reflected on, ought to lead us to doubt God's existence. Many others have as well.

Hume does not say that evil positively shows that God does not exist. But some philosophers have done so, one of the most lucid and sophisticated being J. L. Mackie (1917–81). In a highly influential essay ("Evil and Omnipotence") he concludes: "In its simplest form the problem is this: God is omnipotent; God is wholly good; and yet evil exists. There seems to be some contradiction between these three propositions, so that if any two of them were true the third would be false. But at the same time all three are essential parts of most theological positions: the theologian, it seems, at once must adhere and cannot consistently to all three."[3] Mackie (though he later came to modify his position somewhat) is here offering a *disproof* of God's existence based on evil.[4] The argument just quoted is saying that those who believe in God and the reality of evil are contradicting themselves. In "Evil and Omnipotence" Mackie notes ways in which such people can escape the charge of self-contradiction by abandoning some of their essential beliefs about God (e.g., that God is omnipotent). Assuming that they might not wish to do this, however, Mackie claims that evil *proves* the nonexistence of God.[5]

That is a pretty strong position to take. With an eye on the evil in the world, however, some have preferred a weaker one—something now commonly referred to as the "evidentialist argument" against God's existence.[6] The best known defender of this is, perhaps, William Rowe, who suggests that evil is good evidence for not believing in God even if it does not *prove* that there is no God. I might, in fact, be a saint, but things that I do might be taken as evidence to the effect that I am no such thing. Rowe argues in a similar way when it comes to God. Maybe God exists, says Rowe. But the evidence suggests otherwise—the evidence in question being examples of evil. Here is the core of Rowe's approach to the topic of God and evil:

1. There exist instances of intense suffering that an omnipotent being could have prevented without thereby losing some greater good or permitting some evil equally bad or worse.
2. An omniscient, wholly good being would prevent the occurrence of any intense suffering it could, unless it could not do so without thereby losing some greater good or permitting some evil equally bad or worse.

3. [Therefore] there does not exist an omnipotent, omniscient, wholly good being.[7]

So, we can say, critics of theism have claimed that evil proves God's nonexistence or renders God's existence unlikely.[8]

God and Evil: Defenders of Theism

God, however, has not lacked defenders in discussions of evil and his existence. Some notable contemporary ones (all in many ways drawing on people writing in previous centuries) include Alvin Plantinga, Richard Swinburne, and John Hick. At this point, therefore, let me briefly try to give you a sense of ways in which they have argued.[9]

Plantinga distinguishes between what he calls a "theodicy" and a "defense."[10] A theodicy is an attempt to *explain* the place of evil in a world made by God. It typically seeks to give reasons for evil in the light of belief in God so as, in the words of Milton's *Paradise Lost* (1667), "to justify the ways of God to men." With an eye on authors like Mackie, however, Plantinga offers something more modest: arguments to show (and this is what he means by the word "defense") that evil does not *disprove* God's existence, even if such arguments do *nothing* to *explain* how evil and God fit together, so to speak. Plantinga's main question is: "Can it be *proved* that the existence of God is *logically impossible* given the reality of evil?" His answer is "no." His main reasons for this answer take the form of a series of (quite complicated) arguments intended to show that we cannot demonstrate that God could have made a world that does not contain evil. One of them goes like this:

1. God knows all possible worlds.
2. People in possible worlds may have the property of "transworld depravity."
3. A person in a possible world suffering from transworld depravity is someone who would freely do something wrong in the actual world.
4. So perhaps God could not create an actual world in which people do no wrong.
5. So perhaps there is no way of proving that the actual occurrence of evil disproves God's existence.[11]

Unlike Plantinga, Swinburne and Hick engage in theodicy.[12] They seek to explain why God allows evil. More specifically, they engage in a moral defense of God given the reality of evil. For them (as, indeed, for Plantinga), "God is good" means "God is morally good," and their basic line is that God has good moral grounds (or morally sufficient reasons) for permitting the occurrence of evil. Hence, for example, Swinburne argues that great naturally occurring evil (evil that occurs regardless of what we choose to do) is necessary if we are to have the chance to do great good or harm.[13] The idea here is (a) that it is good that we should be able to do great good; (b) our ability to do great good is bound up with our ability to do great harm; (c) we can know the range of our options regarding good and harm only because evil occurs naturally (we can, for example, strive to cure people of cancer only because they have been struck down by it in the first place). In his own way Hick takes a similar line, one that he ascribes to Irenaeus of Lyon (c. 130–200).[14] He suggests that the world is what he calls "a vale of soul making" in which naturally occurring evils provide us with the opportunity to become better people. According to Hick, if we were created in God's immediate presence, we would have no creaturely independence in relation to him. We would be cowed into worship. Not so as things are, however. In the world that God has made, Hick stresses, God is not overwhelmingly evident to us. Furthermore, he provides us with problems, difficulties, perils, and so on, in order that we might grow spiritually. Hick thinks that this provides God with some considerable moral exoneration when it comes to evil. Like Swinburne (and many others both past and present), Hick is suggesting that there are certain *means* by which God is *constrained* while aiming to do what is morally good.

But should we think of God as constrained in any way? Should we think of him as morally good? And should we approach the topic of God and evil on the assumption that constrained and morally good is what God is if he exists at all? As we shall see, Aquinas does not talk about God and evil by trying to defend God morally. For now, though, I should simply like to stress that discussions of God and evil frequently (and these days almost always) concern themselves with God's moral goodness or lack of it. Simply put, advocates of belief in God have commonly argued, for one reason or another, that God is well behaved (or cannot be proved to be badly behaved) while those critical of belief in God have commonly taken the opposite position and have, therefore, concluded that there definitely is no God or that there probably is no God.

Something else worth noting about approaches to God and evil that seek to defend God is their having frequently tended seriously to entertain the idea that something that happens might not be caused to happen by God. This idea is particularly evident in a move known as the free-will defense, which typically goes as follows.

1. It is good that people should have freedom to choose what to do.
2. To be able to choose freely is to be able to act in various ways and not to be forced into acting in one particular way. To be able to choose freely is to be able to act thus-and-so while also being able to refrain from acting thus-and-so.
3. Being good, God wants a world in which people have freedom.
4. But if people have freedom, then they are free to do what is bad as well as what is good.
5. Therefore, in making a world that contains free people God runs the risk of some people acting badly. He could avoid this risk by removing their freedom and causing them to act just as he wishes. But that would be a morally bad thing for him to do since human freedom is good and something to be protected.
6. Much evil or badness in the world consists in, or is the result of, people freely choosing badly. But God is not to blame for this. It is the freely acting people who are to blame.
7. When people freely act badly, that is because God stands back and allows them to act of their own accord. So our bad actions freely committed actually count as signs of God's goodness. They do so because they are instances of God permitting a great good: the good of human freedom.

Plantinga expresses this line of thinking by saying: "Of course, it is up to God whether to create free creatures at all; but if he aims to produce moral good, then he must create significantly free creatures upon whose cooperation he must depend. Thus is the power of an omnipotent God limited by the freedom he confers on creatures."[15]

Here is the same idea in Swinburne's words: "It is a great good that humans have a certain sort of free will which I shall call free and responsible choice, but…if they do, then necessarily there will be the natural possibility of moral evil.… A God who gives humans such free will necessarily brings about the possibility, and puts outside his own control whether or not it [moral evil] occurs."[16]

Quotations such as these are clearly saying that there are times when people act in causal independence of God. And this idea is to be found in many discussions of God and evil. We shall later see that Aquinas rejects it. For now, though, I content myself with simply drawing attention to it.[17]

Aquinas, Evil, and God

At one point in his *Summa Theologiae* (perhaps his greatest work, and one to which I shall often refer in what follows) Aquinas presents an argument for

God's nonexistence that reads remarkably like Mackie's case for this in "Evil and Omnipotence." Aquinas writes: "It seems that there is no God. For if one of two contraries were infinite, the other would be completely destroyed. But by the word 'God' we understand a certain infinite good. So, if God existed, nobody would ever encounter evil. But we do encounter evil in the world. So, God does not exist" (ST 1a.2.3 [Davies and Leftow 2006: 24]). This argument, which purports to disprove God's existence, is one with which Aquinas disagrees. However, his referring to it shows him to be perfectly aware of the possibility of atheism based on the fact of evil.[18] So Aquinas can be viewed as a participant in discussions of God and evil such as those offered by the authors cited above. Yet his approach to the topic of God and evil is also vastly different from what can be found in them.

His reply to the *Summa Theologiae* argument just quoted is very brief and, you might well think, not very helpful. It goes thus: "As Augustine says, 'Since God is supremely good, he would not permit any evil at all in his works, unless he were sufficiently powerful and good to bring good even from evil.' So it belongs to the limitless goodness of God that he permits evils to exist and draws good from them" (ST 1a.2.3 ad 1 [Davies and Leftow 2006: 26]). This, you might think, is hardly an adequate solution to what is now commonly called "the problem of evil."[19] In a serious sense, however, Aquinas has *nothing* to say on this topic. I mean that he never offers a stand-alone discussion of what contemporary philosophers have come to call the problem of evil. He has no book or essay on it. He offers no full-length treatment starting along the lines "God is X, Y, Z, etc.; yet evil exists; so how can we reconcile evil with God's existence?" In this sense, what now passes as the problem of evil goes unmentioned in Aquinas's writings.[20] These engage in no sustained theodicy or defense of belief in God written with an eye on evil. Compilers of anthologies on the problem of evil will never be able to include in them anything from Aquinas comparable, for example, to the essays by Mackie and Rowe quoted above.[21]

On the other hand, however, Aquinas has a lot to offer with a bearing on what authors such as these are concerned with as they, and others, write about God and evil. The trouble is that what he has to say comes scattered throughout almost the entire corpus of his writings and needs to be brought together if one is to understand his take on the problem of evil. My aim in what follows is to engage in such bringing together so that you can see what Aquinas actually does think with respect to the topic of God and evil. Does he think that evil disproves God's existence? Of course, he does not. And we shall see why he does not. Along the way we shall also see what he takes the world to be, what he takes God to be, how he thinks of God's relation to the world, how he approaches the notion of divine providence, and how he thinks of God's goodness (both in itself and in relation to us). Effectively, therefore, we shall be following the central aspects of Aquinas's teachings about God in general. Such a procedure is needed if we are to understand Aquinas on God and evil since, as I have said, his thoughts on this topic need to be pieced together from what he has to say about God in general and from a number of other questions he discusses (such as "What is a being?" "What is a cause?" "What kinds of beings are there?" and "What kinds of causes are there?")

I should add, however, that this piecing together needs also, and crucially, to take account of things that Aquinas writes with an eye on what he takes to be Christian revelation. Authors concerned with God and evil have often dealt with the topic while ignoring much that Christians have written or taught when it comes to specifically Christian teachings. They have, as we might put it, turned to the topic of God and evil by concentrating on monotheism rather than monotheism in its Christian form. Aquinas did not do so, though he has sometimes been attacked for doing just this. His approach to God and evil, insofar as we can piece it together from his many writings, involves him in talking about this matter in the light of what he took to be some fundamental Christian truths—not just truths arrived at by philosophical inquiry.[22] We will not understand what Aquinas thinks about God and evil if we do not pay attention to what he has to say about Christian theism, which includes belief in the doctrines of the Trinity and the incarnation.

Great thinkers generally turn to difficult topics by exploring them from various angles and bringing many different points into their discussions. This is how it is with Aquinas on God and evil (and goodness). His approach to the topic will not be understood by someone unwilling to follow his thinking on a whole range of issues, some of which might not immediately seem relevant to it. I shall turn to these issues in chapters 2–4. My hope is that, having finished reading this book, you will end up with an overall sense of Aquinas's thinking on God and evil, one that pays attention to both his philosophical and theological views (though these in fact are almost inextricably entangled with each other). I also hope that you will be able to see how some of it compares and contrasts with the writings of authors other than Aquinas. I should stress that I am not here offering an exhaustive account of all that Aquinas says with respect to God and evil. And, with the exception of what I offer in chapter 10, which is a philosophical and theological reflection on the previous nine chapters, I do not intend to defend or attack anything that Aquinas has to say on the topics on which I report him as teaching. To do so, as I said in the preface, would take a volume very much longer than the present one. My aim is simply to give you a general or introductory account of Aquinas's take on God and evil. Many people seem to have lost sight of what this take amounts to, or to be unaware of it, or misinformed about it. And some things, of course, are best forgotten. Yet Aquinas's views on God and evil are, arguably, not things to be forgotten. Aquinas was a remarkable Christian thinker, and since his views on God and evil differ so radically from much that we find in the writings of many others, this book will, I hope, prove to be of some interest to anyone with a taste for philosophy of religion, a concern with the topic of God and evil, an interest in Christian theology, or a desire to understand the mind of Aquinas.

2

Aquinas, Philosophy, and Theology

Authors writing on God and evil today are mostly philosophers, and their tendency is to ask whether evil proves God's nonexistence or is evidence for it. Professional theologians rarely turn to the topic of God and evil in the way that philosophers have done, which is, perhaps, hardly surprising since they are, presumably, committed to belief in God to start with. When theologians write about God and evil they typically assume that God exists.[1] So, rather than worrying about evil and the existence of God, they are much more likely to ask questions like "What is sin?" "How does evil fit into God's plan?" "What are our reasons for extolling God's goodness?" or "In what ways does God show his love for us?" To understand Aquinas on God and evil, however, it helps to recognize at the outset that his treatment of the matter includes both strictly philosophical elements as well as purely theological ones. People have often asked whether Aquinas was a philosopher or a theologian. So I would briefly like to say something about this question immediately. My motive, of course, is to help you to see how Aquinas is to be thought of as approaching the topic of God and evil—to place what he says in a genre, so to speak. As we shall see, Aquinas is not easy to place, which perhaps accounts for his having been characterized as a thinker in some very different ways.

Aquinas as a Thinker

Some commentators on Aquinas have maintained (often quite vehemently) that he should be thought of as nothing but a theologian. Roughly speaking, they have argued along these lines:

1. Unlike pure philosophers (as traditionally understood), Aquinas never wrote anything without presupposing the truth of what he took to be Christian revelation.
2. Aquinas never had a purely philosophical audience in mind when producing any of his writings. He was always talking to Christian believers.
3. In his professional teaching role Aquinas worked as a theologian, not as a philosopher, and this fact is reflected in all of his writings.

These observations are perhaps most famously brought together in some often quoted remarks of Bertrand Russell (1872–1970). According to him, "There is little of the true philosophical spirit in Aquinas. He does not, like the Platonic Socrates, set out to follow wherever the argument may lead.... Before he begins to philosophize, he already knows the truth; it is declared in the Catholic faith.... The finding of arguments for a conclusion given in advance is not philosophy, but special pleading."[2]

Other people, however, have spoken of Aquinas as though he should be taken as compulsory reading for philosophy students today and as very much a philosopher. Histories of philosophy written during the last sixty years or so almost always include a chapter on Aquinas that treats him on a level with such famous philosophical figures as Plato (c. 428–347 B.C.), Aristotle (384–322 B.C.), Descartes (1596–1650), or Wittgenstein (1889–1951). And collections of essays on Aquinas frequently focus on him in philosophical terms.[3] Speaking in a way completely different from that of Russell, Anthony Kenny (one of the most distinguished of contemporary analytical philosophers) writes: "Aquinas is...one of the dozen greatest philosophers of the western world.... His metaphysics, his philosophical theology, his philosophy of mind, and his moral philosophy entitle him to rank with Plato and Aristotle, with Descartes and Leibniz, with Locke and Hume and Kant."[4]

In my view, neither of the positions I have just summarized captures Aquinas with complete accuracy, though each of them can be defended on various counts. Let me try to explain why I think this, starting with the emphasis on Aquinas being a theologian as opposed to a philosopher.

Aquinas, Philosophy, and Theology

Aquinas the Theologian

All of the points I noted above coming from those who want to view Aquinas as a theologian are entirely right. There are many journals filled with articles with titles like "What Is Theology?" and "What Is Philosophy?" On a fairly simple understanding of the word "theology," however, Aquinas was most definitely first and foremost a theologian. Abstracting from what theology might be taken to mean in non-Christian contexts, I (uncontroversially, I hope) take it to mean "what Christians write or say while seeking to expound and comment on what they take to be Christianity as those who believe in it." On this definition, paradigm examples of theologians would be St. Augustine of Hippo (354–430), Martin Luther (1483–1546), John Calvin (1509–64), or Karl Barth (1886–1968). And Aquinas can be grouped with such figures for various reasons (even though he does not agree with everything that they say; indeed, he disagrees with all of them in various ways).

To begin with, as item 3 in the list above notes, Aquinas formally worked as a theologian, and one should, of course, remember that he was a Dominican friar, a member of the Order of Preachers founded by St. Dominic Guzmán (c. 1174–1221), an order specifically founded to promote the teachings of the Christian church by educational and pastoral activities.[5] Aquinas taught at the University of Paris from 1252 to 1259 and from 1268 to 1272. The University of Paris at this time had a Faculty of Arts in which what we might nowadays call "philosophy" was taught. But Aquinas ended up holding a chair of theology and never delivered what would today be thought of as philosophy lectures. For some of his time in Paris he taught (or, rather, commented on) a text by Peter Lombard (c. 1100–1160) known as the *Sentences*, a work largely dealing with explicitly Christian issues. Otherwise he lectured on the Bible, on which he wrote a number of commentaries.[6] When he was not teaching in Paris, Aquinas was providing theological training to Dominican friars in Dominican priories and, again, concentrating on Scripture or on matters to do with explicitly Christian doctrines. As Mark D. Jordan rightly observes, "Aquinas was by vocation, training, and self-understanding an ordained teacher of an inherited theology."[7] For most of his teaching life, and abstracting from his time as a professor in Paris, Aquinas functioned in what Leonard E. Boyle calls "the normal stream of the Dominican educational system in the order's Roman Province." Boyle goes on convincingly to argue that Aquinas's most famous work, the *Summa Theologiae*, was most likely written, not to provide a philosophical text book (as some seem to suppose), but in order to provide working Dominicans with a better alternative to certain theological manuals currently available to them as they prepared themselves for preaching and pastoral care, especially the hearing of confessions.[8]

Then again, what would Aquinas have made of the word "philosophy"? Not what your average current philosopher would make of it. Such a person would take philosophy to be a good thing, something to promote in universities, something to think of as a vocation to which to devote one's life. Aquinas, however, does not think in these terms. In his day, and in the context in which he worked, "philosophy" and "philosopher" were not terms to be noted with particular respect. If anything, they had a pejorative sense. For Aquinas and his contemporaries, a philosopher was basically a pagan—someone who did not accept Christian revelation.[9] Aquinas never uses the term "philosopher" (*philosophus*) when speaking of a Christian author. He often quotes and draws from Aristotle and Plato (and from non-Christian thinkers influenced by them), but it would be quite wrong to describe him as an Aristotelian or a Platonist. Why? Because he took Aristotle and Plato (and other ancient authors) to lack what he thought most important: belief in Christianity. Given his writings, and bearing in mind what is said of him in the biographical texts about him coming from our earliest sources for his life and work, Aquinas was quite definitely a Christian theologian.[10]

Finally, it is not philosophy with which Aquinas is most concerned in most of his many writings. Rather, it is what he refers to as *sacra doctrina*, which, for him, is basically equivalent to the central teachings of the Bible.[11] These, he thinks, come to us by divine revelation, not rational inquiry. For Aquinas these central teachings comprise what he calls the "articles of faith," none of which he takes to be philosophically demonstrable. You can find this line of thinking surfacing very clearly in the very first question of the *Summa Theologiae*:

> It was necessary for human salvation that there should be instruction
> by divine revelation in addition to the philosophical sciences pursued
> by human reasoning—chiefly because we are ordered to God as an
> end beyond the grasp of reason.... In order that our salvation might
> be effected more suitably and surely, we need to be instructed by
> divine revelation concerning God.... Sacred doctrine... proceeds
> from principles made known by a higher science—that of God and
> the blessed.... Sacred doctrine is nobler than all other sciences.
> (ST 1a.1.1,2, 5 [Davies and Leftow 2006: 4, 6, 9])

And it is sacred doctrine with which Aquinas is concerned from beginning to end in the *Summa Theologiae*.[12] He discusses it with considerable philosophical expertise and even with an eye to what we might call its philosophical grounding, offering an account of why it can be truly believed that God exists and is what Christians take him to be essentially (an account of which can be found in an even more austerely philosophical form in SCG 1). But *sacra doctrina* is the topic of the *Summa Theologiae*, in which Aquinas describes himself as *doctor catholicae veritatis* (a teacher of Catholic truth).[13] The *Summa Theologiae* is a work that, starting with an account of God's existence and nature, moves on to deal with notions such as the nature of people as creatures of God, their final end, the teaching that God is three in one (the doctrine of the Trinity), and the teaching that God became human so as to draw people to himself (the doctrine of the incarnation). And, one might add, this structure of the *Summa Theologiae* is also present in one of Aquinas's last works, the "Compendium of Theology" (*Compendium Theologiae*). In this volume, which is an excellent introduction to Aquinas's mature thinking, Aquinas begins by saying:

> The eternal Father's Word, comprehending all things in his immensity, in order to recall human beings weakened by sin to the height of divine glory, willed to become small by taking on our smallness, not by laying aside his majesty. He compressed the teaching on human salvation in a brief summary for those who are busy. He did this in order that no one would be excused from grasping the teaching of the heavenly word, something that he had extensively and lucidly transmitted in the various books of sacred Scripture. (CT 1)[14]

Aquinas goes on to say that his *Compendium* is, as it were, a summary of a summary: "A summary instruction on the Christian religion." And here, without question, Aquinas is writing as a theologian (in my sense noted above). He writes in the same vein in the inaugural lecture he delivered as a new professor in Paris in 1256. The lecture is about teaching *sacra doctrina* and speaks of the teacher of *sacra doctrina* as "watered by the things that are above in the wisdom of God." Aquinas makes it clear that he takes such watering to derive from divine revelation and as being "exalted" and above human reason.[15]

Aquinas the Philosopher

With all of that said, however, Aquinas had a considerable respect for philosophy and engaged in it at some length.[16] At this stage I take philosophy to be what it is for people working in university philosophy departments today; so I take philosophers to be people trying to think about certain topics (such as human nature, knowledge, God, or ethics) without invoking any theological authority (as determining the right answer to a philosophical question) and while arguing with respect to what can be defended on the basis of reason alone.[17] On this understanding of philosophy, paradigm examples of philosophers would be Aristotle, Plato, Descartes, Hume, and Wittgenstein.[18] And, in spite of what I have said above, Aquinas can also be counted among them. Mark Jordan says that "Aquinas chose not to write philosophy."[19] But this comment is misleading, or at least amounts to an overstatement (though it is defended by Jordan with some pertinent observations), for Aquinas in an obvious sense *did* write philosophy.

For one thing, he wrote several texts that do not focus on Christian doctrines but can be read as philosophical essays in the modern sense. Obvious examples are his *De Principiis Naturae* (On the Principles of Nature) and his *De Ente et Essentia* (On Being and Essence). The first of these works is, with a lot of debt to Aristotle and Avicenna, chiefly concerned with what is going on when causation happens.[20] It deals with questions such as "What is change?" "What is involved in something existing?" and "What is going on when something acts?" The second of these works, which admittedly refers to theological issues (chiefly, the existence of angels), is mostly concerned with what, and without believing in God, we might mean by words such as "essence" and "existence." And, of course, we need to remember that Aquinas wrote commentaries on the works of Aristotle. A contemporary of Aquinas, Tolomeo of Lucca, tells us that Aquinas "expounded almost all of the philosophical works of Aristotle, whether natural or moral, while in charge of the *studium* at Rome, and wrote his lectures up in the form of a *scriptum* or commentary on each work, particularly on the *Ethics* and the *Metaphysics*."[21] Aquinas was never formally required to lecture on Aristotle when holding his chairs of theology in Paris, and, in spite of what Tolomeo of Lucca says, we have no definite reason to think that he systematically lectured on Aristotle while in Rome (though he did at that time work on his Commentary on Aristotle's *De Anima*).[22] Be that as it may, though, Aquinas has left us some pretty hefty commentaries on Aristotle.[23] And thoughts of Aristotle much influence the way in which Aquinas approaches the topic of God and evil.

That Aquinas was anything but hostile when it comes to philosophical reasoning with respect to God emerges fairly early on his *Summa Contra Gentiles*. In 1.4 he refers to "truth" concerning God "to which the inquiry of reason can reach."[24] He quickly goes on to stress that some truths about God "surpass the whole ability of the human reason" and that even what can be known of God by reason is hard to acquire. But he does not deny that there are truths about God to be gleaned from purely philosophical reasoning. And he then goes on to spend a lot of time arguing for "truths" about God without invoking divine revelation. "There exists," he observes, "a twofold truth concerning the divine being, one to which the inquiry of reason can reach, the other that surpasses the whole ability of the human reason" (SCG 1.4). Aquinas does not mean that there are two ways of being true. As he goes on to say: "I am speaking of a 'twofold truth of divine things,' not on the part of God Himself, Who is truth one and simple, but from the point of view of our knowledge, which is variously related to the knowledge of divine things" (SCG 1.9). Aquinas's point is that some truths about God are open to philosophical investigation and defense while others are not. And, he maintains, some truths about God can be arrived at by arguments that do not presuppose their truth. Readers of the *Summa Contra Gentiles* will find Aquinas often stressing the need for divine revelation (so the *Summa Contra Gentiles* is not, as some have suggested, simply a *Summa* or summary of philosophy). But they shall also find him arguing at length for conclusions about God that do not appeal to divine revelation. Indeed, the bulk of the *Summa Contra Gentiles* consists of such arguments.[25] It is worth noting that, while again stressing the truth to be learned from divine revelation, its very first chapter says that Aristotle (no Christian thinker) rightly declares that "the wise man" should "consider the highest causes." The implication of this comment is that God is not above philosophical inquiry. Indeed, so Aquinas goes on to say while anticipating his manner of proceeding in the *Summa Contra Gentiles*: "among the inquiries that we must undertake concerning God in Himself, we must set down in the beginning that whereby His Existence is demonstrated, as the necessary foundation of the whole work. For, if we do not demonstrate that God exists, all consideration of divine things is necessarily suppressed" (SCG 1.9). Given what he says elsewhere, Aquinas cannot here mean that nobody can profitably consider "divine things" without being personally able to demonstrate God's existence. He does, however (and to put things in as open-ended a manner as possible), certainly seem to be saying that his project in the *Summa Contra Gentiles* requires him to spend time on what we can recognize as philosophical arguments concerning God. Not surprisingly, therefore, we find him at SCG 1.12 asking whether it is true to say that the existence of God cannot be demonstrated but is held by faith alone. His answer is "no."

In the *Summa Contra Gentiles*, but also in the *Summa Theologiae* and other writings, Aquinas shows himself to be someone happy to engage in what is now referred to as "natural theology"—meaning "attempts to present arguments for the existence and nature of God without relying on supposedly authoritative texts which presume that God exists." Considered as such, natural theology is obviously (in today's sense of 'philosophy', anyway) a philosophical enterprise, one that has been condemned *in principle* by some extremely famous thinkers, both philosophical and theological. Notable theological critics of natural theology who insist that its arguments should not even be engaged with include Søren Kierkegaard (1813–55) and Karl Barth.[26] "The idea of demonstrating that God exists," says Kierkegaard, "could scarcely suggest itself to the Reason.... For at the very onset, in beginning my proof, I would have presupposed it, not as doubtful but as certain."[27] And according to Barth:

> Natural theology does not exist as an entity capable of becoming a separate subject within what I consider to be real theology—not even for the sake of being rejected. If one occupies oneself with real theology one can pass by so-called natural theology only as one would pass by an abyss into which it is inadvisable to step if one does not want to fall. All one can do is turn one's back upon it as upon the great temptation and source of error, by having nothing to do with it.[28]

Yet Aquinas is most certainly an advocate of natural theology. He thinks that human reason is deeply flawed when it comes to knowledge of God, and he holds that, in a serious sense, we cannot know what God is (more on this below). Yet he frequently engages in what can only be called strictly philosophical argumentation concerning God's existence and nature. And we need to be aware of this fact as we try to get a sense of his take on God and evil.[29]

Placing Aquinas on God and Evil

Aquinas's commentaries on the Bible contain discussions that can be regarded as examples of philosophical writing. And his commentaries on Aristotle contain discussions that can be regarded as examples of theological writing. Works like the *Summa Theologiae* and the *Summa Contra Gentiles* present philosophical arguments (not relying on revelation) and theological ones (relying on revelation) in an almost seamless fashion. The *Summa Theologiae*, as Rude Te Velde has said,

> marks itself off against the whole of philosophical disciplines, not by excluding and rejecting them as being foreign to its own revelation-based approach to the truth, but by incorporating philosophical (metaphysical) reason and at the same time limiting its scope from within. The *Summa* incorporates philosophy, not only in the sense that it contains much philosophical argument and analysis, but also and in the first place in the sense that philosophy (metaphysics) assists the theological reflection on the teachings of the faith by providing it with an intelligible account of the reality of God as presupposed by faith.[30]

When it comes to the topic of God and evil, Aquinas clearly does not write in the manner of a contemporary secular philosopher. He does not doubt the existence of God. Nor does he doubt what he calls the "articles of faith." So he does not think that there is a problem of evil to be discussed on the assumption that discussions of it might lead us to conclude that God certainly or probably does not exist. As we shall see, much that he says about God and evil (and the goodness of God) draws on what he takes to be revealed by God and is thus part of what he thinks of as *sacra doctrina*. On the other hand, however, he has serious philosophical interests of a kind that distance him greatly from figures such as Kierkegaard and Barth. Aquinas, though much insisting on the importance of divine revelation, also thinks that there are truths about God to be known philosophically and cogently argued for. And he takes some of these truths to have a bearing on what is now commonly called the problem of evil. We shall not fully understand his thinking on God and evil if we do not grasp what he has to say with what, we might call, his philosophical hat on. Most especially, we shall not begin to understand it without a sense of why Aquinas thinks that we can believe in God on philosophical grounds and what he thinks belief in God amounts to, considered philosophically. Even before we get to that topic, however, we need to see how Aquinas (philosopher and theologian that he was), thinks of the world in general, both as philosopher and theologian. This is what I am concerned with in the following chapter.

3

What There Is

As I have said, Aquinas wrote philosophically as well as theologically. So we now need to note some of his philosophical views, which underpin a great deal that he has to say when writing as a theologian. Here I am thinking of what we might call his basic understanding of the world, one that he most certainly does not derive from what he takes to be revelation, but one that can be seen at work (either explicitly or implicitly) even when he is deep into discussions of topics to do with *sacra doctrina*. In order to get a sense of how Aquinas thinks about God and evil we need to be very much aware of this worldview (or metaphysical picture, as we might call it) since it contains some of Aquinas's deepest convictions about the nature of things, what I have elsewhere called the "building blocks" of his intellectual system.[1]

Beings

What is there? An obvious answer is "things that exist" or "beings." And Aquinas would certainly agree with this answer. Yet he has different ways of understanding what it is for something to exist or to be a being. He does not, for instance, take all sentences of the form "X exists" to signify that X is a being at all (on certain construals of "being," anyway). The Latin word used by Aquinas for what we might call "a being" is *ens* (plural *entia*). Straight off, however, we need to recognize that *ens* does not bear a single sense for Aquinas. He distinguishes between *entia* of different kinds, for he thinks it important to note a difference between what he calls an *ens per se* and an *ens per accidens*. Let me explain.

Think of a cat. And then think of a house or the president of a country. Do you take them to differ in any way? Well, Aquinas certainly does. He takes a cat to be a naturally occurring unit, an entity (*ens*) in its own right. For him, cats are *substances*, subsisting things with an identity of their own in the natural world. But he does not think of houses or presidents in this way. In an obvious sense, of course, houses and presidents *are* individual entities to which we can point and even give names. So we can nod in the direction of the White House in Washington, DC or to Barack Obama (currently president of the United States of America). But, thinks Aquinas, these are not beings as cats are. You might think it really odd if someone were to suggest that Barack Obama is not a being or a naturally occurring unit, but Aquinas would deny that Obama is, *by nature*, a president and would also deny that Obama is a naturally occurring thing *considered as president*. He would say that Obama is a human being *by nature* (and, therefore, an *ens per se*) but a president only *accidentally* (and, considered as a president, only an *ens per accidens*).

Lying behind this thought of Aquinas (and it is, I should emphasize, one that does not depend at all on any of his theological beliefs) is that we live in a world in which there are things to be classified in certain ways. Indeed, thinks Aquinas, all of our knowledge derives from our sensory contact with these things (ST Ia,12,12).[2] He also thinks that our sensory contact with things in the world allows us to identify some of them as *entia per se*. Typical examples of *entia per se* would, for Aquinas, be living things, such as people or cats or trees. These, he thinks, are naturally occurring things with *essences*. They are substances, meaning that they are things of which we affirm predicates (e.g., "—— is human" or "—— is pale" or "—— is mammalian") but do not predicate of other things (we do not, for example, say that Peter is Paul or that this cat is affirmable of that one).[3] The word "substance," says Aquinas, "means that which is possessed of an essence such that it will exist of itself, even though to exist is not its essence" (ST Ia.3.5 ad 1). Some philosophers have taken a substance to be some unknowable underlying "what not" that holds together a collection of phenomena, like color and shape and the like. Note, though, that this is not Aquinas's view. For the most part, he thinks of substances as knowable individuals in the world (such as particular cats or particular dogs), things that, he says, have essences.[4]

Essence

What does Aquinas mean by the word "essence"? He thinks of an essence as what something (a substance) has to have in order to exist as the kind of thing it is. The best way to approach Aquinas at this point is simply to see him as doing what natural scientists do these days as they try to inform us about the world. They pick out naturally occurring individuals (such as cats) and then try to tell us what they consist of, how they normally behave, and how we might expect them to behave. So does Aquinas, and his notion of essence has its home here. Essence, he says, is that which is signified by the definition of a thing (cf. *De Ente et Essentia* 2). In his view, the world is full of things with essences, things to be investigated. Some people have thought that by "essence" Aquinas only means "the meaning of a word," largely because in his *De Ente et Essentia* he speaks of being able to know what something is without knowing that it exists: "I can understand what humans or phoenixes are without knowing whether such things really exist."[5] Since one might doubt the existence of phoenixes, this statement might seem to suggest that what Aquinas means when he talks of understanding an essence can only be a matter of understanding the meaning of a word. And, reading Aquinas along these lines, one might be inclined to agree with him. We might say that, for example, the essence of a phoenix can be expressed by saying that a phoenix is a beautiful bird that bursts into flames and rises to life from its ashes. And we might do so because we have looked up the word "phoenix" in a dictionary. But Aquinas does not think in these terms at all. In his view, we can offer dictionary definitions of various nonexisting things (phoenixes, wizards, unicorns, Santa Claus, the tooth fairy, and so on). But, thinks Aquinas, none of these dictionary entries are real definitions of anything. So he does not take any of them to report that anything has an essence or what the essence of anything is. "If there is nothing to have its essence signified by a definition," he observes, "then the definition is no different from the explanation of the meaning of a term" (*Sententia Super Posteriora Analytica* [Commentary on Aristotle's "Posterior Analytics"] 2.6).[6] For something to have an essence, thinks Aquinas, it actually has to exist. For Aquinas, there is no essence without existence, which, among other things, means that he has no time for the notion of nonexisting things with natures existing in purely "possible worlds." That there are somehow unreal things that exist in such worlds has been philosophically defended in recent years.[7] Aquinas, however, does not share this view. He takes an essence to be had only by something that actually exists. For him, all essences are actual.

When Aquinas uses the word "definition" he typically takes it to mean what we provide when we try to explain what something actually is by nature. And he typically takes it to mean what we provide when we try to say what something is essentially, what it is as a thing in its own right, which takes me back to his *ens per se* and *ens per accidens* distinction. Cats are naturally occurring individuals, but presidents are not. Barack Obama, a president though he is, had to *become* a president; he did not occur naturally as a president. To start with he was a human being, one who developed an interest in politics. To repeat, by nature or essence, thinks Aquinas, Obama is a human being considered as the substance that he is; he is a president only *accidentally*.[8]

Up to now I have been employing a distinction between substance and accident, one that Aquinas uses. Substances, for him, are naturally occurring individuals belonging to many different genera and species, things with distinct natures or essences.[9] Accidents, by contrast, are, for Aquinas, features had by substances that should not enter into an account of what they are by nature, features that they can acquire or lose without ceasing to be what they essentially are. Consider the philosopher Bertrand Russell. Among other things, he once worked at Cambridge University and taught philosophy there. At one time he had dark hair while later he had white hair. He also smoked a pipe and demonstrated against nuclear weapons. These are all things that can truly be said of Russell. But, for Aquinas, they tell us what Russell was accidentally, not substantially. If he had ceased smoking a pipe (which he obviously did when at least asleep) or ceased to have white hair (if he had gone bald perhaps), he would not have ceased to be what he was essentially, a human being. Hard though it might be not to think of Bertrand Russell as a white-haired and pipe-smoking philosopher, he was neither of these things, or comparable ones, simply considered as what he was essentially. Or so Aquinas thinks. So he would say that the truths just mentioned about Russell tell us about accidents of Russell, not about his essence or nature. He would also say that these accidents, though once perfectly real (since Russell *did* once live in Cambridge, teach philosophy, smoke a pipe, and so on) are sharply to be distinguished from anything we should call a substance.[10] Or as he would also say, they lack *esse* even though they *in est*—a statement that might seem totally unintelligible and, therefore, needs some explanation.

Being

When Aquinas talks about genuine substances that actually exist he says that they have *esse*.[11] Here you need to take very seriously the word "actually" in the phrase "actually exist." I actually exist as I write these words, and you actually exist as you read them, but Napoleon does not actually exist. Napoleon *used* to exist, but he does not exist now. Aquinas would put this point by saying that I, as writing, and you, as reading, have *esse* while Napoleon does not.[12] Aquinas believes that people survive death, but only when their bodies are raised. He does not think that they survive death as *people* between their death and their resurrection, though he thinks that their souls survive. For Aquinas, therefore, it is true that the soul of Napoleon now exists, but not that he does. On Aquinas's account, Napoleon's soul is a *part* of Napoleon, not the living individual that Napoleon was. Hence, in his Commentary on St. Paul's First Letter to the Corinthians, we famously find Aquinas saying, "My soul is not me" (*anima mea non est ego*) (*Commentarium Super Epistolam I ad Corinthios* 15). Now you as a reader and I as writing actually exist, while it was true only in the past that Napoleon actually existed. So Aquinas would say that you and I have *esse* (that we actually exist). He would not, though, say the same when thinking of you currently reading this book or I writing it. Your existence (your *esse*) does not depend on your reading this book. You *are* reading this book, so "——— is reading *Thomas Aquinas on God and Evil*" can truly be said of you and is clearly telling us about something real (as, say, reports of Harry Potter killing Lord Voldemort do not). For Aquinas, though, your reading this book is something that you might not have done without ceasing to be what you are by nature— just as my writing it is something I might not have done without ceasing to be what I am by nature. Your existence as a human being happily does not require that you should ever read this book, as mine does not depend on my writing it. Aquinas often makes this point by saying that, considered as human beings, you and I have a "substantial form" and that, as currently reading this book, you have an "accidental form," as do I while writing it. Alien to many contemporary readers as this language might seem, its sense can be conveyed fairly simply. "Form" is the word Aquinas uses when thinking of what we might refer to when we ask what something is. Is it a human being? Is it a human being who smokes a pipe? And so on. As we have seen, though, Aquinas thinks that being human and smoking a pipe differ significantly. You and I, he would say, are essentially human. Whether or not we smoke is accidental to us. So he always distinguishes between what he calls "substantial forms" and "accidental forms." Since you are a human being (a naturally occurring substance or individual, an *ens per se*), Aquinas would say that you have a substantial form— meaning that you are an *ens per se* with an essence. Since your reading or not reading this book does not interfere with your being what you are essentially, he would speak of it as being an accidental form had by you (or existing in you). Hence his notion that accidents exist in (*in est*) substances and need to be distinguished from them and from their having *esse*.

For Aquinas, then, the world contains *entia per se* (e.g., human beings) and *entia per accidens* (e.g., presidents). And the former are naturally occurring substances that actually exist. Evidently, therefore, Aquinas thinks that it makes sense to say that, for example, my cat Smokey exists. Some other thinkers have taken a different line. They have argued that "——— exist(s)" is not properly predicated of individuals, that sentences like "Smokey exists" are somehow malformed or unintelligible. Perhaps the best and most recent detailed defense of this view comes in C. J. F. Williams's book *What Is Existence?*[13] According to Williams, it makes no sense to say that any individual exists. Why not? Because, says Williams, (a) the suggestion that it does leads to paradox, and (b) because existence is a property of concepts, not individuals.

The paradox to which Williams refers hinges on the notion of what philosophers would call "negative existential statements." Examples of these would be "honest politicians do not exist" or "residents of the Antarctic do not exist." If "—— exist(s)" is sensibly ascribed to an individual, says Williams, then statements like these are (unbelievably) false of necessity. Why? Because if "—— exist(s)" serves to mark a property of something, then "—— does not exist" denies that something or other has that property. But how can something be thought of as lacking a property if it does not exist to start with? If one says that honest politicians do not exist, then is one not denying that they lack a certain property? In that case, however, must they not exist in order to lack this? Hence the paradox. On the assumption that "X exists" tells us that an individual has a particular property (that of existing), then, says Williams, negative existential statements are all false of necessity, which cannot be true.

Yet negative existential statements do not have to be thought of as assuming the existence of that of which they speak. To assert that "honest politicians do not exist" is not to tell us anything about anybody at all (in Williams's language, it is not to ascribe a property to an individual). It is simply to state (whether truly or falsely) that nothing is describable as an honest politician. And as Aquinas, and medieval philosophers in general, thought, negative existential statements are true if their subject refers to nothing. By this I mean that they would have said (a) that "Santa Claus lives at the North Pole" is false, not because he lives somewhere else, but because he does not exist and lives nowhere, and (b) that "Santa Claus does not live at the North Pole" ("it is not the case that he lives at the North Pole") is true for the same reason. So perhaps there is no paradox arising from negative existential statements that forces us to abandon the view that we speak significantly when saying that something or other (e.g., my cat) exists.

I stress this point (and do so in defense of Aquinas) since his notion of *esse* is, as we shall see, crucial when it comes to his overall take on God and evil. And, Williams notwithstanding, there are contemporary philosophers who support what I have just been saying. Peter Geach and Anthony Kenny are good examples. Geach reminds us that there is a sense of "exists" in which it should be understood with respect to sentences like "John still exists though Fred has died."[14] Kenny observes that there is a distinction to be made between sentences of the form "cats exist" (meaning that "—— is a cat" is truly affirmable of something) and "Smokey exists" (meaning that Smokey has what Kenny calls "individual existence"). In Kenny's words:

> Since Kant, many philosophers have quoted with approval the slogan "existence is not a predicate." Here...it is important to distinguish between specific and individual existence. It is correct to say that statements of specific existence are not to be regarded as predications about any individual. Statements of individual existence, on the other hand, are genuine predications about what their subject-term stands for—as in "The Great Pyramid still exists, but the Library of Alexandria does not."[15]

It makes perfect sense to say of an individual substance such as Smokey that it exists. In Aquinas's language, it makes sense to say that Smokey has *esse*. But what does this fact imply?

Ultimately, Aquinas takes it to imply that Smokey is a *creature*, that he is made to be by God. I shall be returning to this notion later. In rounding off the present chapter, however, I now need to say something else about Aquinas on what there is. Specifically, I need to note that, in his view, there are causes.

Causes

Actually, Aquinas thinks that there are causes of different kinds, for, following Aristotle, he distinguishes between (a) agent causes, (b) material causes, (c) formal causes, and (d) final causes (ST 2a2ae.27.3; cf. *De Principiis Naturae* [On the Principles of Nature] 3). As you may suspect, therefore, his notion of "cause" is wider than the one we now most commonly employ in everyday language. Translations of Aquinas that give us the English word "cause" are always seeking to translate the Latin word *causa*. Aquinas's use of this term, however, is, I think, better translated into modern English as "explanation."[16]

When we say that "X caused Y" we typically mean that X is something in the world (or maybe several things acting together) that produced some kind of change in it.[17] We may wonder, for example, what is causing the painful symptoms from which John is suffering, or who caused the events of 9/11 to occur. Our most common use of the word "cause," which corresponds to Aquinas's understanding of what he calls "agent causes," carries with it the notion of accountability in terms of something other than that for which we are trying to account. It is, you might say, closely bound up with the notion of blame.[18] When we blame others for doing something we are accusing them of accounting for a change in the world. When we say that "X caused Y" we are usually doing exactly the same thing. "What is causing John's symptoms?" "Oh, it is a particular virus." "Who caused the events of 9/11?" "Well, it must have been someone or a group of people." For Aquinas, however, to refer to a *causa* can also be to refer to what something is made of (as accounting for what happens to it), what something is by nature (as accounting for what it does or what course its career takes), and what good it is seeking (as again accounting for what goes on with it). For this reason Aquinas also takes a *causa* to be what we might reference in answer to questions like (1) "Why did the china cup break when dropped while the plastic one did not?" Here Aquinas speaks of "material" causation: one explains how a china cup breaks while a plastic one does not by noting the difference between china and plastic. Or (2) "Why is that feline animal making purring noises?" Here Aquinas speaks of "formal" causation: one explains why a cat is purring while a dog does not by noting the difference between cats and dogs. And (3) "Why is John being so nice to Mary?" Here Aquinas speaks of "final" causation: one might explain that John is being nice to Mary because he is attracted to her. As I say, Aquinas's *causa* is closer to our use of the word "explanation" than it is to our use of the word "cause."

Be that as it may, though, our common notion of "cause," which, as I have said, corresponds to his notion of *agent cause*, is very prevalent in Aquinas's writings, and if we are to understand him on God and evil we shall need to get a handle on it. In particular, we need to note the following:

(1) As I have said, we commonly think of a cause as something (or a collection of things) in the world that accounts for ways in which certain other things change. When Aquinas speaks of agent causes he frequently does the same. For him, therefore, paradigm examples of agent causes would be me icing a cake or some novocaine making my mouth numb.

(2) Unlike some people, however, Aquinas does not want to make a sharp distinction between cause and effect when he thinks about agent causation. It seems, perhaps, natural to make such a distinction, to say, for example, that agent cause X (me, say) is utterly different from what it produces (the appearance of icing on a cake, say). Indeed, this distinction is one famously emphasized by David Hume, according to whom (a) "all distinct ideas are separable from each other," which means (b) that "the ideas of cause and effect are evidently distinct."[19] Hume is here clearly thinking of a cause along the lines of Aquinas's "agent cause" (insofar as he thinks of a cause as something in the world that produces an effect in the world), and he goes on to argue that, because of the distinction between cause and effect, what we take to be an effect could arise without a cause. Aquinas, however, has a different view. For him, an agent cause is only such *insofar as* it is producing an effect. He does not think of the phrase "agent cause" as designating some natural kind. He does

not think that, as well as there being cats, dogs, and people, there are *also* agent causes. For Aquinas, nothing is naturally an agent cause. He thinks that something is an agent cause only insofar as it is having an effect.

(3) Elaborating on this point, Aquinas, following Aristotle, sometimes uses the example of teaching (cf. *In Libros Physicorum* [Commentary on Aristotle's "Physics"] 3.5). How does one teach someone? One might naturally reply. "By talking, by writing on blackboards or whiteboards, and so on." Of course, though, one can go through the mechanics of teaching until one is blue in the face without one's students actually *learning* anything. And that is because teaching occurs only as *learning* occurs. For Aquinas, teaching is a classic example of how agent causation links cause and effect in a seriously strong way. But he thinks of it only as a classic example illustrating what is always going on when agent causation occurs. As he writes in his Commentary on Aristotle's *Physics*: "Action and passion are not two changes but one and the same change, called action insofar as it is caused by an agent, and passion insofar as it takes place in a patient."[20] What Aquinas means here is that the effects of an agent cause are the *doing* of the agent cause and, therefore, not something to be thought of as distinct from it (in the way that Hume seems to suppose). Aquinas is not, of course, suggesting that an agent cause and what it produces are identical. His point is that *being the effect* of an agent cause is *being what the agent cause is producing.*

(4) When it comes to agent causation Aquinas often insists that the effects of agent causes resemble their causes, which seems a pretty peculiar notion. When I wash some clothes I do not look like them when they are clean. Again, when I feed a hungry cat, I do not look like a fed cat. Aquinas, however, does not deny any of this. His point is that agent causes (not, in a serious sense, to be thought of as distinct from their effects) produce what is like them since they reflect what they are. "What a thing produces reflects what it is," says Aquinas (*omne agens agat sibi simile inquantum est ens*) (ST 1a.4.3). The idea here is that when agent causation occurs what we have is a cause exerting itself and expressing itself in what it produces (as just noted). Sometimes, thinks Aquinas, agent causes produce what resembles them strongly—as, for example, when two human beings copulate and produce another human being. Yet he also thinks that agent causation does not (and most frequently does not) result in such visible replication. Always, though, and relying on his view that the effect of an agent cause is the cause *in action*, he concludes that the effects of agent causes resemble their causes. His meaning here is that the effects of agent causes display the natures of their causes as acting in things other than them- selves. I do not look anything like a clean floor as I make a floor to be clean by washing it. But the coming to be clean of the floor reflects what I am (and what

I use to clean the floor is) as it comes to be clean by me. That is because I and the floor-cleaning products I use are at work and, therefore, showing ourselves forth, exerting ourselves, in the coming to be clean of the floor. Or so Aquinas thinks. In his view, agent causes impose their character on other things and—in this sense, and in this sense only—resemble them.

Where is all of this leading when it comes to Aquinas on God and evil? You shall, I am afraid, have to be patient and read on. In this chapter I have briefly tried to explain some of Aquinas's ideas on being and causation. These are ideas that are part and parcel of Aquinas's overall view on God and evil. In the next chapter I shall try to elaborate on what Aquinas has to say about them.

4

Goodness and Badness

In the last chapter I tried to explain some of Aquinas's basic (or metaphysical) views, ones that we need to understand in order to follow him when it comes to his approach to God and evil. As I said, they are not theological views. They are ones that Aquinas thought defensible by reasonable argument without recourse to divine revelation. In this chapter I need to add to my account of such views by turning to what Aquinas thinks in general about "goodness" and "badness." These are terms that always feature prominently in discussions of God and evil, but how does Aquinas understand them? He does not do so by drawing on beliefs about God. Rather, and as we shall later see, some of his beliefs about God depend on what he thinks of goodness and badness without reference to God, thinking that forms a critical backdrop to his overall position on God and evil. That is why we need at this stage to be clear as to what it amounts to.

Goodness

It has been said that nothing is objectively good or bad. People who make this claim seem, for various reasons, chiefly to be denying that statements of the form "X is good" or "Y is bad" genuinely *inform* us about X or Y. They have no such problem with statements like "John is bald" or "Mary has cancer." They would take these statements to describe John or Mary (or, perhaps, to misdescribe them should John not be bald or Mary not have cancer). When it comes to "good" and "bad," though, they deny that either description or misdescription enters into the equation. For, so they argue, "good" and "bad" are not descriptive terms (and, therefore, not even *possibly* misdescriptive ones). This conclusion has a long history and has been defended on a variety of grounds. Basically, though, what it boils down to is something like the thesis that beauty is in the eye of the beholder, that to call something good or bad is just to express one's reaction to something (one's liking or disliking it).

There is an important sense in which Aquinas agrees with this thesis. For he frequently insists that "good" fundamentally means "attractive" or "desirable." He writes, for example, in ST Ia.5.1: "The goodness of something consists in its being desirable" (*Ratio enim boni in hoc consistit quod aliquid sit appetibile*).[1] Aquinas evidently does not think of "is good" and "is bad" as strictly on a level with "is bald" or "has cancer." He takes "is good" and "is bad" to have what we might call an "evaluative" meaning as opposed to a "purely descriptive" one. For him (at one level, anyway), our use of "good" and "bad" is unintelligible apart from our likes and dislikes. For this reason Aquinas on "good" and "bad" might even be compared with what we find in the writings of Hume (not someone with whom Aquinas is often connected). As J. L. Mackie once put it, Hume thought that "motivation for or against any action requires...what he would call a passion or sentiment, and more particularly a desire."[2] Hume's various discussions of goodness and badness hinge on this thought. Yet so do those of Aquinas. As I have said, he thinks that to call something good is first and foremost to say that it is desirable.

Unlike Hume, however, Aquinas holds that to call something good is to describe it just as much as we describe John by saying that he is bald or just as much as we describe Mary by saying that she has cancer. Hume takes goodness to be in the eye of the beholder alone. As Mackie reports him: "His doctrine means that moral distinctions do not report any objective features at all."[3] Yet this is not Aquinas's view. Also, and it is *important* to notice this, Aquinas does not confine his use of the word "good" only to contexts in which he is talking about moral distinctions (as Hume seems to do). And with good reason. That is because we talk about things of all sorts as being good or bad—reasons being an example. There are good reasons and bad reasons. There are also (and this list could go on almost forever) good/bad opera singers, good/bad computers, good/bad meals, good/bad doctors, good/bad teachers, good/bad eggs, good/bad wine, good/bad desks, good/bad weather, and good/bad airlines.

Aquinas takes "good" to be an adjective, which is not, perhaps, surprising given that it *looks* like one in sentences in which we commonly use it. That we are not somehow describing something when calling it good is, perhaps, a thesis that only someone with a very particular philosophical agenda would want to support. Be that as it may, Aquinas takes "good" to be adjectival and never suggests that "X is good" should be taken only to mean something like "I approve of X" (a statement about me, not about X). But what kind of adjective does he take "good" to be?

As Peter Geach has noted, we can distinguish between logically attributive adjectives and logically predicative ones.[4] Consider the sentence "X is a blue chair." This says two distinct things about X: that it is blue and that it is a chair. Without any change of meaning it can be rewritten as "X is blue *and* X is a chair." But now consider "X is a big flea." That does not neatly break down into "X is big" and "X is a flea." Or, as Geach puts it, "'X is a big flea' does not split up into 'X is a flea' and 'X is big', nor 'X is a small elephant' into 'X is an elephant' and 'X is small'; for if these analyses were legitimate, a simple argument would show that a big flea is a big animal and a small elephant a small animal."[5] As is not the case with "—— is blue," "—— is big" can be understood only with reference to what we are ascribing this predicate. We can clearly understand what X is like when told that it is blue, even if we do not know what X is. Not so with "big." A big flea is vastly different from a big elephant. In Geach's terminology, "blue" is a *predicative* adjective while "big" is an *attributive* one.

Now, Aquinas generally thinks of "good" as an attributive adjective. To be sure, he thinks that to call anything good is to say that it is attractive or desirable in some way. But he does not think of goodness as a property or attribute common to all good things in the way in which being blue is a property or attribute common to all blue things. And that is because he thinks that what is attractive or desirable when it comes to things of one type can differ from what is attractive or desirable when it comes to things of other types. If I am looking for a good bed, I am looking for something that gives me a good night's sleep by supporting my spine properly, something that has what physicians and experts on beds take to be desirable when it comes to beds. Not so, however, when it comes to my looking for a good doctor. Here I am not looking for physical support at all. I am looking for someone who knows about medicine and is able to cure people. Of course it is true that when I call a bed or a doctor good I am declaring them to be desirable or attractive, but for very different reasons. And so on for many other cases you might care to mention. Thus, for example, what we take to make for goodness in an opera singer is not the same as what we take to make for goodness in a computer, teacher, parent, desk, apartment, holiday, or air-traffic controller. As Geach again says, "There is no such thing as being just good or bad, there is only being a good or bad so-and-so."[6]

As we shall see, Aquinas thinks that there is such a thing as unqualified goodness, goodness that is not that of a good such-and-such. His word for this is "God." Generally, though, he agrees with what Geach says. For him, therefore, goodness is objective but also relative: objective in the sense that to call something good is to say something true or false about it; relative in the sense that to understand what "X is good" means involves an understanding of what X is.[7] And here I need to emphasize the word "is," for Aquinas strongly connects goodness and being. In his view, to be good is *to be* somehow, meaning that a good X positively or actually has certain desirable attributes. As he says at one point, "Goodness and being are really the same. They differ only conceptually....Something is obviously good inasmuch as it is a being" (ST 1a.5.1 [Davies and Leftow 2006: 52]). This remark needs explaining, of course, if only because we do not, these days, commonly equate "X exists" with "X is good." Indeed, most people, I suspect, would naturally say that something can exist without being good.

But what has to be the case for something to exist at all? What has to be the case for there, for example, to be a human being? The obvious answer is, "There has to be a human being." There has to be what can be truly thought of as something that is human. So there has to be what *succeeds* in being human for there *to be* a human being in the first place. In other words, the notion of existing is bound up with the notion of achievement or success, which is what Aquinas thinks. His line is that, insofar as something actually is a such-and-such, then it must have what is needed to be a such-and-such and is, therefore, good. Or, as he puts it himself:

> The goodness of something consists in its being desirable....But desirability evidently follows upon perfection, for things always desire their perfection. And the perfection of a thing depends on the extent to which it has achieved actuality. So, something is obviously good inasmuch as it is a being....So good clearly does not really differ from being, though the word "good" expresses a notion of desirability not expressed by the word "being."...Every being, considered as such, is good. For every being, considered as such, is actual and therefore in some way perfect....So, every being, considered as such, is good.
> (ST 1a.5.1 and 1a.5.3 [Davies and Leftow 2006: 52, 56])

Aquinas is not here saying that something is good only insofar as somebody desires it. His meaning is that something is good insofar as it possesses what is desirable for it considered as what it is by nature.[8] And with this thought in mind he concludes that being and goodness are seriously equivalent. He does not think that the terms "being" and "goodness" are synonymous.[9] He does, however, hold that for something to exist at all is for that thing to possess features that make for goodness in it—a conclusion that he takes to be perfectly compat-ible with many existing things being defective or thwarted in various ways. Aquinas always distinguishes between "perfect" and "good." On his account, a perfect X lacks nothing that it could have in the way of attributes or properties fulfilling it (perfective of it), considered as what it is. By contrast, so he says, something can be good without being perfect. Cashed out in terms of a concrete example, what I have just been reporting can be reduced to this: a healthy and happy cat is a perfect cat while a sick cat is not; however, even a sick cat is a cat and, therefore, (a) has enough of what belongs to feline perfection to make it to be a cat at all and (b) is, therefore, good. Here, once again, we need to remember the distinction noted above between logically attributive and logically predicative adjectives and Aquinas taking "good" to be logically attributive.[10]

Badness

For Aquinas, then, to speak of something as good is to say that it at least has what it needs to be what it is by nature. And this, of course, means that Aquinas thinks of goodness as involving the actual existence of something: a substance with what it needs in order to exist as the thing that it is. When it comes to bad-ness, however, Aquinas takes a completely different line. As with "good," he regards "bad" as an attributive adjective. So he thinks that we shall not under-stand statements of the form "X is bad" unless we know what X is. But, though he takes "X is good" to signify that X actually possesses some real attribute or property, he does not think in the same way when it comes to "X is bad."

That is, perhaps, not the best way to report Aquinas at this point since he does not actually speak about attributes and properties as I have just done. In saying so I mean that he does not speak of naturally occurring things in the world (entia per se) as having attributes or properties. As I noted earlier, he speaks of them as having substantial and accidental forms. That said, however, Aquinas's view of badness contrasts sharply with his view of goodness. For him (and to enter more into his mode of discourse than I have so far done in this chapter), something good possesses a substantial form together with various accidental forms, while this is not the case when it comes to badness. According to Aquinas, badness has no actual existence (esse) and is neither something with a substantial nor an accidental form. Rather, it consists in the absence of anything actually existing (formally or accidentally). On Aquinas's account, to say that my cat Smokey exists is to say that he is a cat (to say that a particular nameable feline can be pointed out and truly described as being a cat). Also on Aquinas's account, to say that Smokey is warm is to say of something actual (something that has *esse*) that it is what it does not have to be in order to be what it is essentially (on the assumption that a cold cat is no less of a cat than is a warm one). When it comes to badness (*malum*), however, Aquinas thinks that we are not dealing with existence (*esse*) in either of the above senses. Something with *esse* is for him an actually existing substance. And something with an accidental form is an actually existing substance that is really thus-and-so (though not essentially thus-and-so). As I have noted, an accidental form, for Aquinas, does not so much *est* (exist in its own right) as *in est* (exist as belonging to what exists in its own right); it has no reality as a substance, but is real as belonging to an existing substance. When it comes to badness, however, Aquinas denies that this has *esse* at all, either as a substance or as an accidental form possessed by a substance. He thinks that badness is a lack of being (*esse*).

It has sometimes been suggested that in taking this view Aquinas is saying that badness (or evil) does not exist or is an illusion of some sort. That is not his view, however, and how could it be, given that he is a Christian theologian who acknowledges the reality of sin and believes in someone (Jesus of Nazareth) who was unjustly crucified following a ministry in which he acknowledged and tried to deal with suffering of different kinds? Aquinas recognizes very well that there is a lot of badness around, that all sorts of things are thwarted or suffering in all sorts of ways. He is also aware that there is sense in saying that badness (or evil) exists. But Aquinas does not think that all sentences of the form "X *est*" (X is) should be analyzed in the same way. To be more specific, and adding to what I have already noted, Aquinas recognizes a distinction to be made between true statements and statements telling us what something actually is.

Consider the statement "Smokey exists." As I have said, Aquinas would take this to tell us something about an actually existing substance (that Smokey is a cat). What though of "blindness exists"? How can anyone deny that this is a true statement, for are there not many blind people? And might we not truly say of someone that he or she is blind? Obviously we might. But what would we be ascribing to such a person when saying that he or she is blind? Presumably, "is blind" gets its sense from "sees." By this I mean that our concept of blindness is parasitic on our notion of seeing, just as our notion of sickness is parasitic on our notion of health. We identify people as blind or sick while starting from the understanding that people are not normally either of these things. We do not proceed the other way around, by noting that blindness and sickness are the norm and that sight and health are the exceptions. So to say that someone is blind or sick is to draw attention to an anomaly, to something not working as we would expect and hope it to. In that case, however, is not the word "not" here crucial? Should we not be saying that "X is blind" or "X is sick" tells us what X is *not* rather than what it is? Aquinas's reply to this question would be "yes, in one sense, and no in another."

Since we can, for example, truly say that someone or other is blind, Aquinas would agree that "X is blind" can be thought of as a true proposition (with some name substituted for "X"). He would say the same with respect to "X is sick." And in this sense he would be happy with statements like "blindness exists" and "sickness exists." Yet he would not be happy with them if construed as asserting that there are any such substances as blindness or sickness.[11] He would say that neither blindness nor sickness are substances. He would also say that their reality consists in the absence of something and not the presence of any actually existing accidental form. His view is that to call something blind or sick is simply to draw attention to what it lacks, to what does not actually exist. And this is what he thinks when it comes to all instances of badness or evil. In other words, he subscribes to a view going back at least as far as St. Augustine of Hippo (354–430) according to which badness or evil is always a privation or absence of goodness, not a substance or an accident that anything actually has (one that has the *esse* of accidents that inhere in the substances in which they *in est*).[12] Aquinas's view is that to think of something as bad or evil is always to think of it as *lacking* existence (*esse*) in some respect. Or as he puts it himself:

> Like night from day, you learn about one opposite from the other. So you take good in order to grasp what evil means. Now we have accepted the definition that good is everything that is desirable. Well then, since each real thing tends to its own existence and completion, we have to say that this fulfils the meaning of good in every case. Therefore, evil cannot signify a certain existing being, or a real shaping or positive kind of thing. Consequently, we are left to infer that it signifies a certain absence of a good. (ST 1a.48.1 [Blackfriars edition, 8.109])[13]

Note that Aquinas does not simply say here that evil or badness is merely an absence of good. He says that it is a *certain* absence of a good (*quaedam absentia boni*). If my apartment has nobody in it at a given time, then the goodness involved in being a human being is absent from it. But Aquinas would not therefore conclude that my apartment is bad or evil. As he writes:

> An evil means the displacement of a good. Not that every absence of good is bad, for it can be taken in a negative and in a privative sense. The mere negation of a good does not have the force of evil, otherwise it would follow that wholly non-existents were bad, also that a thing

was bad because it did not possess the quality of something else, a man, for instance, who was not swift as a mountain goat and strong as a lion. The absence of good taken deprivatively is what we call evil, thus blindness which is the privation of sight. (ST 1a.48.3)

For Aquinas, badness or evil is not the absence of some good *period*. It is the absence of a good that belongs to an existing substance by nature. Just as he thinks that we shall not understand what "X is good" means without knowing what kind of thing X is, he also thinks that understanding that X is bad involves knowing what X is. My apartment is not bad if nobody is in it. Human beings are not bad because they lack certain abilities belonging to things of a different kind (such as being able to fly). On this account, badness involves the absence of what is fulfilling or perfective of something in particular as the kind of thing it is. Hence the example of blindness as used by Aquinas with respect to people. When it comes to human beings, not being able to see is a privation of what belongs to them by nature, as is not the case with, say, a stone or a book. For Aquinas, therefore, "bad," just like "good," is "contextually dependent," as Herbert McCabe puts it.[14] For Aquinas, just as there is no specific property of goodness, there is no specific property of badness. In his view, something with a particular nature is good insofar as it possesses the nature that it has and the accidental forms perfective (or potentially perfective) of this. By the same token, something bad possesses a nature but lacks what is perfective of it in some way, as is the case with someone who is blind. This, in turn, means that, for Aquinas, badness (or evil) always exists in some good. Or in his words: "Every privation is founded in a subject that is a being [*ens*]; and in the same way all evil is founded in some good" (ST 1a.17.4 ad 2 [Blackfriars edition, 4.113]). To put matters another way, Aquinas thinks that nothing is unreservedly or purely bad.

With this point in mind, let me make three final observations before proceeding to the next chapter of this book.

The first is that Aquinas clearly thinks that something rightly called bad (or evil) might be positively good under a certain description and even without reference to its merely existing. Consider the case of a really successful serial killer who continually evades capture. Most of us, I presume, would regard such a person as objectively bad, as would Aquinas. Note though that such a killer has to have a serious degree of intelligence in order to do what he or she does and to get away with it. Considered as a strategist, therefore, even a serial killer might be thought of as good. Aquinas allows for this thought since, as I have said, he takes "good" and "bad" to be attributive adjectives, which allows him to distinguish between the goodness of something considered as an X (e.g., a human being) and the goodness of something considered as a Y (e.g., a strategist).[15]

My second observation concerns what Aquinas thinks about presence and absence when it comes to badness. As we have seen, he thinks of evil as a privation, as an absence of due good, as a lack of being (and chiefly with an eye on what something is essentially). Yet, so we should note, he also recognizes that badness might be due to the presence of something. If you manage to inject embalming fluid into me while I am still alive, I shall quickly start dying. Yet the badness involved here is due to the presence of something in me (the embalming fluid). In short, it is not Aquinas's view that badness or evil is always a matter of something being absent *simpliciter*. For him, badness or evil is often the result of the presence of perfectly real things. Seeking to defend Aquinas, McCabe writes: "A washing machine may be bad not only because it has too little, as when there is no driving belt on the spin drier, but also because it has too much, as when someone has filled the interior with glue."[16] As presenting a contemporary example so as to illustrate what Aquinas thinks, McCabe is quite right here.

And, finally, I need to emphasize that Aquinas does not take "good" or "bad" to be terms only to be used when expressing moral approval or disapproval. It should be obvious from what I have said that he does not suppose that "X is good" always means that X is good as a human being to be evaluated on moral grounds. Aquinas thinks of "good" as signifying what medieval thinkers in general, and under the influence of Aristotle, referred to as a "transcendental"—a term to be used when talking about all sorts of different things. There are few terms that we can think of as applicable to everything that exists. Aquinas, though, thinks that one of these is "being." He also thinks that another one is "good." In his view, everything that exists has being (whether substantially or accidentally). And everything is good in some sense. But Aquinas does not presume that everything is good insofar as it is morally good (insofar as it is a well-behaved human being).

This is a matter to which I will be returning.

5

God the Creator

We have now seen something of what we might call Aquinas's basic metaphysics and something of his general take on the terms "good" and "bad." The question we need to ask at this point is how, for Aquinas, does God fit into what I have so far been reporting? In one sense, the answer to this question is "not at all," for what I have been reporting makes no mention of God. Yet, and without abandoning what I have described him as saying (quite the contrary), Aquinas certainly believes that God exists and that what I have been noting so far is relevant when trying to think about him. In what sense is this true, however? I take this question to bring us to a thought that governs or at least hovers over everything that Aquinas has to say about God: that God is the Creator. In this chapter, therefore, I want to say something about Aquinas and the notion of God as Creator. As is the case with almost everything I have noted in the previous chapters, what I say here does not take us to the heart of Aquinas's view of God and evil. But anyone with an interest in Aquinas needs to be aware of it in order to understand Aquinas's approach to God and evil (and goodness) as a whole.

Knowing That God Exists

Unlike some authors, Aquinas does not hold that anyone who believes that God exists is obliged, on pain of intellectual vice of some kind, to be able to offer arguments for the truth of the claim "God exists." He has no problem with many who believe in God's existence doing so on the basis of faith, not reasoned argument.[1] Faith, by which Aquinas roughly means "belief without knowledge" (belief without what he calls *scientia*), is not, for him, automatically to be dismissed as intellectually unrespectable. On the contrary, there is a sense in which he takes it to be a virtue.[2] He does not, of course, think that it is always good to believe without having reasons for doing so. He does, however, hold that it is always good to believe what God has revealed, and he takes the truth of the proposition "God exists" to be presupposed by the notion of God revealing anything. So belief in God's existence is not, for Aquinas, something that cannot respectably be had by someone unable to argue in its defense. In his own words: "There is nothing to stop people from accepting on faith some demonstrable truth that they cannot personally demonstrate" (ST Ia,2,2 ad 1 [Davies and Leftow 2006: 23]).

On the other hand, however, much that Aquinas himself says about God rests on what can only be called philosophical arguments. And this is so when it comes to the question of knowing that God exists. When it comes to this question, Aquinas is definitely talking with a philosophical hat on his head.[3] You can see this best from his general treatments of the question, "In what way can we know that God exists?" Is it, for example, self-evident to us (*per se notum quoad nos*) that God exists? Aquinas's answer to the question is "no." Citing several arguments to the effect that "God exists" is "self-evident" to us, and distinguishing between different senses of "self-evident," he rejects all of them on philosophical grounds while moving to a conclusion that is obviously very important to him. This conclusion is that the only knowledge we can have of God has to be derived from causal reasoning based on what God has brought about.[4]

Hence, for example, Aquinas denies that "God exists" is what we might call an analytic truth, on a level with propositions like "all triangles have three sides." Once we have understood what the word "triangle" means, we can immediately see that "all triangles have three sides" is true. But we cannot, Aquinas argues, comparably see that "God exists" is true.[5] We can, he thinks, intelligibly assert "there is no God." Why? Because we do not have a grasp of what God is, one that would allow us to say that "God does not exist" is as nonsensical as "no triangles have three sides." Aquinas thinks that "God exists" *is* in one sense "self-evident" (*per se notum*) since, in fact, God cannot but exist. Yet he also thinks that God's being unable not to exist is a conclusion we can currently know to be true only on the basis of causal arguments and inferences from them.[6]

You might suppose that we can know that God exists on the basis of direct experience. I might know that Fred is on the street because I see him there. So might one not know that God exists by something analogous to my seeing Fred? Aquinas thinks not. That is because he takes very seriously the idea that we are human animals whose knowledge depends heavily on our senses even though it also depends on premises that really are self-evident to us. We might, he thinks, know a lot about Fred, but only because we can single him out as an item in the physical world to which all of us belong. Yet, thinks Aquinas, God is not an item in the physical universe. In the sense in which we commonly speak of knowing of the existence of something by direct experience, Aquinas denies that we can know of God's existence. In some places he speaks of Moses and St. Paul as having a direct awareness of God or as seeing God's essence (cf. ST 2a2ae.174.4). But he clearly regards this seeing as miraculous, not as something available to people by nature. By nature, he thinks, we can arrive at *scientia* only on the basis of what we know by means of our senses (together with what is indeed self-evident to us). That is why he concludes that any knowledge we have of God has to derive from what is there in front of us at a sensory level.

We can put all of this by saying that, for Aquinas (and abstracting from the notion of faith), any knowledge we might have of God as the Creator has to derive from what he has brought about. It is an inference from what are taken to be effects. In particular, it is an inference based on the notion that there is in creatures a distinction between essence (*essentia*) and existence (*esse*).

Essence, Existence, and God

Some people have argued for God's existence from what they have called the contingency of creatures. Their idea is that all beings apart from God are contingent and need to be accounted for in terms of something noncontingent or "necessary" (i.e., God).[7] This is not Aquinas's position, however. As is clear from, for example, ST 1a.2.3, he thinks of contingency and necessity as a distinction that can be made with respect to different *creatures*, some of which he takes to be contingent and others of which he takes to be necessary. What is the distinction in question? It is that between (a) being able to acquire or lose a substantial form in the course of nature and (b) not being able to do so. For Aquinas, something is contingent if it is caused to exist by what already exists in the material world and/or if it can cease to exist by the action of what exists in the material world. And something is necessary if, though part of God's created order, such is not the case with it. Hence, for example, Aquinas thinks of cats as contingent. These come into being and pass away, and they do so because of the actions of other physical things. On the other hand, thinks

Aquinas, angels are necessary beings. For Aquinas, angels (which he certainly takes to exist) are nonmaterial. So they cannot be produced or generated by material things; nor can they be destroyed or obliterated by such things or by any material factors in them leading them to perish in the course of nature.[8]

If the distinction between God and creatures does not, for Aquinas, lie in all creatures being contingent while God alone is necessary, then in what *does* it lie? According to Aquinas, it lies in all creatures being such that their existence and essence (or nature) differ while such is not the case with God. On this account, knowing *what* a creature is does not come with a knowledge that it (considered as the particular thing that it is) has to exist. On this account also, knowing what God is *would* come with the knowledge that he cannot but exist. Indeed, says Aquinas, what distinguishes God from creatures is his being *ipsum esse subsistens* (subsisting being itself). That conclusion may sound very murky. So let us try to see how Aquinas arrives at it.

He typically begins by noting what seems to be evident in the world of our experience—that, for example, things undergoing change depend on other things that cause them to change, or that things that come into being depend on causes that bring it about that they do so. He then tends to suggest that, as well as asking what in the universe accounts for this or that change, or this or that coming into being, we should ask what accounts for the existence of the universe as a whole (including all of the causes that operate within it). Suppose we agree that the existence of a particular cat, Smokey, say, raises the causal questions, "How come it exists?" or "How come it has come to be as it is now but once was not?" In seeking to answer these questions we are looking for something or several things in the world (whether currently existing or not) that can be thought of as accounting for (or as having accounted for) the coming to be of Smokey or that he is now what he once was not. But can we not also ask how come the existence of a world in which things in it, and the changes undergone by them, can be causally accounted for in terms of other things in it? Aquinas thinks that we can. His view is that, as well as asking causal questions of the kind "What in the universe accounts for this, that, or the other?" we can and should ask "What accounts for there being any universe at all rather than nothing?"

Aquinas presents this line of thinking in a number of places, a good example being ST 1a.44.2:

> The ancient philosophers entered into the truth step by step and as it were haltingly. Somewhat raw to begin with, they reckoned that the only realities were sensible bodies.... Later others climbed higher to the prospect of being as being and observed the cause of things

inasmuch as they are beings, not merely as things of such a kind or quality. To be the cause of things in that they are beings is to be the cause of all that belongs to their existence in any way whatsoever, not merely as what they are like by the properties which shape them [*per formas accidentales*] or what kind they are by their substantial forms. (Blackfriars edition, 8.11, 13)

What Aquinas is doing in this passage is to distinguish between causal questions to be asked and answered with respect to what exists in the universe (all that I reported him as talking about in chapter 3) and a question that asks how any such questions can be asked or answered at all. For him, that question is, "How come *anything* in the universe *at any time?*"

Notice that this is not a question about what brought it about that the universe began to exist. Aquinas believed (on the basis of his reading of Genesis 1) that the universe had a beginning. Philosophically speaking, however, he thought it impossible to prove either that the universe had a beginning or that it did not.[9] To repeat: Aquinas's question is "How come *anything* in the universe *at any time?*" His thought is that the existence of nothing in the universe is explicable in terms of its nature and therefore requires a cause that is not part of the universe to account for its existing. This thought emerges in Aquinas's *De Ente et Essentia*, where he asserts that one can understand what humans or phoenixes are without knowing whether such things really exists (an assertion to which I drew attention above).[10] As I have noted, it has been said that all that Aquinas is saying here is that we can know what the words "human" and "phoenix" mean without knowing that there are any human beings or phoenixes.[11] Yet that is not what Aquinas is driving at in the text just quoted. His point is that one can know what the nature of any *existing* thing in the universe is without knowing that any nameable individual having that nature actually exists—that, for example, one can know what a cat is (cats being existing things with a nature) without knowing that *Smokey* actually exists.[12] For Aquinas, the existence of any particular existing individual in the universe is not to be read off from a knowledge of the nature it has, this being something had (or potentially had) by other things.[13] For this reason Aquinas thinks that the *esse* of *any* given thing in the universe, at any given time, is not explicable solely in terms of the nature it has (albeit that he does not think that anything can exist without having the nature that it has).

So Aquinas holds that everything in the universe is at all times dependent for its existence on, or is caused to be by, what is not part of the universe. And this is what he means when saying that things are created by God—since he takes it as obvious that "God" is the natural word to use when referring to what accounts for the existence of the universe as a whole and at all times. "Natural" because of the way in which Aquinas reads the Bible and the Christian tradition preceding him, according to which God is "the Maker of heaven and earth."[14] Hence, for example, we find him saying this:

> God is in everything; not indeed as part of their essence, or as an accident, but as an efficient cause is present to that in which its action is taking place. For every efficient cause must be connected with that upon which it acts and must touch it by its power.... Now since it is God's essence to exist, created existence must be his proper effect, as burning is fire's proper effect. But God causes this effect in things not just when they begin to exist but all the time they are maintained in existence, just as the sun is lighting up the atmosphere all the time the atmosphere remains lit. During the whole period of a thing's existence, therefore, God must be present to it, and present in a way that accords with the way in which the thing possesses its existence. Now, existing is more intimately and profoundly interior to things than anything else.... So, God must be, and be intimately, in everything. (ST 1a.8.1 [Davies and Leftow 2006: 79])

One will never understand Aquinas on what matters most to him unless one recognizes the seriousness with which he takes comments such as these, insisting, as they do, on the total and absolute dependence of creatures on God.

What God Is Not

With that understood, however, we need to note some other points that Aquinas thinks it worth making with respect to the notion of God and creation, the first of which is that there might have been nothing created, and not just in the sense that, for Aquinas, the essence of a particular creature does not guarantee its existence. For Aquinas thinks that God does not have to create creatures that depend on him for their existence from moment to moment. Granted that God has created, one might ask if he is compelled to do so either because of what he is by nature or because of something apart from him forcing him to create. With an eye on this question Aquinas replies "no," and he does so because he thinks that will can be ascribed to God.

Aquinas regularly starts his various discussions of will by taking it to be a faculty by which we are attracted to what we take to be good (Aquinas's reflections on talk about God always start from the ways in which we speak when referring to creatures). So, for example, he takes voluntary or willed human behavior to be goal-directed. The question "Why are you doing that?" is for Aquinas always one that invites an answer referring to what the person addressed regards as desirable or attractive. Now, Aquinas takes God to know.[15] Indeed, he thinks of God as omniscient, which, in turn, leads him to think that God knows and loves what is actually good. He also thinks that a knowledge of what is good without reservation is something that cannot but lead one with will or desire to will or desire that thing. This thought, in turn, leads Aquinas to conclude that God cannot but will or delight in himself since God is good without reservation (a matter to which I shall be returning). In other words, and in a manner of speaking, Aquinas believes that God necessarily delights in himself. This delight, though, does not, for Aquinas, involve God *doing* anything, where "doing" means "acting so as to obtain a good not presently enjoyed." One might seek a good of some particular kind, and, in doing so, one might be constrained to act with an eye on means by which to obtain it. For Aquinas, however, God by nature enjoys (and is) the perfect good.[16] So his nature is not such as to compel him to create insofar as he essentially wills (delights in) what is good. Or, as we find Aquinas himself writing:

> [God] wills his own goodness necessarily, rather as we cannot but
> wish our own happiness.... By willing an end we are not bound to
> will the things that lead to it unless they are such that it cannot be
> attained without them (as when to preserve life we must take food or
> to cross the sea we must take a boat). Other things, however, without
> which the end can be attained, we do not will of necessity (thus a
> horse for a journey we can take on foot, and the same holds good in
> other cases). Hence, since God's goodness subsists and is complete
> independently of other things, and they add no fulfilment to him,
> there is no absolute need for him to will them. (ST 1a.19.3 [Blackfriars
> edition, 5.13, 15])

What Aquinas is saying here is that God has no need of creatures as contributing to his happiness or well-being. And, for this reason, he does not think that God has to create considered as what he is by nature. One might think that God, perhaps, yearns for and needs the creatures he produces, in something like the way in which many people yearn for and need to have children. Yet Aquinas would not be able to make sense of this idea. For him, God lacks nothing as God, so he cannot be understood as creating things to satisfy some unfulfilled desire on his part. Aquinas would think of the contrary supposition as dragging God down to the level of a creature.

Aquinas also denies that God has to create because something external to him forces him to do so. By now, though, it should be obvious why he thinks in this way. Given his notion of God as Creator, Aquinas takes anything other than God to be or to have been a creature of God. And he thinks that there can be no causal effect from creatures to God. His view is that everything that creatures of God are and do derives from God and that there is, therefore, no possibility of creatures acting so as to modify God in any way. That, to repeat, is because he thinks that *everything* that creatures of God are and do derives from God. In Aquinas's view, their doing is, therefore, always something caused by God (as making it to be). Many people have wanted to say that creatures can exert a causal influence on God. Abstracting for the moment, however, from what he thinks about Jesus of Nazareth (whom he takes to be God incarnate, as I stress in chapter 9), Aquinas is adamant that, with an eye on agent causality, the causal direction always has to be from God to creatures. One might, of course, produce something that goes on to have a causal effect on one. I might, for example, make a cuckoo clock that subsequently falls from my wall and renders me unconscious. Or I might father children who go on to have all sorts of causal effects on me (many, perhaps, wished for by me). But examples such as these are positively misleading when it comes to understanding the causal relationship between God and creatures, or so Aquinas thinks. For he does not think of God as a member of the universe able to be acted on by things in it as I can be acted on by a cuckoo clock or my children. He thinks of God as completely transcending the universe and as (although not of necessity) causally making *to be* all of its inhabitants and their operations.

So Aquinas thinks that God is not *essentially* the Creator of things. Something else he maintains is that God is not something that brings about any change or modification in creatures. He certainly thinks that all real changes undergone by creatures can be attributed to God as the cause of the *esse* of creatures and of their operations.[17] Yet he does not think that for God to create is for him to change anything. Why? Because he takes God's creative act to make something to be from nothing without acting on anything preexistent so as to change or modify it. We sometimes use the verb "create" when talking about people and what they produce. Hence, for example, we might speak of the "creations" of great painters or architects. Yet painters and architects need materials with which to work (paint, canvases, stones, and so on). And their creating always amounts to altering something. According to Aquinas, however, such is never so (and could never be so) when it comes to God creating. He thinks that God creates *ex nihilo* (from nothing). He does not, of course, think that there is some peculiar stuff called "nothing" on which God acts when creating. Nor does he conceive of "nothing" as some real alternative to there being things with *esse* (he would, I am certain, have recognized and appreciated the humor and the nonsense in chapter 7 of Lewis Carroll's *Alice through the Looking Glass* and its talk about nobody walking faster than someone else and therefore, of necessity, arriving beforehand).[18] His point is that God, as Creator, brings it about that things have *esse*, period. When a virus makes me sick, it brings it about that I am sick. When I close a door, I bring it about that a door is closed. In cases like this, thinks Aquinas, we have agent causation that brings about a change in something. For Aquinas, though, this is not what we have as God creates. We have a case of agent causation that is unique: one in which something receives the forms that it has (both substantial and accidental) without any change in it being caused by what accounts for its having these forms. Or as Aquinas puts it: "To be created is not to be produced through a motion or mutation which works on something that already exists, as is the limited causality which produces some sorts of being" (ST 1a.45.3 [Blackfriars edition, 8.00]). Aquinas, so we might say, takes God to make no *difference* to anything insofar as he creates. You make a difference to something only insofar as it exists as something for you to encounter as you tinker with it or modify it in some way. When thinking of God as Creator, however, Aquinas is not thinking of creatures as preexisting God or as being tinkered with or modified by him in any way (as we shall see, this thought is one on which Aquinas relies on in a big way when talking about God and human freedom).

Finally, and for present purposes, we need to note what Aquinas thinks that God is not as he presents his views on the topic of divine simplicity.

Divine Simplicity

A presiding teaching of Aquinas is that God is entirely simple. Here I am merely going to explain what he means by that teaching in (forgive the pun) simple terms.[19]

First, that God is simple is, for Aquinas, something that follows from the notion that God is the unchangeable source of the *esse* of created things. It is not an obviously biblical teaching, but Aquinas regards it as one to which we should be lead as we reflect on what the Bible says about God and on what we can say about God even without reference to divine revelation.[20]

Second, when Aquinas says that God is simple he is most certainly not attempting to *describe* God as having an intelligible property called "simplicity." He is concerned only to *deny* that God is complex in certain specific ways. This is obvious from, for example, the *Summa Theologiae*, in which Aquinas turns to the notion of divine simplicity just after saying, "We cannot know what God is, only what he is not. We must therefore consider the ways in which God does not exist rather than the ways in which he does" (ST 1a.3, prologue [Davies and Leftow 2006: 28]).

In saying that God is simple Aquinas means three things: (a) that God is *not* changeable, (b) that God is *not* an individual belonging to a natural kind, and (c) that God is *not* created.

Not changeable since, as the source of the *esse* of all changing things (as the Creator of a world in which things undergo substantial and accidental changes), God, for Aquinas, has to lie beyond any possibility of change on pain of being part of his created order. Real change is, for Aquinas, always a matter of something in the universe that is potentially thus-and-so coming to be actually thus-and-so, and always by virtue of agents within the universe (and by virtue of God).

Not an individual belonging to a natural kind since Aquinas takes all such things to be materially distinguishable (as in "this dog as opposed to that dog" or "this tree as opposed to that one"). Hardly being original, given what we read in the Bible, Aquinas takes God to be nonmaterial.[21] He therefore concludes that God is no individual belonging to a natural kind. What accounts for it being true that, say, two cats are *two* cats and not one cat? It cannot be their nature as felines since this is something they share. Could it be that cat A and cat B are different because of different accidental forms had by them? Aquinas thinks not since this suggestion would already presuppose a distinction between A and B (on the surely correct principle that what Aquinas means by "accidental forms" cannot serve to distinguish between A and B unless they are already distinct to start with). For Aquinas, we can distinguish between A and B only insofar as we can take them to be materially distinct. The numerical difference between A and B is, for Aquinas, grounded not in differences of form (substantial or accidental) but in matter, which Aquinas does not take to be a form. What does he take it to be? That is hard to explain since he does not take it to be a form and since he takes only forms to be intelligible. He does not think of matter as being what we might call "stuff" (as in the stuff left in a test tube after an experiment). Such stuff would, he thinks, always have form. His view seems to be that matter, considered as what individuates things, is something we can only point to rather than conceptualize. Let me give an example. Suppose that we are looking at a sofa. A cat walks behind it from the right and then emerges at the left. Is it the same cat that emerges? How are we supposed to know? Aquinas thinks that we can know that it is the same cat only by tracking it materially, by living with it, by stroking it, and by recognizing it as something able to change in various ways. Tracking a cat, of course, cannot intelligibly be thought of as (a) tracking a cat, and (b) tracking its matter (as we might distinguish between tracking Bill and tracking Ben). In Aquinas's view, however, we can and do distinguish between objects in the universe, and we do so only insofar as we can (at least potentially) lay hands on them in some way, what I have called "tracking" them. And with this thought in mind Aquinas denies that God is one of many objects on which we might get our hands and take to be one of a natural kind.[22]

Not created because not existing as derived from anything. If God is the source of the *esse* of all things whose nature (*essentia*) can be distinguished from their existence or being (*esse*), then, Aquinas reasons, God cannot be thought of as something able not to be. God, says Aquinas, "is not only his own essence but also his own existence" (ST 1a.3.4). Aquinas does not here mean that "existing" is a term that we can understand as *describing* God, as we can, for example, understand "agile" as describing a particular human being. His point is that, considered as the Creator, God cannot be thought of as having existence derived from another—a thought that Aquinas often expresses by saying that, if asked what God is, we can say that God is *ipsum esse subsistens* (subsisting being itself). Again, though, I emphasize that this phrase is not offered by Aquinas as a *description* of God (in the ordinary sense of "description" according to which a description of X picks something out and notes what Aquinas would have called its substantial and accidental forms or features). In Aquinas's view, to call God *ipsum esse subsistens* is primarily to assert that, whatever else we say about God, we should deny that he is something the existence of which is caused by what is not God. Aquinas, of course, does not mean that God's existence is caused by God himself. He means that God is not caused to exist by anything. And he means nothing more than that. In this sense, his teaching that there is no distinction in God between *essentia* and *esse* is very much an exercise in negative theology—talk about God intended to say what God is not.[23]

Moving On

Yet Aquinas does not think that we are confined only to saying what God is not. We have already seen that he takes "God is an agent cause" to be literally true (albeit that he does not think that God is *essentially* an agent cause since he believes that God does not *have* to create in order to be what he is by nature). And he argues in various places that we cannot regard all talk of God as telling us that God is not this, that, or the other. An obvious text to note is ST 1a.13.2, where Aquinas maintains that, for example, "God is living" cannot be construed along the lines "God is not something inanimate." And he thinks the same when it comes to "God is good." In Aquinas's view, this statement is not merely saying "God is not bad." Aquinas takes it to be saying something true and positive with respect to God. In the next chapter I shall try to explain how he develops this thought.

6

God's Perfection and Goodness

If God is the Creator of everything that has *esse*, if God is *ipsum esse subsistens*, and if God accounts for there being any universe at all (for there being something rather than nothing), how can we seriously think of ourselves as being able to know what he is? Or how can we take ourselves to say anything about God that is literally true? Aquinas is acutely aware of these questions. Indeed, you might say that he has set himself up for them to be posed to him. There have been theists who have spoken about God as if he were a part of the universe, something to be thought of as an individual that we can single out among many other individuals. To be sure, such thinkers always insist that God is unique in various ways. But the ways in question always seem to amount to a matter of degree—along the lines: I know some facts; yet lots of people know more than I do; and God knows even more than them. For people thinking in this way there is no obvious problem when it comes to our knowledge and talk about God. For them, God is just one more object alongside others. As we have seen, however, this is not how Aquinas thinks of God. So he has questions to answer that other theists do not, which is why I say that he might be thought of as having set himself up for them. In the present chapter I am chiefly concerned with what Aquinas has to say about the propositions "God is perfect" and "God is good." To start with, however, I need to say something about what Aquinas has to say about what we might call "God-talk in general."

Talking about God

In *The Coherence of Theism* Richard Swinburne suggests that in Aquinas's view terms used when talking of both God and creatures have the same meaning or sense. Aquinas's position, says Swinburne, "boils down to that of Scotus," whom Swinburne describes as teaching that "the meaning of words such as 'good' and 'wise' is learnt by seeing them applied in mundane situations. The only difference when we use them in theology is that we combine them in unusual ways or suppose the properties denoted to exist in higher degrees than in mundane objects to which we originally applied the words."[1] And there is a sense in which Swinburne is right in what he says of Aquinas here. For Aquinas certainly does not believe that "—— is F," said of both God and a creature, does not in each case mean the same thing, that in "John is good" and "God is good," for example, the phrase "is good" is to be regarded as equivocal (as not signifying anything at all similar, as when we speak of a bank when talking of both a place in which we keep our money and of what can be found alongside a river).[2] According to Aquinas, not all terms are said of God and creatures in a purely equivocal manner. "A name," he observes, "is predicated of some being uselessly unless through that name we understand something of the being. But if names are said of God and creatures in a purely equivocal way, we understand nothing of God through those names; for the meanings of those names are known to us solely to the extent that they are said of creatures. In vain, therefore, would it be said or proved of God that He is a being, good, or the like" (SCG 1.33).[3]

In other words, Aquinas thinks that, in some sense of "same sense," there are words that we can use when speaking of both God and creatures that bear the same sense. "Bank" in "HSBC bank" and "riverbank" does not in any sense have the same sense. It is a mere accident of language that the same word has come to be used with respect to completely different things.[4] But there are, Aquinas holds, terms or words properly used to talk of both God and creatures that are not in this way unrelated in sense or meaning. Aquinas, I should note, allows for the propriety of speaking of God in ways that are not literally true. He does not, for example, object to sentences like "God is a mighty fortress," though he certainly does not believe that God is really made of stone or that he has some particular spatiotemporal location. For Aquinas, one can usefully and truly speak of God by means of metaphors or similes (cf. ST 1a.1.9). Yet he also thinks that it is possible to speak literally of God.[5] And, since he takes all our talk of God to employ words that we first of all use when speaking of creatures (at one point he writes "we cannot speak of God at all except in the language we use of creatures"; ST 1a.13.5), he concludes that some of these words can be used to speak truly and literally of God. Most commonly he does so when dealing with arguments to the effect that God is X, Y, or Z. His practice here emerges from the quotation from him provided in the paragraph above. You can also find the same approach exemplified in ST 1a.13, which is devoted to a discussion of what Aquinas calls "the divine names" (de nominibus dei) and which is, perhaps, the best introduction to Aquinas's general approach to talking about God (since it is one of his last discussions of the topic).[6] Here he insists that "we are not merely equivocating" when we use the same word of God and a creature "for if this were so we could never argue from statements about creatures to statements about God." By the same token, thinks Aquinas, we cannot conclude from what we know about creatures to truths about God if we are assuming that all words used of God and of creatures are to be understood equivocally. And we have now seen how Aquinas works with this thought when speaking of God as Creator. For Aquinas, God creates by causing. Yet can we think of "cause" when predicated of God as having no meaning in common with its use when, for example, we speak of an explosion as causing the deaths of certain people? Obviously not. Or, at least, not if we are concerned to argue for the existence of God by invoking the term "cause" as it is usually used without reference to God. If the word "cause" when applied to God bears no meaning in common with its use when talking of creaturely causes, then why use it with respect to God?

Yet, as Swinburne seems not to have grasped, Aquinas holds that there is a serious sense in which words used to talk about creatures do not have the same sense as they do when used to speak truly of God.[7] Remember what I noted earlier concerning Aquinas on God's simplicity. Swinburne seems to take sentences like "God is good" as ascribing a property to God. Indeed, Swinburne's whole approach to God, in common with that of many contemporary philosophers, seems to be property-oriented. For him, God has various properties. Aquinas, however, does not speak in these terms. As I have noted, he prefers to talk about forms (accidental and substantial). And he denies that God has any accidental forms. He also denies that there is in reality anything distinct when it comes to what is variously affirmed in talk of God's essence (as in "God is good," "God is alive," "God knows"—all, for Aquinas, being true statements concerning what God is essentially). In modern English you might fairly put this by saying that God has no properties. To say that something has a property is surely to say that what it is can be distinguished from the individual that it is, that properties (whether substantial or accidental) are had by individuals and are not identical with them. Yet, as we have seen, Aquinas denies that there is any distinction in God between the individual and its nature. For him, there is no question of God having properties distinguishable from himself or distinguishable from each other. Given the way in which we normally talk of things, we will inevitably often speak of God as if this were false—as if God had properties that really are distinguishable from each other and from himself. Yet, Aquinas thinks, it cannot be so. Or as he says in one place, "God is both simple, like a form, and subsistent, like something concrete. So, we sometimes refer to him by abstract nouns (to indicate his simplicity) while at other times we refer to him by concrete nouns (to indicate his subsistence and completeness)—though neither way of speaking measures up to his way of being, for in this life we do not know him as he is in himself" (ST 1a.13.1 [Davies and Leftow 2006: 140]). What Aquinas means here is that, for example, the proposition "God is goodness" is no less true than "God is good," that each is as appropriate to advance as the other. And this thought, derived from what Aquinas thinks of divine simplicity, is what lies behind his insistence that we cannot apply terms to God and creatures univocally. As he makes the point himself:

> The words denoting perfections that we use in speaking of creatures all differ in meaning and each one signifies a perfection as something distinct from all others. Thus when we say that a man is wise, we signify his wisdom as something distinct from the other things said about him—his essence, for example, his powers, or his existence. But when we use the word "wise" when talking about God we do not intend to signify something distinct from his essence, power or existence. When we predicate "wise" of a human being we, so to speak, circumscribe and define the limits of the aspect of human beings that it signifies. But this is not so when we predicate "wise" of God. What it signifies in him is not confined by the meaning of our word but goes beyond it. So, it is clear that we do not use "wise" in the same sense of God and people, *and the same goes for all other words.* So we cannot use them univocally of God and creatures. (ST 1a.13.5 [Davies and Leftow 2006: 148, emphasis added])

Aquinas does not here mean that different terms used to say what God literally is are, in fact, synonymous. He does not, for example, think that "wise" and "good" when used to speak of God mean exactly the same thing, as is the case with, for example, "sick" and "ill," or "student" and "pupil," or "buy" and "purchase" (cf. ST 1a.13.4). His point is that when it comes to what God is, terms or phrases that are not synonymous can be used to speak truly about what is really one and the same thing, as when we speak of "the Morning Star" and "the Evening Star" when referring to the planet Venus, or as when we speak of Mark Twain and Samuel Clemens when thinking of the author of *Huckleberry Finn.*

What I have just been saying can be summarized by observing that Aquinas takes us to be able to speak of God without doing so either univocally or purely equivocally. His view is that we can truly speak of God in nonmetaphorical ways, and that in doing so we are neither univocally nor equivocally using words that we apply to both God and creatures. We can, says Aquinas, use familiar words that we employ when referring to creatures to talk of God *analogically.*

Aquinas's notion of analogy has been discussed at great length by many of those who have commented on him.[8] Yet it is not, I think, something very hard to explain, in its mature form anyway—as we find it, for example, in the *Summa Theologiae.* Here Aquinas speaks of "univocal," "equivocal," and "analogical" as a way of distinguishing between our uses of certain words. We have "dog," as in Fido and Rover: univocal. We have "bank," as in where I put my money and what is alongside a river: equivocal. And we have, for example, "good." When it comes to "good" as predicated of God and creatures, Aquinas thinks that the word is to be understood analogically. Aquinas does not think that everything we call good is exactly like everything else that we call good. He does not, as I have said, take "goodness" to be a single property had by all good things (as, say, being plastic is a single property had by all plastic things). On the other hand, he does not think that we are always necessarily punning or equivocating when describing different things as good, or when speaking of God as good. In his view, and as I noted above, things like good doctors, good weather, good health, and good children do not have any obvious property in common. But neither are they wholly unalike. This notion, of course, is merely picking up on our, in fact, often using one and the same term or word on different occasions without meaning exactly the same by it and without meaning something completely different either. An example would be "love" as in "I love my wife," "I love my job," and "I love fried bacon." The love of spouses for each other is, presumably, not exactly like (or, perhaps, not desirably like) the love that someone might have for a job or for bacon (each of these, in turn, being distinguishable from each other). But neither is it completely different. There are, as one might put it, threads of connection that can be teased out.

God Is Perfect

With all of that behind us, let me now turn to Aquinas's approach to the proposition "God is perfect." What might he take that proposition to mean? Could he, for example, take it to mean that God is a perfect example of the kind to which he belongs, a perfect specimen, so to speak? Obviously not. Aquinas denies that God belongs to a (natural) kind of any sort as, for example, you and I do.[9] As we have seen, for him God is simple or noncomposite. What God is cannot be distinguished from the individual that he is. In terms of this account, and as Aquinas well sees, there can be no question of God being a perfect X, Y, or Z.

Actually, Aquinas acknowledges a possible and general objection to speaking of God as perfect. He writes: "'Perfect' does not seem a suitable term to apply to God. Its literal meaning is 'thoroughly made', but we would not say that God is made. So we should not say that he is perfect" (ST 1a.4.1).[10] Given that Aquinas does want to speak of God as perfect one might expect him to give this argument very short shrift. But he does not. Instead he says: "What is not made cannot properly be called perfect. But as Gregory says, 'stammering, we echo the heights of God as best we can'" (ST 1a.4.1 ad 1).[11] This remark is a telling one and squares well with Aquinas's whole general approach to God— one that continually distinguishes between creatures and God, and between the knowledge that we have with respect to each of them. At any rate, it clearly shows that Aquinas certainly does not think of God's perfection as an attribute of some sort around which we can get our minds (as we can, for example, get our minds around the attributes of a piece of pasta).

Instead, he approaches the topic of God's perfection in rather formal terms. For Aquinas, "perfect," like "good," does not single out any particular empirical (or nonempirical) property. Generally speaking, so he thinks, it signifies "not being able to be improved" or "being fully actual." For Aquinas, something is a perfect X insofar as there is no gap between what it actually is and what it could be, and could desirably be, but is not. And, so he adds, God can be said to be perfect because he is fully actual (because he is not something with untapped potential that could be actualized). His meaning here is what he is declaring in his teaching that God is *ipsum esse subsistens*—that God is the source of everything having *esse* and therefore has to be thought of as lacking potentiality or as being unchangeable. Or as Aquinas himself observes: "The first origin of all activity must be the most actual, and therefore the most perfect of all things. For we call things perfect when they have achieved actuality (a perfect thing being that in which nothing required by its particular mode of perfection fails to exist)" (ST 1a.4.1).

Aquinas is not here saying that perfection is an intelligible attribute predicable of God (as in "focus on the particular property that all perfect things have, insofar as they are perfect, and then think of God as having it"). Rather, he is saying something *negative*: that, whatever God is, he cannot be thought of as subject to improvement, that there is with God no "could and would desirably be thus-and-so, but is not."[12] This observation is subject to qualification since

Aquinas also argues that God is perfect as containing in himself the perfections of creatures. But I am now going to put that thought on hold as I turn to what Aquinas says about "God is good," since the thought is contained in his reflections on that proposition.

God Is Good

From what we have seen, you will, I hope, realize that Aquinas does not take "God is good" to assert that God has a certain property distinguishable from himself and from other properties had by him. For Aquinas, "God is good" tells us what God is essentially or by nature, and, for Aquinas, God *is* his essence or nature (or, better, God *cannot be thought of* as something other than his essence or nature).[13] My cat might be gray, but his grayness can be distinguished from him (he would not cease to exist if he became completely bald). For Aquinas, however, God's goodness and God himself are not similarly distinguishable. Indeed, so he also wants to say, and as we have seen him saying, God's goodness and God's existence (*esse*) are not distinguishable either. We can, therefore, take it for granted that Aquinas takes "God is good" to mean something very different indeed from what we have in mind when picking out objects in the universe and calling them good. He certainly thinks that serious connections of meaning can be traced between "God is good" and "X, some creature of God, is good." But Aquinas also wants to bear in mind that there have to be certain important differences between what it is for God to be good and what it is for anything else to be so. That is why I had to talk above about Aquinas on univocity, equivocity, and analogy.

So what is Aquinas's basic take on "God is good"? As I have said, Aquinas regards "good" as an attributive adjective, not one that picks out some particular property had by all good things. And this thought comes into play when Aquinas turns directly to the question of God's goodness, as does his claim that the fundamental meaning of "good" is "desirable" or "attractive." Aquinas thinks that, regardless of what we are talking about, to speak of it as good is always to say that it is somehow desirable or attractive. In this sense, though in this sense *only*, he thinks that calling things good is always to say the same thing of them. He does not, as I have noted, suppose that a good opera singer looks like a good holiday, or that a healthy (and, in this sense, good) cat looks like a healthy (and, in this sense, good) cactus. Nor does he think, as some have done, that goodness is a nonnatural property had by all good things while perceptible only to something called intuition.[14] Yet he does think that by focusing on what he takes to be the basic meaning of "good" (i.e., "attractive" or "desirable") we can say something significant and true when it comes to God's goodness. To appreciate how this is so, we can turn to ST 1a.6.1.[15] Here Aquinas asks whether we can associate goodness with God. Quoting the sentence "the good is what everything desires," he first raises the argument that God cannot be good since "not everything desires God, because not everything knows him, and one can only desire what one knows." Yet, so Aquinas goes on to say, "we should especially associate goodness with God" and he reasons to this conclusion as follows:

> Something is good insofar as it is desirable. But everything desires its perfection, and an effect's perfection and form consists in resembling its efficient cause (since every efficient cause produces an effect like itself). So an efficient cause is desirable and may be called good because what is desired from it is that the effect share its goodness by resembling it. Clearly then, since God is the first efficient cause of everything, goodness and desirability belong to him.[16]

Perhaps the key sentence here is "every efficient cause produces an effect like itself," which seems palpably false since we can think of efficient causes that do not produce effects like themselves. By "efficient cause" here Aquinas is referring to what I spoke about earlier when talking about "agent causes," yet what Aquinas means by an "agent cause" surely does not always produce its like. A house does not look like a builder, does it? And a devastated city does not look like the earthquake that leveled it, does it? Obviously not.

Yet, and as I have tried to explain, we should not assume that Aquinas supposes otherwise. In the above quotation, "every efficient cause produces an effect like itself" is translating the Latin *omne agens agat sibi simile*, which can be most accurately translated as "every agent makes its like" but which is not asking us to believe that, in the sense in which, for example, human babies resemble their parents, all effects of agent causes resemble their agent causes.[17] Rather, it is asking us to view the effects of agent causes as the agent causes expressing themselves in something other than themselves, as showing forth what they are insofar as they operate in or on something else. Aquinas thinks that the effects of some agent causes really do resemble them as closely as children and their parents do (this being an obvious example of agent causation in which effects literally look like their causes). Frequently, though, he does not presume that such will be the case. When dying from the effects of sulfuric acid, I do not look like sulfuric acid, and so on. What can, however, be said, thinks Aquinas, is that my dying from the effects of sulfuric acid can be accounted for in terms of sulfuric acid and its nature and, therefore, shows us what sulfuric acid is *when at work in me*. Generally speaking, thinks Aquinas, we learn about the nature of agent causes by studying their effects.

So in the passage from ST 1a.6.1 noted above, Aquinas is suggesting that, insofar as creatures aim and attain to what is desirable for them, they reflect what God is as bringing it about that they do so, since he is the source of all that they are and all that they succeed in being. The idea here is that the good at which creatures aim and sometimes obtain is in God as their maker before it is in them. Or, as Herbert McCabe writes, Aquinas's position can be expressed as follows:

> God is the ultimate maker, and, as such, the ultimately desirable, the ultimate good. Every creature, just in naturally tending to its own goodness, is seeking God as what ultimately intends it as its maker. And this is what, for Aquinas, the goodness of God is first of all about: it is the goodness, the attractiveness or desirability inseparable from being Creator. God is the *omega* because he is the *alpha*, the end because he is the beginning. God is good because he is Creator...in the metaphysical sense that, being Creator, he must be the ultimate object of our desire, without which we would have no desires.[18]

Aquinas is not saying that God is good just because he produces good things. Indeed, he expressly denies that we can properly argue that God is F only because God produces things that are F. God produces rocks, but should we, therefore, conclude that God is a rock? Evidently not, at least for Aquinas (cf. ST 1a.13.2). But we can, he thinks, sensibly say that, as the Creator of all creatures, God accounts for all the perfections that they have and aim for, and that these reflect him as their Maker. Or, as Aquinas sometimes says, the perfections of creatures exist in God in a "higher" (i.e., noncreaturely) way.

God's Moral Goodness

At this point you might well be wondering how Aquinas thinks of what has often been said of God's goodness: that it amounts to moral goodness, that to call God "good" is to commend him as being morally so. Indeed, and as we saw in chapter 1, for many people (both critics and fans of belief in God) "God is good" simply and obviously means that God is morally good. This is not how Aquinas thinks, however—or at least not in any straightforward sense.

What does Aquinas think that we are doing when we commend people morally?[19] His answer is that we are ascribing virtues to them. What does he mean by "virtue"? He means a disposition or settled way of acting (in his language, a *habitus*) that leads us to make choices that generally contribute to our well-being or happiness considered as human beings.[20] Virtues, Aquinas thinks, are what we need in order to flourish as animals of the particular kind that we are, and (as did Aristotle) he identifies four of them in particular: prudence, justice, temperance, and fortitude. He thinks that people can possess other virtues comparable to (though not as important as) those just mentioned. As I shall later explain, he also thinks that there are theological virtues (faith, hope, and charity), which fit us for living with God. At the level of what we might call "philosophical ethics," however, it is the four so-called cardinal virtues that Aquinas takes chiefly to be present in morally good human beings. He takes their presence in people to enable them to make choices that contribute to their fulfilment as people. In this sense, Aquinas is a classic exponent of what moral philosophers today refer to as "virtue ethics." And he takes moral goodness in people to consist in them doing well as human beings living in the world and choosing to act in particular ways.

Now, Aquinas certainly does not think of God as a human being. Nor does he take God to live in the world. And he does not take God to choose in the way that people do. He thinks that we choose by going through a process of reflection leading us to act with respect to what we take ourselves to want and need. For Aquinas, our moral life is that of changeable beings ever seeking goods that they lack at various times. Yet God, he thinks, is the simple, unchangeable source of all the perfections of creatures. So it never occurs to Aquinas to consider whether God is morally good as having the virtues that make for our moral goodness. He turns to the topic of virtues in God in SCG 2.92. But here he merely makes explicit what is implicit in what he writes elsewhere—that moral goodness cannot be ascribed to God as it can to people. He says, for example, that one cannot rightly ascribe dispositions (Aquinas's *habitus*) to God, that there can be no moving to a better state when it comes to divinity, and that what contributes to human flourishing cannot possibly contribute to that of God. In SCG 2.93–94 Aquinas goes on to accept that what we think of as virtue in people can somehow be ascribed to God. He says, for example, that there is nothing preventing us from speaking of God as just. I shall return to this point below. For the moment, however, what needs to be stressed is that Aquinas is not easily to be cited as holding that God is morally good.

You might naturally assume that Aquinas must, therefore, conclude that God is morally bad. But he does not do this, and I presume that he does not do so since he is aware that to say that something is not thus-and-so is not to say that it is positively thus-and-so. An American citizen might say "I am not a Democrat." This does not imply that the person in question is a Republican. Someone else might say "I am not French." This does not imply that the speaker is Italian or Russian. Some have suggested that to speak of God as unchangeable is to say that God is inert (like a stone). But this, again, does not follow. And Aquinas seems to be perfectly aware of all of this. In denying that God is morally good as people can be morally good, he is not asserting that God is morally bad. As he strives to do in almost all of his writings, he is drawing attention to what God *cannot* be if he is, indeed, the Creator. When it comes to the issue of moral goodness, he is saying that we are bound to go wrong if we start by thinking of God as having (or even as accidentally lacking) human moral virtues. Given the *omne agens agat sibi simile* principle, Aquinas is happy to agree that human moral virtue, since it is caused to be by God, reflects God's nature. Yet Aquinas thinks that *all* instances of created goodness reflect what God is, which, in turn, means that *none* of them are to be taken as anything like what we might call a picture of God. For Aquinas, God is unpicturable and incomparable. And he is certainly not to be thought of as having human moral virtues as human beings have them. In this sense, Aquinas denies that God is morally good.

Some people would focus on moral goodness by taking it to amount to obedience to moral imperatives or obligations by which both people and God are presented and constrained. The idea here seems to be that we can somehow see that we (and God) are obliged to act thus-and-so and that moral obligations can be referred to by quoting sentences expressing necessary truths. Again, though, such is not Aquinas's view. He does sometimes speak of people having an obligation (*obligatio*), and he says that an obligation implies that a deed should be performed or refrained from (ST 2a2ae.89.7). But he does not have a notion of moral obligation at the heart of his ethical theory concerning human beings. As I have said, his key term here is "virtue" (and, correspondingly, "vice"). And he never suggests that God is bound by any obligations at all. Aquinas thinks of obligations as deriving from law, which he defines as "an ordinance of reason for the common good made by the authority who has care of the community and promulgated" (ST 1a2ae.90.4 [Blackfriars edition, 28.17]). Generally, therefore, Aquinas thinks of obligations as binding on human beings with respect to a human legislator (and therefore as not binding on God). To be sure, with the notion of natural law he famously extends the sense of law to speak of what is promulgated by God. But he never suggests that there is any law to which God should or does conform. In this sense, also, he is not of the view that God is morally good. Swinburne tells us that "all theists hold that God is perfectly good"—meaning that God "does whatever it is of overriding importance that he should do."[21] For Swinburne, "God is so constituted that he always does the morally best action (when there is one), and no morally bad action."[22] Swinburne also observes that a (morally) good act is one that is obligatory, one that an agent ought to do or has a duty to do.[23] Applied to God, however, such a way of talking is very foreign to Aquinas (regardless of how natural it may seem to theists such as Swinburne). He positively never talks about divine goodness with mention of duties or obligations had by God. The notion of God as subject to duties or obligations (and as acting in accordance with them) would, I think, have been thought of by him as an unfortunate lapse into anthropomorphism, as reducing God to the level of a human creature.

Divine Justice

Yet there are terms that Aquinas (a) would have recognized as designating human virtues and (b) is happy to use with reference to God. Does this undermine what I have been saying above? The answer I think is no, as we can see by turning to one telling example—the proposition "God is just," a proposition that Aquinas certainly endorses (as one might expect him to if only on biblical grounds).

Here, so one might think, we have a clear case of Aquinas bringing God within the realm of what might be thought of as that of moral agents, since justice is one of the key human virtues highlighted by Aristotle. If Aquinas thinks that God is just, is he not presuming that God is indeed subject to familiar moral evaluation and that his goodness lies in him being so and behaving well by a standard to which he manages to conform? In approaching this question, let me turn to ST 1a.21.1, which asks, "Is God just?" (*utrum in Deo sit justitia*).[24]

Aquinas's answer to this question starts by distinguishing in Aristotelian fashion between two kinds of justice: commutative and distributive. He takes commutative justice to consist in "mutual giving and receiving." Here he has in mind what is involved in, for example, my purchasing a car from you and then paying you for it, or my borrowing money from you and then returning it. If I buy a car from you, justice requires that I pay you what I owe you (all things being equal).[25] And if I borrow money from you, justice would seem to require that I pay you back (all things being equal). Yet, says Aquinas, "this kind of justice does not belong to God." Why not? Because, Aquinas argues, God is not in debt to any human being, because God has not received anything from any creature, and because the "receiving from" relation always has nothing but creatures at the receiving end when it comes to God and creatures. In this context Aquinas quotes St. Paul: "Who has given him anything first, and shall there be a recompense for such a person?"[26] He might, of course, also have quoted himself and what he says (and what we have seen him saying above) about God as Creator.

What, though, of distributive justice? "This kind of justice," says Aquinas, "consists in sharing out." It is "the justice by which a ruler or administrator distributes to each on the basis of merit" (*secundum suam dignitatem*). Here Aquinas seems to be thinking of a giving from one who is not in debt, a giving that somehow befits one or many on whom it is bestowed. An example would be the way in which parents provide for their children. Parents are not in debt to their children, but they rightly strive to provide for their needs. They aim to enable them to flourish considered as what they are. And, with this sense of justice in mind, says Aquinas, God can be thought of as just. But how so?

Certainly not because God is just in exactly the same sense as human parents caring for their children might be thought of as just. We have already seen that, for Aquinas, attributes ascribed to God do not really signify anything other than God's essence, which is his individual self. So, for him, God is not a just X or a just Y—something that Aquinas takes for granted by the time he writes ST 1a.21. Again, in this text Aquinas makes it clear that he does not take God to be just as obeying some law requiring justice from him. As he writes: "He does justly what he does according to his will (as we do justly what we do according to law). But we, of course, do things according to the law of someone superior to us, while God is a law unto himself [*Deus autem sibi ipsi est lex*]."[27] For Aquinas, God's justice is in no sense a matter of obedience. What, then, does it amount to? According to Aquinas, it amounts to (a) God creating things ordered to him (and therefore befitting him) and (b) God creating things ordered in a way that befits them. Or, as Aquinas himself writes at 1a.21.1 ad 3:

> We can mark a double order in things: the ordering of all creatures to God, and their being ordered among themselves (e.g., parts to wholes, accidents to substances, and everything to its end). So, throughout God's work we can consider a double due: what is owing to God, and what is owing to creatures, and under both respects God gives what is due. It is his due that things should fulfil what his wisdom and will require for them, and that they should manifest his goodness. In this way his justice regards what befits him, as he renders to himself what he owes himself. There is also a creature's due to have what is ordered to it—that, for example, people should have hands and that animals should serve them. In this way God works according to justice in giving to each what its constitution and condition require. Yet this due is based on the first. For to each is owing what is settled for it in the plan of God's wisdom. Though God renders what is owing on this count, he is not anyone's debtor. For everything is ordained to him, not he to anything else.

The argument here seems to be: (1) it is right that creatures should act as God wills and reflect his goodness; (2) God brings it about that they do so and, in this sense, brings about what is owed; (3) it is right for parts of creation to be ordered to other parts in certain ways; (4) God brings it about that parts of creation are ordered to other parts in certain ways and, in this sense, brings about what is owed; (5) so justice is attributable to God.[28]

Now, whatever the merits of this argument may be, one thing seems abundantly clear: Aquinas is not thinking of divine justice as on a level with the justice ascribable to just people. He conceives of that as an accident and as one had by us as we pay what we owe or do as some law requires us to do. In ascribing justice to God, however, all Aquinas retains of this notion is that of bringing about what is owed, and he does so on the assumption that what is and what is not owed always derives from God's will. Whether you describe the result as employing a highly attenuated notion of justice (given the contexts in which we normally speak of people being just) or as ascribing justice to God in a higher sense than it has when possessed by people does not matter for my present purposes. What matters is that we should recognize that, at a point where someone (e.g., Swinburne) might expect Aquinas to attribute justice to God just as one might attribute it to a right thinking high court judge, he does not. Or, to put matters another way, God's justice is not, for Aquinas, a matter of him being morally well behaved.

And yet, so one might say (and as many have), God seems responsible for a terrible amount of badness. Does this not force us to regard him as bad? Or does it not force us to conclude that he cannot exist? These questions take us to the topic of God and causation, to which I now turn.

7

The Creator and Evil

We have seen that Aquinas takes God to be the cause of the *esse* of everything *having* (as opposed to *being*) *esse*. We have also seen how he maintains that there is no internal or external compulsion leading God to be this. In other words, Aquinas does not think that God has to create. He puts this point by saying that God's creative act is free. "Free choice," he writes, "is said in relation to the things that one wills, not of necessity, but of one's own accord.... But God wills things other than himself without necessity.... Therefore, to have free choice befits God" (SCG 1.88).[1] Aquinas, as you might now expect, takes willing in God to be seriously different from willing in creatures. We will to do things (or to produce things) as changeable and temporal individuals. And we do so on the basis of some reflection, and with an eye on some good we are seeking but have not obtained. As we have seen, however, Aquinas does not think of God as a changeable and temporal individual. So he does not take God's action to follow from any reflection. Nor does he take it to spring from a desire on God's part to obtain a good that he lacks. Be that as it may, Aquinas thinks it proper to speak of God's creating as free. That is because he thinks that God *does* create and that nothing in his nature, or anything acting on him, *forces* him to do so.[2]

Yet if God is the Creator in Aquinas's sense, must he not be causally responsible for evil or badness in any form? And if God is this, can anything be salvaged of the claim that God is good? Given what I said in the previous chapter you might imagine Aquinas replying, "Well,

God's goodness is not moral goodness, so even his causing of what is bad does not tell against it." But he does not take this line. He seems to think that directly to will evil as an end in itself is indicative of badness, for he often says that what is good (or goodness in general) produces only what is good. And, when it comes to creation and God's causing of evil or badness, the approach he adopts is simply to deny that God causes evil directly and as an end in itself.

Philosophers other than Aquinas have defended this way of thinking by arguing that much that is evil or bad should be thought of as a necessary means to goods aimed at by God. The idea here is that God wants to produce certain goods, but cannot do so without also permitting certain evils, and there is, as we shall soon see, a sense in which Aquinas does buy into this argument. He does not do so, however (and this is a point I should stress), insofar as the argument is construed as suggesting that God's creating what is good ever involves him in having to put up with there being evil. We shall, perhaps, best understand why this is the case by noting what Aquinas takes God's omnipotence to involve.[3]

Omnipotence

Aquinas holds that God is omnipotent or all powerful.[4] In doing so, he does not mean (although others have meant) that one can tack onto the phrase "God can" any string of words signifying a logically possible feat. "Catch a train" seems to signify a logically possible feat. I, at any rate, can and often do catch trains. But it would obviously be ludicrous to suppose that God can catch a train. And there are many other things that it would be ludicrous to suppose that God can do (e.g., go for a summer holiday, climb a mountain, run a mile, eat roast beef, speak on the telephone, ride a bicycle, bloom in the springtime, and so on). I doubt that theists of any persuasion would deny any of this, and for obvious reasons (one being that God is traditionally taken to be essentially noncorporeal).

Some theists have seemed to suggest that God is omnipotent in that he can somehow override logic so as, for example, to make it to be true that what we would take to be a logical contradiction is not so. But Aquinas is firmly set against this way of thinking. Indeed, his whole approach to divine omnipotence rests on the assumption that logical contradictions cannot be true. More specifically, it rests on the assumption that there can be nothing describable by a phrase that is logically contradictory.[5] Aquinas takes it for granted that there cannot, for example, be people who are also iguanas, or dogs who are also cats, or tigers who both exist and do not exist. So he does not take God's omnipotence to extend to the making (creating) of such "things."

His view is that God is omnipotent in that he can make *to be* anything *the existence of which* does not involve a logical contradiction. Can God create wooden cotton candy? Can he create mammalian trees? Aquinas thinks not (though these are not examples that he uses). He does, however, think that if something can be intelligibly thought to be, then God can make it to be. Or, as he writes in the *Summa Contra Gentiles*:

> God's power is through itself the cause of being, and the act of being
> [*esse*] is his proper effect.... Hence, his power reaches out to all
> things with which the notion of being is not incompatible; for if
> God's power were limited to some particular effect, he would not be
> through himself the cause of a being as such, but of this particular
> being. Now, the opposite of being, namely, non-being, is
> incompatible with the notion of being. Hence, God can do all things
> which do not essentially include the notion of non-being, and such
> are those which involve a contradiction. (SCG 2.22)[6]

Created things with different natures have, thinks Aquinas, characteristic effects that reflect these natures (effects that sometimes allow us to infer particular causes from particular effects, as, for example, when we infer that someone died because of being poisoned by arsenic). Yet God, Aquinas maintains, can be said to have a "characteristic effect" only insofar as he makes all creatures to be—implying that, if we want to speak of anything as God's characteristic effect, we shall have to refer to *esse*. And thus, Aquinas holds, if something can be thought to be, then God can make it to be and, in this sense, is not constrained by means when it comes to his causal activity. Aquinas does not, for example, think that God must (absolutely speaking) put up with something bad in order to make something good. He thinks that God can produce a world that consists only of things that are good (albeit not things that are good as God is).

Evil Suffered and God's Causation

Yet there is a sense in which Aquinas does think of God as causally constrained. This is because of what he takes to be an implication of God having made a world of a certain kind. Aquinas finds no absurdity in the suggestion that God might have made a world in which nothing at all is bad (albeit that, as I have said, he does not think that God can make a world that is perfect as God is so).[7] But he does hold that, on the supposition that God has made a world of interacting things with certain definite natures, then certain goods willed by him shall necessarily derive from, or be bound up with, certain evils. Here we come to his notion of evil suffered.

By "evil suffered" I mean what Aquinas calls *malum poenae*. Literally translated, this phrase means "evil of punishment" and can be fully understood only in the light of things that Aquinas says concerning the origins of the human race.[8] For present purposes, though (getting an overall sense of Aquinas on the topic of God and evil), we need not, I think, dwell on these. Rather, we can note that Aquinas's notion of *malum poenae* corresponds to a high degree to what authors other than Aquinas have referred to as "naturally occurring evil"—that is to say, instances of badness that are not directly willed by people (hence my phrase "evil suffered").[9] Examples here would be human illness or animal suffering, or even the wilting of a plant (certainly bad for the plant).[10] To be sure, all of these things can sometimes be brought about because of choices that people make. My choosing to smoke, for example, might make me ill. And people can be responsible for the suffering of animals or the wilting of plants. But the occurrence of badness such as this, even as chosen by people, is part of a system in which effects come about naturalistically and not as determined by us. And, thinking about this fact, Aquinas (not someone who thinks that all that we do is determined by natural causes), concedes that God is somehow causally constrained. His view is that if, for example, God makes a world containing people and viruses of certain kinds, then people are inevitably going to become sick, or that if God creates carnivores, then there will be animals that get gnawed at and eaten, or that if God produces plants in our atmosphere, and with a lack of water, then the wilting of plants will occur.

Aquinas's idea here should seem fairly easy to understand, I would think, and should also seem uncontroversial. For all he is saying is that, as things are, some evil or badness is naturally explicable. Aquinas does not think that this evil has to be (anymore than he thinks that the universe has to be), but he does think of it as representing a constraint on God of a "given that" kind. God does not have to make people or viruses, but *given that* he has done so, human sickness is only to be expected. God does not have to make carnivores, but *given that* he has done so, they are going to have victims. God does not have to make plants, but *given that* he has done so, some are going to perish. At this point, however, an obvious question arises: is God causing evil insofar as he creates a world in which evil suffered can be found?

Aquinas thinks that God is not doing this. Or, more precisely, he thinks that, as author of a world containing evil suffered, God is not causing evil or badness directly and as an end in itself. Quite the contrary. In Aquinas's view, as the Creator of a world containing evil suffered, God is causing only what is good. Why does Aquinas reach this conclusion? Because of what he thinks about evil as a privation of *esse* (for which see chapter 4). The evil in evil suffered is not, thinks Aquinas, something made to exist, something with *esse*. Aquinas does not take it to be an illusion. Nor does he hold that evil suffered does not exist *period*. For him, people really do become sick, carnivorous predators really do squeeze the lifeblood out of other animals, and plants fall victim to pests, weather conditions, or a lack of water. But the badness in each of these cases is not, thinks Aquinas, something created by God. Rather, it amounts to a privation or lack of being explicable in terms of a good that is created. According to Aquinas, evil suffered occurs only insofar as there is a concomitant good in the light of which it can be explained. It is, he thinks, due to something that by being good in its way, causes something else to be bad in its way.[11] When confronted by an example of evil suffered (someone sick, say), we do not suppose a complete lack of causation. Rather, we look for something the action of which is to be found in something else exemplifying evil suffered. We look for something that is just doing well at the expense of something else. And this is how Aquinas thinks, which means that he takes evil suffered to be nothing but a matter of goodness and in no way a matter of badness being caused by God.

This may sound utterly paradoxical, but it is not so on reflection and with an eye on Aquinas's notion of *esse*. Consider the case of someone who is sick because of a virus of some kind. Here we have (a) a human being, (b) a human being ailing in some way, and (c) a virus at work. Now even a sick human being succeeds in being a human being and, in this sense, is good (in Aquinas's sense of "good"). And a virus able to make someone sick is also good considered as what it is. So where is the evil or badness in this scenario? For Aquinas, the evil here does not have the *esse* of a substance or a positive attribute or accident. For him, the evil in this scenario has no *esse* at all. The existing human being, considered as such, has *esse*. So does the virus (even if it itself should be ailing in some way, albeit not so much as to prevent it making someone sick). Hence the conclusion that with evil suffered there is (as in "has *esse*" or *in est*) only what is good (given the equation of "is good" and "has *esse*" or *in est*). As I have indicated, Aquinas has no problem with statements like "the evil of sickness exists," which is why he does not think of sickness and the like as an illusion. In the sense of *est* in which to say that something *est* is just to say that a certain true proposition can be formed (e.g., "there is sickness"), Aquinas most certainly holds that evil suffered can be spoken of as being. But not, he wants to add, as being a substance or a positive attribute or accident.

Hence, he concludes, evil suffered is not something creatively caused by God. Indeed, so he thinks, it cannot be this since it consists in a certain absence of what God as Creator causes—*esse*. Aquinas, of course, does not think that

God is causally unrelated to the occurrence of evil suffered. For him, evil suffered occurs as God creatively makes to be things that have *esse* and act in various ways. But this fact, Aquinas holds, does not imply that God causes evil
suffered as an end in itself (it does not mean that God *creates* the evil of evil
suffered). Evil suffered, he says, is caused by God *per accidens*. It is, so to speak,
a by-product of the good that God is causing to be.[12] One might ask whether
God cannot produce good without the occurrence of evil suffered. Here, though,
I refer you to what I said above with respect to the notion of a constraint on
God. Aquinas thinks that God can make a world that contains no evil suffered.
But he does not think that God can make a material world such as ours without
material agents interacting and causing damage to each other. To summarize
him somewhat crudely: Aquinas's view is that God cannot make lions and
lambs without the lambs having something to worry about.

Evil Done and God's Causation

It is central to Aquinas's account of evil suffered that there is always a concomitant good involved. But this is not at all what Aquinas thinks when reflecting
on evil done—by which I mean bad choices that people make, ones that lead to
badness of a kind that arguably sometimes exceeds what naturally occurring
and nonhuman things manage to bring about when left to their own devices.
When talking of evil done, Aquinas recognizes that he cannot appeal to concomitant good of any kind. If I wrongly cause you pain, he thinks, there is no
flourishing to appeal to by way of explanation. For where is the flourishing
here? Certainly not in you. And neither in me, or so Aquinas thinks. Bad moral
choices do not, for him, add to or express the goodness of any human agent
(though they might accidently sometimes result in bad moral agents benefit-
ting in some way). They are instances of failure—failure in the people who
make these choices. Such people, Aquinas holds, do not exemplify human
goodness. They are examples of things that fail to be what they ought to be.

One might wonder if there is goodness even in the most horrid of human
actions. And Aquinas would say that there is. He would, for a start, say that
there is goodness simply insofar as there is an existing human being acting at
all. He would also say that, under certain descriptions, even a fiend can be
thought of as good. Consider the case (noted above) of really expert serial killers
who continually escape the detectives trying to capture them. Bad people, you
might say. But pretty good in some ways: good at tracking people, good at
killing them and figuring out how to get away with it. Regarded from certain
points of view, even moral monsters, thinks Aquinas, can be thought of as

exhibiting goodness (or success) of *some kind*. Yet it is not success with which Aquinas is first of all concerned when talking about evil done. It is failure. With evil done we have a lack of goodness, and one without concomitant good explaining it or accounting for it.

So is God creatively responsible for it? Here Aquinas says that God is not, and by now you will probably realize why. His position is that the evil in evil done is not created by God because it is not a created thing. Evil done, Aquinas argues, "comes about because the [human] will by tending to an improper end fails to attain its proper end" (QDM 3.1 [Regan 2001: 143]).[13] In creating, Aquinas thinks, God makes to be only what is good (and what reflects him somehow). And Aquinas does not view the evil in evil done as good or as reflecting God in any way. But he is anxious to add that all that is real (all that has *esse*) when it comes to the occurrence of evil done is caused creatively by God. Hence, for example, while saying that God does not cause sin he also observes that God causes the existence of sinners and their sinful acts: "Since God is by his essence being, for his essence is his existing, everything existing in whatever way derives from himself. For there is nothing else that can be its own existing.... But acts of sin are evidently beings and classified in the category of being. And so we need to say that the acts are from God" (QDM 3.2 [Regan 2001: 147]).[14]

In other words, Aquinas takes morally bad human choices to be as real as anything else in the world is, and, therefore, made to be (created) by God. But he does not think that God can be deemed to create the evil of evil done as he creates a badly acting person. The evil in evil done, he holds, consists only in the gap between what exists and what should exist but does not. There being a badly acting person, he thinks, consists in the existence of a substance acting in particular ways. The evil in evil done, he concludes, does not involve divine creation (is not created by God). The existence of a badly acting person, he thinks, does involve this (is created by God). One might think that if God causes the existence of someone acting badly then God *is* causing evil done. But Aquinas does not accept this conclusion. He argues that evil done (or sin) "can be called a being and an action only in the sense that something is missing. And this missing element comes from a created cause, that is, the free will in its departure from order to the First Agent who is God. Accordingly, this defect is not ascribed to God as its cause, but to the free will, just as the limping by people who are lame comes from a physical malfunction and not from their power to move, even though this power enables them to limp" (ST 1a2ae.79.2 [Blackfriars edition, 25.211]). What Aquinas is saying here is that the evil in evil done has a cause only in the sense that it can be accounted for in terms of someone not choosing to act well, not in the sense that it is something made to exist by God. Or, to put it another way, Aquinas's view is that while God causes those actions that we freely choose, he does not choose those actions for us.

God and Human Choices

So Aquinas holds that God is not creatively responsible for either evil suffered or evil done. God, for him, is not an agent cause of evil in either sense. These evils, he thinks, arise and can be said to exist only insofar as there is goodness belonging to things of different kinds or insofar as human beings choose not to aim for what is morally good.[15] As I have said, Aquinas does not deny that God can make a world in which neither evil suffered nor evil done exist. But he also thinks that such a world would not be one remotely like ours—ours being a material world in which some things flourish at the expense of others, and one in which there are people able not to choose well.[16] One might respond to Aquinas at this point by saying that God ought to have made a world without evil suffered or evil done. As I explained in the previous chapter, however, Aquinas does not think of God as bound by anything we might think of as an obligation. For Aquinas, God's goodness does not consist in anything so creaturely as doing what one ought to do while conforming to a standard of goodness binding on one. God's goodness does not consist in him being "well behaved."

When it comes to God and evil, though, how should we think of God's causation and human freedom? We have just seen how Aquinas maintains that God can be said to be the cause of the act of sin. Yet how can he take this view without embracing some kind of theological determinism? Should he not be saying that God *permits* human choices (whether good or bad) but does not *cause* them? As I noted in chapter 1, many theists have said that this is all that God does and that belief that this is the case is required by anyone who espouses both belief in God's existence and belief in human freedom. Hence the so-called free-will defense according to which God can be morally exonerated from the evils resulting from human free choices since these are things with which he simply has to put up if he wishes to make a world containing people who are genuinely free. At this point, therefore, I need to say something about Aquinas on God and human freedom. For, as people sometimes seem astonished to discover, the free-will defense plays no role in what Aquinas has to say about God and evil. That is because, though not mentioning it by name (the phrase "free-will defense" became popular long after his lifetime), Aquinas makes it clear that he rejects what it proposes.

Given what I have been noting in previous chapters, you might now realize why I say this. Aquinas's approach to God as Creator absolutely prohibits him from supposing that any real thing in the universe (whether a substance or an accident or an activity) is not caused to be by God. Yet a human free choice is an activity of a substance in the universe. So Aquinas concludes that it is caused to be (and not merely permitted) by God. Here is a typical passage in which he does so:

> God is the cause enabling all operating causes to operate....
> Therefore, every operating agent acts through God's power.... Every power in any agent is from God, as from a first principle of all perfection. Therefore, since every operation results from a power, the cause of every operation must be God.... Just as God has not only given being to things when they first began to exist, and causes being in them as long as they exist, conserving things in being...so also has he not merely granted operative powers to them when they were originally created, but he always causes these powers in things. Hence, if this divine influence were to cease, every operation would cease. Therefore, every operation of a thing is traced back to him as to its cause.... In the order of agent causes, God is the first cause...and so, all lower agent causes act through his power. But the cause of an action is the one by whose power the action is done rather than the one who acts: the principle agent, for instance, rather than the instrument. Therefore, God is more especially the cause of every action than are the secondary agent causes.... Hence it is said: "Lord, thou hast wrought all our works in us" (Isaiah 26.12) and "without me you can do nothing" (John 15.5) and "it is God who works in us both to will and to accomplish according to his good will" (Philippians 2.13). And for this reason, the products of nature are often attributed, in Scripture, to divine working, because it is he who works in every agent operating naturally or voluntarily. (SCG 3.67)[17]

The free-will defense supposes that God can sometimes go in for a hands-off approach when it comes to people acting freely, that he can sometimes let something created (and, therefore, caused to be by him) not be so. Aquinas completely rejects this way of thinking.

Is Aquinas therefore committed to the view that there is no such thing as human free choice? He does not think so. In his view God's causation is no threat to us being free, and that is largely because of something else that I noted earlier—the insistence by Aquinas that creation does not involve a change in anything created. When created agent causes effect changes in things, the causes in question, thinks Aquinas, interfere with or modify something else. They "have their way" with them. Yet, Aquinas thinks, God's agent causality (always a matter of him producing *esse*) is not interfering or modifying. Rather, it is enabling. And this is how Aquinas argues when thinking about human free choices. These, he says, are not the result of God tinkering with or imposing himself on us. They are what exists insofar as God makes us to be as freely choosing creatures.

One place in which Aquinas presents this idea is his Commentary on Aristotle's *Peri Hermeneias* (1.14). Here he turns to the claim that "if God's providence is the cause of everything that happens in the world...it seems that everything *must* happen the way it does."[18] One reason why it might be thought that this is so, says Aquinas, derives from the notion of God's will. For might it not be suggested that if something happens because God wills it, and since God's will cannot be ineffective, "everything he wills, it seems, must necessarily happen"? Yet Aquinas rejects the implication involved here. It depends, he says, on thinking of the working of God's will on the model of human production of effects while it is, in fact, different. He continues:

> God's will is to be thought of as existing outside the realm of existents, as a cause from which pours fourth everything that exists in all its various forms [*Voluntas divina est intelligenda ut extra ordinem entium existens, velut causa quaedam profundens totum ens et omnes eius differentias*]. Now *what can be* and *what must be* are variants of being, so that it is from God's will itself that things derive whether they must be or may or may not be and the distinction of the two according to the nature of their immediate causes. For he prepares causes that must cause for those effects that he wills must be, and causes that might cause but might fail to cause for those effects that he wills might or might not be. And it is because of the nature of their causes that some effects are said to be effects that must be and others effects that need not be, although all depend on God's will as primary cause, a cause which transcends this distinction between *must* and *might not*. But the same cannot be said of human will or of any other cause, since every other cause exists within the realm of *must* and *might not*. So of every other cause it must be said either that it can fail to cause, or that its effects must be and cannot not be; God's will, however, cannot fail, and yet not all his effects must be, but some can be or not be.[19]

The first sentence in this quotation can be regarded as a summary of what I reported in chapter 5. The quotation then goes on to note that created things (or processes) can be divided into things (or processes) that may or may not be—meaning (a) things that are not such as to be determined or necessitated when it comes to what they are, and (b) things that are determined or necessitated when it comes to what they are. Aquinas here is clearly thinking that within the universe there are things or processes that are not inevitable and things or processes that are. But, so he wants to say, all such things are creatively caused by God, who is not, therefore, something in the world to be thought of as a cause among others bringing about an effect that is inevitable. What God brings about, thinks Aquinas, is not that something exists as able not to exist or not able not to exist. He brings about a world in which this distinction becomes intelligible in the first place.

Cashed out with respect to human freedom, Aquinas's point can be expressed as follows: (1) some things or processes in the world come about of necessity; (2) some do not; (3) yet both come about because of God's creative activity, which is not to be thought of as like that of a creaturely cause that renders its effect inevitable (or determined or necessitated). If I place olive oil in a pan and put heat under it, and if nothing interferes with what I am doing, the oil will inevitably become hot. It has no choice. But, Aquinas thinks, there are in the world things with choice, albeit things created by God. These things are what they are and do what they do because God makes them to be as they are and to do what they do. But this making to be, unlike oil becoming hot because of a flame under it, does not coerce as a created agent acting on another might be thought to coerce. Or such is Aquinas's view. He thinks that we are free not *in spite of* God but *because* of him. That our freedom can be badly interfered with by items in the universe is something that he does not deny. That it can be interfered with by God, however, is something he finds inconceivable given his view of God as Creator and given that he takes human freedom to be a fact of life (cf. QDM 6).

In various places Aquinas offers philosophical arguments for the conclusion that there is such a thing as human free choice, and, in doing so, he aims to give an account of what there is in the world.[20] But he thinks of what there is in the world to be what it is because of God, whom he, therefore, deems to be no threat to it being what it is. As I should again note, Aquinas does not take God's act of creation to involve a modification of something by something else in the world of change and time. And when it comes to human free choices he pursues this line of thinking so as to conclude that freely acting people, though created by God in all that they are and do, are not being interfered with or coerced by God. They are being made to be the freely choosing creatures that they are (as, thinks Aquinas, all created agents are made by God to be what they essentially are). It has been said (and said, I might add, in favor of the free-will defense) that human actions can be free only if "no causal laws and antecedent conditions determine" that they occur or do not occur.[21] And Aquinas, I think, would agree with this suggestion. But he would not take it as supporting the free-will defense since he does not conceive of God's action as springing from or exemplifying causal laws and antecedent conditions determining anything that comes to pass in time. He takes God to be *ipsum esse subsistens*—the cause of the existence of anything created acting and being what it is. His thinking on this matter has, I believe, been nicely represented by James Ross:

> The being of the cosmos is like *a song on the breath of a singer*. It has endless internal universal laws, and structures nested within structures, properties that are of *the song* and *not* of the singer or the voice or the singer's thought, though produced by them and attributively predicated of them.... The universe is continuously depending, like a song or a light show.... Its being is its own, yet it is from a cause, everywhere, and at no *including* time.... God produces, for each individual being, the one that does such and such (whatever it does) throughout its whole time in being.... God does not make the person act; he makes the so acting person *be*.... The whole physical universe, all of it, is actively caused to be. Still, to say that freedom or human agency is thereby impeded is absurd. Nothing can be or come about unless caused to be by the creator. So the fact that God's causing is necessary for whatever happens cannot impede liberty; it is a condition for it. Similarly, in no way is our liberty impeded by the fact that God's causing is sufficient for the being of the very things that do the very things that we do. Nothing possible can be impeded by its necessary conditions.... God did not make Adam to be the first man to defy God; God made Adam, who was the first man to defy God, to be. God made Adam, who undertook to sin.... God makes all the free things that do *as* they do, instead of doing otherwise as is in their power, by their *own* undertaking. So God does not make Adam sin. But God makes the sinning Adam, the person who, *able* not to sin, does sin. It follows logically that if Adam had not sinned, God would have made a person who, though able to sin, did not. And, surely, God *might* have made a person who, though able to sin, did not.... It is the whole being, doing as it does, whether a free being or not, that is entirely produced and sustained for its time by God.[22]

In the *De Malo* Aquinas puts things in a somewhat drier fashion than does Ross. He observes: "The will when moved by God contributes something, since the will itself acts even though God moves it. And so the will's movement, though from an external source as the first source, is nevertheless not coerced" (QDM 6.3 ad 4 [Regan 2001: 261]). It should, however, be clear how Ross's more graphic comments bring out what Aquinas wants to say. And, to repeat, what he most emphatically wants to say is that, though human choices are part of what God makes to be (and are in this sense caused by God, contrary to what the free-will defense supposes), they remain what they are—choices. It has been said that, for Aquinas, God makes no difference to the universe—the point being not that God is not efficacious but that divine creative willing does not prevent things from being what they are.[23] Aquinas's thinking on God and human choosing is a first-rate indication that this, indeed, is what Aquinas believes.

Moving On Again

At this point, let me briefly summarize some important elements in what I have so far presented Aquinas as thinking when it comes to God and evil:

1. Aquinas takes evil (both evil suffered and evil done) to be something that can truly be said to exist, though he does not take it to be something having *esse* and, therefore, does not regard it as creatively caused by God.
2. Aquinas holds that God is good, but not as subject to duties or obligations and not as exhibiting human virtues as people might be thought of as having them. So he does not even begin to defend the claim that God is good by appealing to "morally sufficient reasons" that God might have for allowing or permitting evil.
3. In fact, he rejects a line of thinking often presented for defending God morally—the free-will defense. For Aquinas, all that is real in the created order is God's doing. Aquinas, however, does not take this truth to entail that there is no human freedom.

These conclusions of Aquinas place him at odds with what many writers have assumed or advocated when it comes to the topic of God and evil. It has been said that God, if he exists, has a moral case to answer, and both theists and nontheists have written on this presumption. Aquinas clearly does not think in such terms. It has been said that God's moral justification for allowing evil partly consists in God taking a risk with people by creating them as free. Again, though, Aquinas does not think in such terms (even abstracting from the notion of moral justification). Considered as such, Aquinas is just not a participant in discussions of the problem of evil as this is commonly understood—the problem being: "How can a morally good God permit the evils that occur even though he knows about them and could have prevented them?" Aquinas would have considered the problem of evil, in this sense, to be based on philosophical confusions—these being reducible to the error of thinking of God as an inhabitant of the universe rather than as what makes for the *esse* of things in the universe.[24]

But what now, if we forget about the problem of evil and ask how Aquinas goes on to talk about God and evil given what I have reported him as saying? Without worrying about God's moral integrity, does he have more to offer concerning God's goodness and the evil or badness with which we are familiar? We shall see that he does.

8

Providence and Grace

When turning to the topic of God and evil many people, as I have
said, have written on the assumption that reflection on the reality of
evil might rightly lead one to conclude that God does not exist.
Aquinas, however, never writes on this assumption. As I have noted,
he acknowledges that one might argue in terms of it—as in the first
objection listed in ST 1a.2.3 (ending: "If God existed, nobody would
encounter evil. But we do encounter evil in the world. So God does
not exist"). Yet Aquinas never seriously takes God's existence as open
to question because there is evil. That is because of his Christian
faith, which rests on the conviction that God exists, and because of
what he thinks can be established by philosophical argument—that
God exists. In other words, when Aquinas concerns himself with
God and evil, his aim is always to strive to provide some account of
what God is and how evil should be thought of in a world created by
God. He is, you might say, never on the defensive when it comes to
the reality of evil and the existence of God. His approach to this
matter is always thoroughly influenced by his confidence that God,
indeed, exists (and, in this sense, is theological).

Some would say that such confidence needs to be justified by an
account of God's morally sufficient reasons for permitting evil. As we
have now seen, though, Aquinas does not think of God as having any
moral case to answer and, in this sense, would reject attempts to prove
that God, if he existed, is morally bad—as he seems clearly to reject the
suggestion that God is morally good (as being virtuous or doing what

he ought to do). For Aquinas, God is *ipsum esse subsistens*, the creative source of all that we can conceive of as being parts of the universe. And, considered as such, says Aquinas, God can in no way be thought of as being in any way bad. Why? Because, to start with, this is what the Bible says (here Aquinas quotes texts such as 1 John 1.5).[1] But also, says Aquinas, considered as *ipsum esse subsistens* God cannot be thought of as lacking being or goodness at all. If being is a matter of actuality, and if goodness is a matter of actuality, then, thinks Aquinas, God cannot lack actuality or goodness (or, as Aquinas obviously intends us to understand, we cannot think of God as being potentially thus-and-so but not actually thus-and-so or as being able to attain a good that he currently does not possess; cf. ST 1a.6.2–3). God, thinks Aquinas, is not a good such-and-such and can (albeit haltingly and obscurely) be best described only as being goodness itself—implying that there cannot possibly be evil in God.[2]

It has been suggested that a question mark might be put against God's existence given the reality of evil and given that God is supposed to be a person, for are persons not required to prevent evil, and so on? But Aquinas does not think that God is a person (though he always thinks of God as an other to be addressed by us in, for example, petitionary prayer).[3] By this I mean that he does not take God to be what he takes human persons to be (animals with minds). He does not even take God to be a person in the sense of being an essentially nonmaterial individual able to think, remember, anticipate, or react (a center of consciousness with a biography). René Descartes (1596–1650) famously claimed that this is what all of us are,[4] and many authors (both theists and nontheists) have supposed that belief in God is a projection of this notion into the heavens, so to speak.[5] Aquinas thinks differently, however, as we have now seen. It might be said that, in spite of appearances, he really does regard God as a person since he ascribes understanding and will to God. But Aquinas clearly does not think of God's understanding and will as distinguishable faculties (as they are in us). Nor does he think of them as subject to change or as in any way dependent on external causation, stimuli, or influence—as understanding and will are in people, who are, after all, what we primarily have in mind when speaking of persons.[6] And Aquinas certainly never employs the formula "God is a person."[7] Something worth noting in this connection is what Aquinas says about the word "God." Does he think of it as a proper name (like "John")? He does not. He says that "God" (*Deus*) is the name of a nature (*nomen naturae*) (cf. ST 1a.13.8). In other words, Aquinas takes "God" to be shorthand for referring to whatever God is by nature (simple, good, powerful, and so on). And, remember, Aquinas regards God's nature as something with respect to which we are seriously in the dark. We are able to make true statements about what God is, he thinks. And we are rightly able to claim to know that God is

X, Y, or Z (e.g., good or powerful). But, thinks Aquinas, we lack a comprehensive knowledge of God or a knowledge comparable to that which we have insofar as we are able to develop (in the modern sense) a scientific understanding of something. "From God's effects," Aquinas writes, "we do not come to understand what God's nature is in itself, so we do not know what God is. We know him...only as being excellent, as being causal, and as lacking in anything merely creaturely. It is in this way that the word 'God' signifies the divine nature: it is used to mean something that is above all that is, and that is the source of all things and is distinct from them all" (ST 1a.13.8 ad 2 [Davies and Leftow: 2006 157]).

Providence

As I say, when Aquinas talks about God's goodness he is not on the defensive. He is not seeking to show that God exists in spite of some supposed evidence against this being so. Nor is he trying to show that God has morally sufficient reasons for what he does or does not do. Rather, he is interested in trying to give some account of what God's goodness amounts to while recognizing that God is incomprehensible. And, we should recognize, one thing he stresses is that God's goodness is displayed by virtue of God's providence. God, he says, acts providentially and thereby shows forth the goodness that he is. This notion of Aquinas needs to be unpacked somewhat, however.

Aquinas takes "providence" to mean "foresight" or "care" or "direction." For him, providence is essentially a matter of *looking after* and, therefore, ties into the notion of goodness—on the supposition that to look after something is to provide for its well-being (or flourishing or goodness). "Are you providing for your children?" is asking, "Do you see to the well-being of your children?" And Aquinas certainly thinks that God provides and, in doing so, brings about well-being (or goodness). Indeed, so Aquinas argues, God does so on a grand, indeed fantastic, scale.

Aquinas takes this view chiefly because of what I noted in chapter 6—his conclusion that all created goods derive from God and reflect (admittedly obscurely) what God essentially is. What I did not perhaps sufficiently emphasize in chapter 6, however, is that Aquinas makes it clear that he takes God's goodness to be displayed and at work in anything you care to think of. As I have stressed, Aquinas takes all things to be good insofar as they succeed in being. But this has to mean that all success when it comes to being derives from God—or so Aquinas thinks. And with this thought in mind he takes it that all things that exist (have *esse*) are good and that this is so because God is making them to be. This conclusion, of course, means that God brings about (makes to be) all created goods. So, thinks Aquinas, God looks after or sees to the good of things in a way that admits of no comparison. Is X (a creature) good? If the answer is "yes," thinks Aquinas, then X is good by God's doing—something that Aquinas takes to mean that the goodness of creatures (and all the goodness of all creatures) is made to exist by him and is also something that gives us reason to think of God as good (though not a good individual conforming to standards to which we look when deciding whether an individual, considered as a member of a natural kind, is good). As I have noted, Aquinas does not take "God is good" simply to mean that God causes things that are good. But he does think that God causes things that are good to be. So he takes God to be, so to speak, the ultimate provider.

One might, perhaps, think that all creaturely goodness derives from a source that cannot but produce it. And one might, therefore, suppose that, if that is the case, then God (considered as the source from which all goodness in the universe derives) does not deserve to be thought of as good. Yet, and as I have already tried to note, Aquinas is clear that the created order is not something that God is compelled to produce. Hence, having asked if God wills of necessity whatever he wills, he replies that God does not. God, he thinks, has to be thought of as drawn to the goodness that is himself, so he can be said to will himself of necessity. But God cannot, holds Aquinas, be said to will (i.e., produce) things other than himself of necessity. Or as Aquinas himself writes:

> We should note that there is something he [God] wills of absolute necessity, but that he does not necessarily will all that he wills. His will is necessarily related to his own goodness, which is its proper objective. So, he necessarily wills his own goodness (just as we cannot but will our own happiness).... But God wills things other than himself insofar as they are set towards his goodness as to their end. Now by willing an end we are not bound to will the things that lead to it unless they are such that it cannot be attained without them (as when we have to will to eat in order to stay alive, or as when we have to will to take a boat in order to cross the sea). Other things, however, without which the end can be obtained, are not things we will of necessity (e.g., a horse is not necessary for a journey we can take on foot). So, since God's goodness is perfect and can exist independently of other things, and since they add no perfection to him, there is no absolute need for him to will them. (ST 1a.19.3)

In Aquinas's view, will is a matter of desire. And desire focuses on what those who have it regard as good (hence Aquinas's use of the slogan "good is what everything desires"). Now when it comes to God, he thinks, there cannot but be desire for what is absolutely good—that is, God, as the ultimate good, cannot be drawn to anything but himself (on the principle that to know what is absolutely good is to be drawn to it or to love it). But, thinks Aquinas, there is no comparable desire in God for anything that falls short of the goodness of God himself. Any such thing, insofar as it exemplifies goodness, reflects what God is, adds no goodness to him, and is not willed (or created) by him of necessity.

In Aquinas's view, all created goodness is produced by God not because he needs it, and certainly not because any agent apart from him coerces him into producing it. This in turn means that Aquinas takes all created goodness to be freely given, that the goodness had by creatures is given to them by one who did not have to give it. Surprisingly, perhaps, Aquinas does not dwell on this point so as to argue for God being good (surprisingly, perhaps, since most of us would, I presume, give praise to people who make for goodness without having to do so of necessity). He does not, I think, dwell on the point because he does not want simply to equate God's goodness with what we might call God's generosity or benevolence. His view is that God is essentially good but is not essentially the Creator of the universe. But we can certainly ascribe to Aquinas the view that God is generous insofar as he produces creaturely goodness (generous as causing the existence of goodness in creatures who display it). And, we might note, Aquinas takes God's production of creaturely goodness as a reason for saying that God loves creatures (a reason that some, at least, might think of as contributing to a case for God's goodness).

When it comes to the question of God's love of creatures I should make it immediately clear that Aquinas does not think that God is emotionally affected by anything he makes to exist. Insofar as love can be thought of as an emotion, then Aquinas does not ascribe it to God. In his view, emotions (feelings) are what we humans undergo as we are affected by (*moved* by) objects in our physical environment. They belong to us as physical inhabitants of the universe.[8] Insofar as love is deemed to be an emotion, then Aquinas excludes it from God, and you might well expect him to do so given what I have so far reported him as saying. Yet Aquinas positively teaches that God loves all creatures. So what does he mean by doing so?

Here, perhaps, I should let him speak for himself as, in the *Summa Theologiae*, he turns to the question "Does God love everything?":[9] "God loves all existing things. For everything that exists is, as such, good, because the very existing of each thing is a certain good. As are each of its perfections. Now I have already shown that God's will is the cause of all things and that everything therefore has to be willed by God insofar as it has any reality or goodness at all. So God wills some good to every existing thing. Since loving is the same as willing good to something, God clearly loves everything" (ST 1a.20.2 [Davies and Leftow 2006: 244]).

In this text, as in comparable ones, Aquinas is thinking of love not as an emotion but as a matter of willing goodness for something. And, since he takes God to be the creative source of all that is good in creatures, he naturally concludes that God loves all creatures insofar as he freely produces all that is good in them. He goes on to say that (and even forgetting about love as an emotion) God does not love things as we do. We will good things for others (whether people or animals or even plants) while not being the creative cause of the goodness to be found in them. As loving, we aim (well or badly) for goodness that is not of our making (not in our power to create). Yet, thinks Aquinas, such is not the case with God. "God's love," he observes, "pours out and creates the goodness of things" (amor Dei est infudens et creans bonitatem in rebus) (ST 1a.20.2).

So Aquinas clearly thinks of God as loving all of his creatures. They exist, so he believes, only because God is willing goodness to them. But he also holds that God loves some creatures more than others—meaning that he wills more good for some creatures than he does for others. "One thing would not be better than another but for God willing it," he writes (ST 1a.20.3). Aquinas takes it as obvious that some things are better (have goodness to a greater degree) than others. But he takes this thought further than you might expect a philosopher to do since he employs it when talking of people and goodness had by some of them in a special way. One way to approach Aquinas on this matter is to start with some things that he says about human happiness.

Happiness

Aquinas certainly believes that people are able to achieve happiness. Indeed, he believes that many people have achieved it. In saying so I am focusing on what Aquinas refers to as felicitas, which he takes to be happiness obtainable by us simply insofar as we are human beings who are not, in various ways, incapacitated or thwarted simply considered as such (insofar as we are not, for example, dying of cancer or in a coma). For Aquinas, we are, all things being equal, able by our natural powers to arrive at the enjoyment of various genuine goods—examples being physical well-being (arising from food, drink, shelter, and health) or certain pleasures involved in our relationships with others (such as the pleasure of being loved or honored by someone). These goods, Aquinas thinks, are things for which we naturally strive or aim. He also thinks that we sometimes succeed in our striving or aiming for them. We can, he holds, indeed be happy. And insofar as we are, he adds, we are so because of God. For Aquinas, all human happiness (in the senses just touched on) derives from God as the Creator of all that is real and positive, of all creaturely success or goodness. As we look around us and note the existence of people who are happy in various ways we are, thinks Aquinas, looking at what God, and only God, is (creatively) making to be. We are literally looking at God at work.

Yet Aquinas has a notion of happiness that goes beyond what he is talking about when referring to *felicitas*. This word as used by Aquinas is most naturally translated by the English term "happiness." But "happiness" is also a natural translation of another Latin word frequently used by Aquinas: *beatitudo*.

Aquinas's approach to *beatitudo* reflects his understanding both of goodness in general and of God's goodness in particular. As we have seen, he thinks that what is good is desirable, so that a reason (though not the primary one) to call God good lies in his producing created goods, and God also being thought of as good since he contains in himself all that is desirable as aimed at by creatures. On this account, any good aimed at by a creature exists, somehow, in God and is reflected in what God brings about. On this account, also, God is good without qualification and without respect to genus and species. And yet, of course, goods that we might obtain in day-to-day life are not this. Or so Aquinas thinks. There is, he argues, goodness to enjoy that is not anything creaturely. There is the goodness of God to enjoy. And this is what Aquinas takes *beatitudo* to consist in: an enjoying of God himself, not of anything that consists in the having of goods that are less than what God is, goods that pass away and are often but means we desire in order to arrive at other goods.

What could Aquinas mean by "an enjoying of God himself"? We have already seen him sharply distinguishing between God and creatures. We have also seen how he takes our knowledge of God to be limited and based on causal inference from what we know much better than we know him.[10] Yet Aquinas does not take us to be condemned only to such knowledge of God. For, he thinks, God can unite us knowingly to himself after death and in a way that he does not presently employ—by bringing it about that we "see" God's essence and delight in it. To be sure, Aquinas does not take himself to be able to prove philosophically that anyone in particular will see God's essence, nor does he claim to understand what doing so would amount to exactly since he does not claim to understand what God's essence is (he speaks somewhat obscurely, though perhaps necessarily so, of seeing God's essence by virtue of "the light of divine glory strengthening the mind" and of God joining himself to a mind as something intelligible to it; cf. ST 1a.12.2, 4). Yet basing himself on biblical texts such as 1 John 3.2 ("we will see him as he is") and John 17.3

("this is eternal life, that they may know you, the only true God"), Aquinas firmly believes in what is sometimes called "the beatific vision."[11] "Our ultimate happiness," he writes, "consists in our highest activity, which is the exercise of our mind, and if a created mind were never able to see God's essence, either it would never attain happiness, or its happiness would consist in something other than God. This is contrary to faith, for the ultimate perfection of the rational creature lies in the source of its being" (ST 1a.12.1 [Davies and Leftow 2006: 114]). So Aquinas actually thinks that God does bring human beings (some of them, anyway) to a state of perfect happiness.[12] And this fact needs to be borne in mind when thinking of his position on God and goodness.[13] When turning to the problem of evil many authors focus exclusively on goods and ills that befall us in this life—as if what happens to us in this life can be thought of as allowing us to understand how God, goodness, and badness fit together in what we might call "the final analysis." Aquinas, however, and without trying to excuse God in what we might think of as moral terms (without, for example, suggesting that beatitude "makes up" for the sufferings of those who arrive at it), does not write on this assumption. When thinking of God's goodness he also wants to draw attention to God's bringing people to beatitude—a state of happiness exceeding any other achievable by us before death and something displaying God's goodness in an excellent way.

Yet Aquinas, as I just noted, does not think that the achieving of *beatitudo* on our part is something we can know to occur (something the reality of which is philosophically demonstrable). For him, it is a matter of faith. We can believe in its occurrence, but cannot know that it occurs. Yet what does Aquinas mean by saying this? What does he mean when he speaks of faith? What does he mean by distinguishing between faith and knowledge? Does he, for example, think of faith as wishful thinking and of knowledge as superior to this? Does he believe that faith can in no sense be thought of as knowledge?

Faith

What might people mean when saying that they take something "on faith"? Even those with no religious beliefs can understand the notion of taking something on faith. It is not a uniquely religious one. It has its home in everyday discourse. Or, rather, it has its home in everyday discourse in which we refer to ourselves as believing people. Suppose I meet someone for the first time at a party. He says, "My name is John." Unless I have some evidence to the contrary, I will believe him.[14] I am not doing so because I already take myself to have grounds for supposing that his name is John. And I am not just believing that what he says is true. I am believing *him*. Or suppose that children go to school and their teacher says, "There was once a queen in England called Anne." And suppose that the children believe the teacher, without having ever heard about Queen Anne before. The children are not believing what the teacher says because they have independent reason to believe that there was a queen called Anne. They are just believing their teacher—as children constantly do.

Is it unreasonable to believe someone in this sense? Arguably not, for what is going on here is something that occurs all the time and actually contributes to ways in which we determine what is and what is not reasonable. As Elizabeth Anscombe has said, "The greater part of our knowledge of reality rests upon the belief that we repose in things we have been taught and told."[15] She continues:

> Nor is what testimony gives us entirely a detachable part, like the thick fringe of fat on a chunk of steak. It is more like the flecks and streaks of fat that are often distributed through good meat.... Examples could be multiplied indefinitely. You have received letters; how did you ever learn what a letter was and how it came to you? You will take up a book and look in a certain place and see "New York, Dodd Mead and Company, 1910." So do you know from personal observation that that book was published by that company, and then, and in New York? Well, hardly. But you do know that it *purports* to have been so. How? Well, you know that is where the publisher's name is always put, and the name of the place where his office belongs. How do you know that? You were taught it. What you were taught was your tool in acquiring the new knowledge. "There was an American edition" you will say, "I've seen it." Think how much reliance on believing what you have been told lies behind being able to say that. It is irrelevant at this level to raise a question about possible forgery; without what we know by testimony, there is no such thing as what a forgery is *pretending* to be. You may think that you know that New York is in North America. What is New York, what is North America? You may say you have been in these places. But how much does that fact contribute to your knowledge? Nothing, in comparison with testimony. How did you know you were there? Even if you inhabit New York and you have simply learned its name as the name of the place you inhabit, there is the question: How extensive a region is this place you are calling "New York"? And what has New York got to do with this bit of a map? Here is a complicated network of received information.[16]

Notice that Anscombe is not here producing an argument for some kind of wholesale skepticism. Nor is she refusing to apply the word "knowledge" to what is believed on testimony, or saying (absurdly) that we should believe everything that anyone tells us. Nor is she denying that what people tell us can sometimes be independently verified by us. Rather, she is drawing attention to the way in which believing people ("believing x that p" as she puts it) is something all pervasive in our starting to learn and our moving on to increase our store of knowledge. As she says herself, she is highlighting the importance of *faith* as something we display and rely on in day-to-day life.

I refer to Anscombe simply as a way of working up to the manner in which Aquinas approaches the topic of faith as a theologian. Like Anscombe, he thinks of faith as not springing from investigation or a process of rational argumentation. He thinks of it as distinguishable from knowledge considered as something demonstrable (as in "I know that p because of premises X, Y, and Z, which are indubitable truths entailing p"). Yet he is also prepared to speak of us "knowing" truths of faith, and he takes people with faith to assent without wavering to what they believe by faith—just as we speak of ourselves as knowing various things that we cannot personally demonstrate and just as we assent without wavering to all kinds of propositions that we cannot demonstrate to be true. And it is to faith that Aquinas appeals when saying that God in his goodness has destined us for union with him beyond death. Very much like Anscombe, Aquinas thinks of faith as a matter of believing what one is taught. Most especially, though, he takes it to be a matter of believing God.

What could be involved in believing God? Aquinas certainly does not think that God is anything like someone we might meet at a party and believe when he tells us something or other—as should be obvious from what I have reported him as saying in this chapter and in previous ones. He does, however, believe that God has addressed us directly because God has become human and has taught us about himself. I shall be focusing on this belief in the next chapter, but the point I want to stress for now is that Aquinas holds that God *has* taught us about himself and that it is perfectly proper to believe him on his say so (so to speak). I also want to stress that something God has taught us, thinks Aquinas, is that (to repeat my phrase above) God, in his goodness, has destined us for union with him beyond death.

These points need to be stressed if we are to appreciate all that Aquinas has to say about God, goodness, and evil—if we are accurately to understand his final approach to this topic. In previous chapters and also partly in this one I have tried to explain his philosophical approach to the existence of God, how he thinks about good and evil in general, why he thinks that God can be called good as the Creator of everything other than himself, how he denies that evil in the universe raises a question when it comes to God's "moral goodness," and how (arguing philosophically) he regards God and evil with an eye on causality. But what we might call the philosophy of Aquinas does not include all that he holds when it comes to God's goodness. Many thinkers have written about the goodness of God while considering only what might be argued about God in the context of a contemporary philosophy seminar. And, to a large extent, Aquinas seems to have been someone prepared to share in discussions conducted in such a context. Yet, philosopher though he is, he also believes in what he takes to be Christian revelation and should not be thought of as thinking of God's goodness without also having an eye on this (and not only as an afterthought).[17] I have just tried to explain how Aquinas thinks that this is so while mentioning his notion of the beatific vision. Now I should like to note how he takes it to be so by saying something about what he calls grace.

Grace

The basic point to make is that Aquinas takes God's goodness to be expressed, among other things, by his raising people to share in what he himself is, and that he does so by grace, which Aquinas calls "a certain participation in the divine nature" (quaedam participatio divinae naturae) (ST Ia2ae.112.1).[18] Given what I have reported when it comes to Aquinas's thinking, it should be obvious that he does not suppose that any human being can become God. But he does think that God can and does make people godlike (a thought that does not seem to enter the minds of many people writing on God and evil).

Aquinas holds that God makes people to be with a distinct nature (human nature). In his view, people have to be human in order to exist simply as people. And, he thinks, they have a definite range of physical and intellectual abilities considered as such.[19] One ability he deems of special importance is that of being able to arrive at settled ways of behaving that make for human flourishing, ways of behaving that Aquinas takes to indicate the presence in people of what he calls virtues—dispositions that incline us to achieve happiness in one way or another considered as human beings. The notion of virtue plays a key role in what we might call Aquinas's "purely philosophical moral philosophy." It has its roots in the thinking of Aristotle, who makes much reference to prudence, justice, temperance, and courage as virtues that we need in order to live well, and it leads Aquinas to say that, simply by being human, we can be happy in various ways.[20] But, he thinks, there is a happiness or well-being that is not referred to in Aristotelian moral philosophy (albeit that it is something open to philosophical discussion). So he writes:

A person is perfected by virtue [*per virtutem*] towards those actions
by which he is directed towards happiness.... Yet man's happiness
or felicity is twofold.... One is proportionate to human nature, and
this he can reach through his own resources. The other, a happiness
surpassing his nature, he can attain only by the power of God, by a
kind of participation of the Godhead [*secundum quamdam Divinitatis
participationem*].... Because such happiness goes beyond the reach
of human nature, the inborn resources by which a man is able to act
well according to his capacity are not adequate to direct him to it.
And so, to be sent to this supernatural happiness, he must needs be
divinely endowed with some additional sources of activity; their role
is like that of his natural capabilities which direct him, not, of
course, without God's help, to his connatural end. Such sources of
action are called theological virtues. (ST 1a2ae.62.1 [Blackfriars
edition, 23.137, 139])

Aquinas here is thinking that a philosophical account of human beings can tell
us a lot about what it is to be human and about ways in which human beings
can be happy given their own natural resources. Yet he is also thinking that we
can gain happiness (or well-being) that is not explicable given what we are by
nature. This is where his notion of grace kicks in.

Aquinas thinks of grace as a matter of God making us to be good (as
raising us to a state of being) in a way that we cannot arrive at given our
nature as human beings (though, of course, he also thinks that all goods we
might end up possessing by nature come to us by God's creative action). No
human being is able, by nature, to fly. Yet, of course, a plane can wing us
from one place to another. No human being is able, by nature, to defy gravity.
Yet, of course, there are always such things as elevators able to take us from
floor 1 to floor 100. In this sense, Aquinas holds, we may say that human
nature can be helped to a state of being that is not to be inferred from a
knowledge of human nature.[21] And, so Aquinas thinks, help such as this is
what grace amounts to.

But what is the good to which Aquinas takes grace to bring us? I shall
have more to say about this question in the next chapter, but for now let me
settle for saying that it is, in a serious sense, God's way of being (or, better,
that it is what is in God).[22] Here, presented very simply (and so that you might
quickly be able to grasp what we might call Aquinas's big picture when it
comes to grace), are Aquinas's main conclusions concerning the good to
which people are raised by grace, a good of which he chiefly talks by speaking
of faith, hope, and charity:

(1) God knows himself and no creature can know God as God knows himself. By grace, however, God shares his self-knowledge with us by the (supernatural) virtue of faith.[23] Those with faith truly believe God to be Father, Son, and Spirit (as proclaimed in the Christian creeds). They also (and again as proclaimed in the Christian creeds) believe that God has become incarnate so as to be one with us and to offer us friendship with him, a friendship meant to lead us to union with him after death. Faith is not wrung from us by argument (as, for example, is the acceptance of the conclusion of a valid argument whose premises we know and accept). In this sense it can be contrasted with knowledge considered as something arrived at on the basis of demonstration. But, for those who have it, faith is a matter of accepting what God has revealed of himself and, in this sense, amounts to a sharing in God's knowledge of himself, albeit an imperfect one.[24] And how has God revealed himself so that those with faith might have it? By the teachings of Jesus, who is God incarnate.[25]

(2) Faith gives rise to hope. By hope we persevere in the world as those with correct expectations that are not confirmable philosophically—the expectation, for example, that we shall be united with God after death, an expectation not grounded in philosophical argument but in the virtue of faith considered as a receiving (and loving) of the person and teachings of Jesus (cf. ST 2a2ae.17.2 and 17.7). As it says in Hebrews 1.1–2: "Long ago God spoke to our ancestors in many and various ways by the prophets, but in these last days he has spoken to us by a Son, whom he appointed heir of all things, through whom he also created the worlds." So hope, produced in us by God, is a good for us insofar it sets us on a path to our own final good. But it is also a good in us with an altruistic element to it insofar as by having it we look to (are concerned with) the final good of others (cf. ST 2a2ae.17.3).

(3) Charity exists in a person insofar as the person loves God for what God is, and not for any gain to be achieved by doing so.[26] So someone with charity loves what God essentially loves (the perfect good that is God himself) and is united to him simply on this basis. By charity we share in the life of the Trinity in which the Father loves the Son and the Son loves the Father. It is the presence of Trinitarian love in us because it is the presence in us of the Holy Spirit, which is the love of the Father and Son for each other. By charity we are raised from being servants of God to friends of God since charity enables us to love God (and, therefore, the goodness of God) for his own sake and not (as is so often the case with us) with an eye on what we might gain (cf. ST 2a2ae.23.2 and 23.6). So charity makes us like God. It raises us to embrace a goodness that is ultimate.

That, indeed, was a *very* brief account of ideas that Aquinas develops over many pages and in various places (it had to be so since this book is not a study of Aquinas on theological virtue). Yet you will, I hope, see how it contributes to an overall understanding of Aquinas on God and goodness. What I have just been reporting clearly rests on beliefs that Aquinas held as a Christian, and philosophers discussing God, goodness, and evil will probably not be interested in such beliefs.[27] For Aquinas, though, they are critical. As we have seen, he has plenty to say about God, goodness, and evil from what we can fairly call a purely philosophical perspective. Yet he also holds that such a perspective gives us but part of the picture. And he takes his views on grace significantly to augment what we might end up thinking without recourse to them, for, as I have said, he takes them to amount to the claim that God's goodness flows into or is communicated to certain creatures as raising them to share in what he is.[28] It is, of course, his commitment to what he takes Christianity to be that leads him to this conclusion. But that commitment is part and parcel of what Aquinas is thinking about when it comes to God, evil, and goodness in general, and it needs to be borne in mind if we are to understand him on this topic. In the next chapter I shall be trying to elaborate further on how this is so. For now, and to round up the present one, I need to say something about a topic connected with what I have spoken of above.

Predestination

Aquinas thinks that some people are raised to union with God in the beatific vision (a great good, in his view). He also thinks that some people are in this life given God's grace so as to share in the goodness that is God (albeit imperfectly since Aquinas does not think that any creature can be literally divine). But he also thinks that some people might fail to arrive at the beatific vision and that not all people have grace. The question therefore arises: how does Aquinas think of those without grace, and how does his view of these people square with his insistence on God's goodness? After all, so one might assume, a good God would deal out the same goodness to all. So how can it be that God does not do this while also being thought of as good?[29] Aquinas's answer to this question is to be found in what he has to say about what he calls predestination.

His discussions of this notion are heavily influenced by some biblical texts, an important one being St. Paul's letter to the Romans, the relevant bit of which reads: "For those whom he foreknew he also predestined to be conformed to the image of his Son, in order that he might be the firstborn within a large family. And those whom he predestined he also called; and those whom he called he also justified; and those whom he justified he also glorified" (Romans 8.29–30).[30] Paul is here clearly thinking that human union with God is brought about by God, and this is what Aquinas thinks. Distinguishing (significantly) between predestination and predetermination (so as to distinguish between God's creative action and action on us that makes us *forced* to do what we do), he holds that God brings to the beatific vision those who enjoy it, that he *sends* them to heaven:[31]

> The function of providence is to arrange things to an end. Now the destiny to which creatures are ordained by God is twofold. One exceeds the proportion and ability of created nature, and this is eternal life, which ... consists in the vision of God and surpasses the nature of any creature. The other is proportionate to it, and can be reached by its own natural powers. Now when a thing cannot reach an end by its own natural power, then it has to be lifted up and sent there by another, as when an archer shoots an arrow to the target. So a creature of intelligence, capable of eternal life, is brought there, properly speaking, as sent by God.... The planned sending of a rational creature to the end which is eternal life is termed predestination, for to predestine is to send. (ST 1a.23.1 [Blackfriars edition, 5.109])

Aquinas thinks of predestination as a matter of grace. By grace God brings it about that some people attain glory. So he takes predestination to be something very good, and something very good that is brought about by God. One might instinctively feel that, if this is what Aquinas thinks, he must also think (and maybe ought to think) that predestination is incompatible with human freedom. But he does not. And that is because of his general approach to God and human freedom as I tried to explain it in the previous chapter. For Aquinas, the free/determined distinction is one intelligibly made only with an eye on created causes and the effects of created causes. In the created world, he thinks, some things act as coerced while others do not. Among things not acting as coerced by created causes, he adds, human beings acting freely stand out. But even these, he thinks, are caused to be what they are by God, whose creative causality makes them to be freely acting people. And some freely acting people are, Aquinas holds, people freely acting as graced by God who is leading them to union with him. Aquinas does not think of grace as any more intrusive or manipulating than he takes divine creating to be. Indeed, of course, he takes the work of grace to be a matter of God creating. God, he thinks, creates (makes to be) some things as graced (saints) and some things as not graced (cats, for example).

Yet what of people who do not end up with the beatific vision? Some theologians and philosophers have suggested that there are no such people, that everyone must finally end up loving God for what he is and enjoying beatitude because of this.[32] Aquinas, however, and grounding himself on biblical texts, takes a different view. He never claims philosophically to know that some people are, in plain English, damned for eternity. But he writes: "Some people God rejects.... Since by divine Providence human beings are ordained to eternal life, it also belongs to divine Providence to allow some to fall short of this goal. This is called reprobation" (ST 1a.23.3). So Aquinas thinks that there are people who fail to arrive at beatitude. But does he take this fact (if fact it be) to count against God's goodness?

Why might it be thought to do so? Perhaps because what Aquinas calls reprobation should be understood as meaning that God actively wills people to be damned. But this is not how Aquinas thinks about the causality of reprobation. His line is that people are created as able to choose what is good. If they do not, then that is something accountable to them since they act freely. To be sure, Aquinas thinks, all of our doings are also God's doings as making us to exist. But, he also thinks, God's way of doing includes creating people who make choices. And so, he assumes, some people might just choose badly. Insofar as God creates what is good, he thinks, then God is the agent cause of what is good. But, he adds, God is not the agent cause of the badness present in one who finally falls short of the goodness that God is—one who is reprobate. He writes:

> The causality of reprobation differs from that of predestination. Predestination is the cause both of what the predestined expect in the future life, namely glory, and of what they receive in the present, namely grace. Reprobation does not cause what is there in the present, namely fault, though that is why we are left without God.... The fault starts from the free decision of the one who is reprobated and deserted by grace.... God's reprobation does not subtract any power from one who is reprobated.... Although one whom God reprobates cannot gain grace, nevertheless the fact that he flounders in this or that sin happens of his own responsibility. (ST 1a.23.3 ad 2–3 [Blackfriars edition, 5.117, 119, with some modification])

Aquinas's point is that though some fall short of God, they do so willingly (and are therefore blamable) even though God makes to be everything that is creaturely, including human choices.

So with an eye on the notion of predestination Aquinas maintains that the raising of creatures to God is a gift of God, one by which he enables people to be drawn to the good that he is. This conclusion, of course, is what Aquinas's whole teaching on grace amounts to. For him, calling God good is partly to say that God leads people to beatitude as his freely acting creatures, that among the effects that reflect the goodness of God one is the existence of graced people who enjoy God after death. To understand him further on this notion, however, we now need to note something I have touched on hardly at all: how Aquinas thinks of God as triune and incarnate. For the good God in whom Aquinas believes is describable not just as the Creator of the universe but as a life of love that has become physically present in the world. Aquinas's talk about grace and beatitude cannot be separated from this belief of his, so I turn to it in the next chapter.

9

The Trinity and Christ

The *Oxford Dictionary of the Christian Church* tells us that monotheism is "belief in one personal and transcendent God."[1] On this account, Aquinas is certainly a monotheist. Yet not all monotheists believe what Aquinas believes when it comes to God. In terms of the definition just quoted, Jews and Muslims are monotheists. But, in spite of his respect for various Jewish and Muslim authors, Aquinas's monotheism takes a different form from theirs, for he believes in the Christian doctrine of the Trinity. For him, God is Father, Son, and Holy Spirit. In keeping with the Athanasian Creed, he does not take this doctrine to mean that there are three gods. He takes it to mean that there is but one God who is Father, Son, and Spirit and, therefore, one to be referred to as the Trinity. And the notion of God as Trinity is, for Aquinas, of considerable importance when it comes to how we should think of God's goodness and of evil. In developing his thinking on this matter Aquinas takes himself to be launching out way beyond what can be established by philosophical arguments. But he also takes what he has to say as noting a series of truths that we need to be aware of when thinking of God, ones that he regards as part and parcel of his approach to the topic of God, goodness, and evil.

Aquinas on the Trinity in General

Aquinas has sometimes been criticized by theologians for not, in texts like the *Summa Theologiae* and the *Summa Contra Gentiles*, talking about the Trinity before discussing what he takes to be the divine nature. The criticism is based on the (I would have thought correct) assumption that, for Christians, God just is the Trinity. It amounts to the charge that reflection on God that abstracts from Trinitarian thinking amounts to some kind of betrayal of true Christianity.[2] Yet Aquinas's thinking about God is profoundly Trinitarian.[3] Anyone reading him carefully, and as a whole, will see this. He does offer discussions of God's nature without recourse to the doctrine of the Trinity, but only because, and as I have noted, he thinks that the Trinity is God and because he thinks (a) that there are things to be known about God without recourse to the doctrine of the Trinity, truths presupposed by the articles of faith, and (b) that these things should be put on the table before we start reflecting about God as Trinity since the doctrine of the Trinity cannot be usefully thought about without a consideration of what can be known of God by reason. As I have said, Aquinas does not think that those who believe in God have to be able to produce reasons for doing so on pain of engaging in some kind of intellectual vice. Nor does he think of human reason as standing in judgment on God in some way. But, and as a theologian, he also does not think that one can fling words like "Trinity" at people without a context—this context being some notion of what God is before it is declared that the Father is God, the Son is God, and the Holy Spirit is God. What might the word "God" mean in such a declaration?[4] Aquinas thinks it possible to say something with reference to this question, which is why (in the *Summa Theologiae* and the *Summa Contra Gentiles*) he talks about the divine nature before turning to the doctrine of the Trinity. But talk about the Trinity he does, and at considerable length.

This is not a book on Aquinas's theology of the Trinity so I am simply going to summarize some of its major emphases:[5]

(1) As I have already indicated, the doctrine of the Trinity is not advanced by Aquinas as a philosophical theory. Aquinas takes it to be revealed in the teachings of Jesus and codified by texts such as that of the Athanasian Creed.[6] So he writes: "Faith concerns what is not apparent to reason, as is clear from Hebrews 11.1. Now it is an article of faith that God is three in one. Therefore reason is not adequate to perceive this" (*Expositio Super Librum Boethium de Trinitate* [Commentary on Boethius's "On the Trinity"] 1.4).[7] As Peter Geach concisely explains when expounding Aquinas, "Since all the propositions of natural theology tell us only what is true of a being by virtue of his being God, they cannot serve to establish any distinction there might be between two Persons both of whom were God and the same God. Thus, so far as natural theology goes, the question whether many distinct Persons can be one and the same God is *demonstrably undecidable*, on Aquinas's view."[8] Now Aquinas thinks that solid philosophical replies can be given to arguments purporting to

prove the falsity of the doctrine of the Trinity (cf. ST 1a.1.8 and SCG 1.6). Yet he does not think that the truth of this doctrine can be *established* philosophically. As he bluntly observes in ST 1a.32.1: "We cannot come to know the Trinity of divine persons through natural reason" (*impossibile est per rationem naturalem ad cognitionem trinitatis divinarum personarum pervenire*).

(2) On the other hand, Aquinas does think that there are models available to us when thinking about the Trinity, ones that can be employed when reflecting on the (ultimately unfathomable) truth that God is Father, Son, and Spirit.

(3) So, with respect to God the Son, and clearly influenced by the first chapter of the Gospel of John and its talk of the Word being God, Aquinas appeals to the notion of conceiving an idea or concept of something (a "word of the heart" or *verbum cordis*, as he calls it). Forming a conception of something is, Aquinas thinks, an intransitive action, one that remains in a knowing subject (as, for example, the *transitive* action of moving a chair does not). Now suppose that we grant that God can be said to know or understand himself. We might, says Aquinas, think of him doing so by (eternally) forming a concept of himself, one that is in him. Since God is entirely simple, however, such a concept cannot be something different from what God is—or so Aquinas reasons. So God's understanding of himself just is God and cannot be an *accident* in him (as, for example, is the existence in me of a conception of myself). Yet, Aquinas adds, God's understanding of himself (should he have it) is something that (albeit eternally) comes to be in God and can, therefore, be thought of as in some way distinct from (or as "proceeding" from) that from which it comes to be (cf. *Expositio in Ioannem* [Commentary on the Gospel of John] 1.25–29 and ST 1a.34.1). So, without wishing to deny that God is simple, and certainly without wishing to imply that there are three gods, Aquinas thinks of God the Son as distinct from God the Father (from whom he "proceeds") just by virtue of the Son proceeding from the Father.[9] The number 4 is nothing but the successor of 3 and the predecessor of 5. It is not an individual substance belonging to a natural kind. Its identity (as distinct from 3 and 5) is secured only by its relation to what precedes and follows it (3 and 5).[10] Without using this example, Aquinas suggests that the Son's distinction from the Father (a real one, he assumes) is a matter of relation, not one of difference within a species (cf. ST 1a.28). The Son is God as known by God the Father. The Father is God as knowing God the Son.[11]

(4) Aquinas thinks that to know God perfectly is to love God, to be drawn of necessity to the goodness that God is.[12] So he suggests that there is love in God that is not a matter of willing the good for something other than God. In knowing each other perfectly, the Son and Father, he says, must also love each

other as being drawn to what each is as God. Yet love in God himself (as opposed to God's love of creatures) cannot, thinks Aquinas, be an accident in God. It has to be what God is essentially. And, so Aquinas says, the love of the Father for the Son, and the love of the Son for the Father, is something that springs from both of them and, like the proceeding of the Son from the Father, can be thought of as distinct from each of them. Aquinas calls this love "the Holy Spirit."

(5) Aquinas is not presenting his account of the Trinity as an explanation of what God is. He does not think that there can be any such explanation (on the assumption that an explanation is something we understand better than what we invoke it to explain). But he does think that God is essentially a life of love between equals, though not one between members of a kind, and not one that we can comprehend. His basic thought is that God is good without reserve (is goodness without qualification) and that, in the light of Christian revelation, we can (without fear of being trounced by philosophical arguments) think of him (insofar as we can think of him) as eternally enjoying the goodness that God is as Father, Son, and Spirit.

But does this life of love remain in God? Or might it be something that goes forth so as somehow to unite creatures to it? Aquinas thinks that it is indeed something that goes forth. Hence his approach to the doctrine of the incarnation.

Incarnation

Aquinas's view of the incarnation is thoroughly orthodox—by which I mean that it accords without reservation to what we find taught by the Council of Chalcedon (451). For Aquinas, to speak of God incarnate is to refer to Jesus of Nazareth considered as being, quite literally, both human and divine. Some Christian thinkers have taken a different view of Jesus. They have suggested, for example, that he should be thought of as a saintly person or as a splendid example to follow, but not as one who is truly divine.[13] This, however, is not what Aquinas thinks. For him, Jesus is truly God and truly human. He is the second person of the Trinity, the Word, united to what is thoroughly human.

One might wonder how Aquinas can think anything like this given his account of the difference between God and creatures. He chiefly does so because he embraces Chalcedonian orthodoxy when it comes to the incarnation and because he takes this to be taught by the Bible.[14] It might be argued, as have some theologians, that such orthodoxy conflicts with a proper notion of

God and is irreconcilable with it. Yet Aquinas disputes this conclusion. He maintains that there is no contradiction in asserting that one and the same subject is all that God is by nature and all that a human being is by nature.[15] As with the doctrine of the Trinity, Aquinas does not believe that the doctrine of the incarnation can be proved philosophically (he denies, for example, that it follows from what we can philosophically know God to be, or that it follows from anything we might know about Jesus at the empirical level; cf. ST 3a.1.2 and 2a2ae.1.4). Aquinas takes the doctrine of the incarnation to be revealed by Jesus (whom he takes to be God). "Our faith," observes Aquinas, "rests on the first truth. And therefore Christ is the pioneer of our faith by reason of his divine knowledge" (ST 3a.11.6 ad 2 [Blackfriars edition, 49.137]).[16] Aquinas does, however, think that the doctrine of the incarnation can be defended against the charge of logical contradiction. Basically, his position is (a) that Jesus is one divine subject, the second person of the Trinity, with two distinct natures, divine and human, and (b) that there is no demonstrable logical contradiction in ascribing two distinct natures to one and the same subject. "The Word," he says, "has a human nature united to himself, even though it does not form part of his divine nature...[and]...this union was effected in the person of the Word, not in the nature" (ST 3a.2.2).

With all of that said, I now pass over the details of Aquinas's treatment of what we might call "the logic of God incarnate," which is something deserving of a book-length discussion in its own right.[17] For present purposes, the point to note is that Aquinas really does think that Jesus is God incarnate. This thought dominates all that he has to say about Jesus and, as we shall now see, significantly adds to what we have noted him to be saying on the topic of God, God's goodness, and evil.

The Purpose of the Incarnation

In his *Commentary on the Sentences* 3.1.1.3 Aquinas accepts that God might have become incarnate even if people had never sinned. And he says the same in the *Summa Theologiae.* "Even had sin not existed," he writes, "God could have become incarnate" (*quamvis potentia Dei ad hoc non limitetur, potuisset enim, etiam peccato non existente, Deus incarnari*) (ST 3a.1.3). Given God's omnipotence, thinks Aquinas, there is nothing to stop God becoming incarnate without the occurrence of sin on the part of people. But should we connect the incarnation with sin? Aquinas thinks that we should largely on biblical grounds. "Everywhere in sacred Scripture," he observes, "the sin of the first man is given as the reason for the incarnation" (ST 3a.1.3). For Aquinas, God became incarnate so as to liberate people from sin.[18] There is, he thinks, no way of showing that God would have become incarnate regardless of the occurrence or nonoccurrence of sin. Yet, he maintains, God has become incarnate and has done so to free us from the effects of sin.

Aquinas certainly believes in the reality of sin. He believes that people in general continually fail to aim at the good that God is. Yet he also believes that sin is something that can be thought of as somehow vanquished by virtue of the incarnation. In his view, the life and death of God incarnate serves to bring people to God in spite of sin. "The work of the incarnation," he says, "was directed chiefly to the restoration of the human race through the removal of sin" (ST 3a.1.5).

Why this emphasis on sin? Aquinas endorses it since, as I have said, he takes it to be scriptural—as in 1 Timothy 1.15: "The saying is sure and worthy of full acceptance, that Christ Jesus came into the world to save sinners." Yet might God not have saved sinners by simply forgiving them? Surprising as it might seem (given some biblical texts, anyway), Aquinas's answer to this question is "yes." In ST 3a.1.2 he asks whether the incarnation of the Word of God was necessary for the restoration of the human race. He then distinguishes between two senses of "necessary" (senses that I have already noted him as recognizing). In aiming for an end, he says, we may have to choose a means without which the end is simply unobtainable—as when we eat in order to keep ourselves alive (we have no option but to eat in order to live). But, Aquinas adds, something can be thought of as necessary for an end insofar as it brings about the end in a particularly good way. He writes:

> We refer to something as necessary for an end in two senses. First, when the goal is simply unattainable without it, e.g., food for sustaining human life. Second, when it is required for a better and more expeditious attainment of the goal, e.g., a horse for a journey. In the first sense the incarnation was not necessary for the restoration of human nature, since by his infinite power God had many other ways to accomplish this end. In the second sense, however, it was needed for the restoration of human nature. (ST 3a.1.2 [Blackfriars edition, 48.11])

Aquinas's view is not that the incarnation is the only way by which people can come to enjoy the goodness that God is. He does, however, think of it as a particularly good way.

The Work of Christ

Aquinas reasons along these lines since he takes the incarnation to unite people to God in an extraordinary manner. That is because of his belief that Jesus Christ is truly God. Human sin could, Aquinas agrees, be simply forgiven by

God. Yet, Aquinas adds, God the Word has quite literally thrown in his lot with us and, so to speak, personally invited us to friendship with him. For Aquinas, the history of Jesus is the history of God uniting himself with us and declaring us forgiven. "The very nature of God is goodness," Aquinas observes. He continues: "It is appropriate for the highest good to communicate itself to the creature in the highest way possible. But, as Augustine teaches, this takes place above all when *he so perfectly joins human nature to himself that one person is constituted from these three: Word, soul, flesh*" (ST 3a.1.1).[19] Aquinas takes the significance of the incarnation to be summarized in the New Testament text that reads, "For God so loved the world that he gave his only Son, so that everyone who believes in him may not perish but may have eternal life" (John 3.16). Aquinas reads the Gospels as telling us that the incomprehensible God has entered our world as one proclaiming forgiveness and as one literally identifying with us and mixing with us. For Aquinas, the incarnation is a matter of God befriending us on the condition that we want his friendship. In this sense, he thinks, it amounts to God as loving us.

Some Christian authors have seen the true significance of the incarnation to lie in Christ dying on a cross.[20] Their idea is that sin requires a penalty of some kind and that Jesus saves people by his suffering—this being deemed by God to "make up" for the sin of others. I shall return to this notion in a moment. For now, though, I think it important to stress that Aquinas presents a number of different reasons for thinking of the incarnation as expressing God's goodness to people, a number of ways for drawing out the purpose of the incarnation. This is nicely highlighted by Romanus Cessario, who draws attention to Aquinas's commentary on Isaiah 9.6, in which we read, "For a child has been born for us, a son given to us." Aquinas, of course, takes the child here to be Jesus, and, focusing on the phrase "given to/for us" (*datus est nobis* in the Latin translation of Isaiah that Aquinas was reading), he writes:

> Noting the phrase "datus est nobis" it can be said that Christ is given to us first as a brother: "O that you were like a brother to me, that nursed at my mother's breast!" (Song of Solomon 8.1); second, as a doctor [i.e., teacher]: "Be glad, O sons of Zion, and rejoice in the Lord your God; for he has given you a doctor of justice" (Joel 2.23); third, as a watchman: "Son of man, I have made you a watchman for the house of Israel" (Ezekiel 3.16); fourth, as a defender: "He will send them a savior, and will defend and deliver them" (Isaiah 19.20); fifth, as a shepherd: "And I will set up over them one shepherd.... And he shall feed them" (Ezekiel 34.23); sixth, as an example for our activities: "For I have given you an example, that you should also do as I have done to

you" (John 13.15); seventh, as food for wayfarers: "The bread which
I shall give for the life of the world is my flesh" (John 6.52); eighth, as
a price of redemption: "The Son of man came not to be served but to
serve, and to give his life as a ransom for many" (Matthew 20.28);
ninth, as a price of remuneration: "To him who conquers I will give
some of the hidden manna" (Revelation 2.17).[21]

Whatever one might make of this passage, it ought to be obvious that Aquinas
shows himself in it not to want to flog one concept or image to death when trying to think of the value of the incarnation to people. When it comes to this, as
Herbert McCabe observes, "he finds a place for all sorts of insights where
others have been hypnotized by one model or another."[22] Among other things,
so Aquinas maintains, the incarnation expresses God's goodness since it provides us, for example, with (1) one who, though God, acts toward us and invites
us to act in return, as a brother, (2) one who teaches us as only God can, (3)
someone concerned for our future, (4) someone on our side, and (5) someone
who is a God-given example to us, someone, indeed, who is God.

Aquinas takes the incarnation to be, as it were, what God looks like as pro-
jected into human history. He does not, of course, suppose that the divine
essence looks like anything (how could it?). Yet he does take the life of Jesus as
revealing to us what God is about when it comes to us. One might think, as
Unitarians seem to do, that God is a very benevolent individual, one who is
concerned about us. Aquinas, however, never thinks of God in these terms. As
we have seen, he does not think of God as an individual member of any kind.
Nor does he think of God as a benevolent despot. He takes God to be the Creator
of all that is good, and he takes the life of Jesus as making for good in a quite
particular way. For he thinks that anything we can say of Jesus we can predicate
of God. So, for example, he thinks that "Jesus welcomed sinners" means that
God welcomes sinners (though not without repentance). And he thinks that,
insofar as Jesus loved people, so God loves people, and that, insofar as Jesus
gave us a good example, so God gave us a good example. And, for Aquinas,
Jesus indeed gives us a good example. For, Aquinas notes, he was obedient to
God unto death.

Aquinas clearly sets great store by the death of Jesus as leading people to
union with God. As I noted above, he does not think that God cannot bring
people to union with him without the death of God incarnate. What stands between people and union with God is, thinks Aquinas, sin. And, he argues, God,
absolutely speaking, can simply forgive this. Human judges, he says, are bound
to demand penalties of some sort for crimes committed. But this, he continues,
is not the case with God since God "has no one above him" and "violates no

one's rights" should he simply forgive sin, "which is a crime in that it is committed against him" (ST 3a.46.2 ad 3). Yet Aquinas, basing himself on his reading of the New Testament, also believes that the death of Jesus has a critical role in human salvation, in God's drawing us to union with him. How so, however?

One thing worth noting is that Aquinas takes every aspect of Christ's life, and not just his passion on the cross, to be a matter of God drawing people to himself. "From the moment of his conception," he says, "Christ merited eternal salvation for us" (ST 3a.48.1 ad 2). His point seems to be that the incarnation as such is a matter of God embracing and accepting people, acting as an elevator raising us to him. So he clearly does not think of the death of Jesus as some kind of mechanism required to shift people into a gear in which they are then automatically headed for the beatific vision. The notion that God's anger against sinners is somehow switched off by Jesus's death (a notion popular in some circles) is not one shared by Aquinas, who, in any case, thinks that talk of God's anger is purely metaphorical.[23] His view is that the death of Jesus can be thought of as leading us to God because it amounts to God, as one like us, canceling all debts between us and himself. Aquinas does not think that this canceling of debts remains in effect regardless of how people behave. He believes that to benefit from it one needs to conform oneself to Jesus, to love what he loved and to hate what he hated. It is not Aquinas's view that human salvation is the result of God waving a magic wand and saying, "Everything is fine, no matter what you get up to" (cf. ST 1a2ae.113.6). But he does have a view of human salvation that allows for the death of Jesus as definitely debt-canceling. In developing this view a term that Aquinas frequently uses is "satisfaction." The death of Jesus, he says, "satisfies" for human sin (cf. ST 3a.46, 48, 49).

"Satisfaction" was a term much used in ancient Roman legal writings. It came to prominence in Christian reflections on the death of Jesus in St. Anselm's *Cur Deus Homo*.[24] And it was a term that Aquinas inherited as he put his mind to thinking about the death of Jesus. If I act unjustly toward you, one might think, then a disorder exists between us. I owe you. How is this debt to be overcome so that we are properly reconciled with each other? You could just say "forget about it" and we could then proceed together in harmony. Yet your saying "forget about it" does not, in spite of your generosity, cancel out that I do, indeed, owe you. So what about the disorder between people and God arising from sin? Let us assume (as Aquinas does) that sin always amounts to a refusal to give God what is his due (love of God as the supreme good and as the agent cause of all creaturely goods). Can God look at sin and say "forget about it"? Aquinas thinks that he can. And here we might say "Hooray!" But he also thinks that God has, in fact, done something to right what we might think of as the wrong done to him by sin, something over and above an act of merely forgiving. Hence his appeal to the notion of satisfaction when thinking of the death of Jesus, a notion that he employs in order to say that Jesus's death was that of God incarnate making up for anything that we might think of as a debt owed by people to God.

St. Anselm argues that human sinners owe God since they have offended against him. He goes on to argue that sin cannot be compensated for unless one who is both God and human satisfies for sin. And, writing with an obvious debt to Anselm, Aquinas says:

> If God were to have restored human beings only by his will and power, the order of divine justice, which requires satisfaction for sins, would not be observed. God does not make satisfaction, nor does he merit, since this belongs to one who is subject to another. Therefore, neither was it proper for God to make satisfaction for the sin of the whole human nature, nor was a mere human being able to do so.... Therefore, it was appropriate that God became a human being, so that the one who was able to repair human nature and the one who was able to make satisfaction for sin would be one and the same. (CT 200)[25]

For Aquinas, forgiveness of sin is possible without satisfaction. For Aquinas, also, the death of Jesus is contingent (and not necessary) in that it resulted from the free actions of those who killed him, from his free choice to do and say what led them to do so, and from his freely choosing to place himself into their hands.[26] Yet Aquinas also thinks that Jesus's death can be thought of as appropriate and desirable in that what it amounts to is pain accepted by one who is both human and divine. Aquinas typically thinks of Jesus as representing the whole of the human race as reconciled to God—an idea he must clearly have gotten from St. Paul (cf. Romans 12 and 1 Corinthians 12). So he regards the freely accepted sufferings of Jesus as restoring right order between sinners and God. And since he takes God to be suffering in that Jesus suffered, he takes the sufferings of Jesus to correct a disharmony between people and God that people, considered simply as such, cannot correct. His point is not that the only remedy for sin is that someone should suffer.[27] Aquinas's position is that God incarnate, and as representing those willing to accept him as such, is, as both God and man, one whose freely accepted sufferings can be viewed as more than compensating for the sins of human beings. In this sense, he thinks, that Jesus should satisfy for sin is more desirable or fitting (though not absolutely necessary) than that God should simply forgive it (a possibility). "One who was merely a man," Aquinas observes, "could not make satisfaction for the entire human race, and how could God? It was fitting, then, for Jesus Christ to be both God and man" (ST 3a.1.2). Or as Aquinas also argues:

> Someone properly satisfies for an offense when he offers to the one
> who has been offended something which he accepts as matching or
> outweighing the former offense. Christ, suffering in a loving and
> obedient spirit, offered more to God than was demanded in
> recompense for all the sins of mankind, because first, the love which
> led him to suffer was great love; secondly, the life he laid down by
> way of satisfaction was of great dignity, since it was the life of God
> and man; and thirdly, his suffering was all-embracing and his pain so
> great.... Christ's passion, then, was not only sufficient
> superabundant satisfaction for the sins of mankind; as John says,
> "He is a propitiation for our sins, not for ours only but also for those
> of the whole world" (1 John 2.2). (ST 3a.48.2 [Blackfriars edition,
> 54.79, with emendations])

Once again, it is not Aquinas's view that God cannot simply forgive sin. As Romanus Cessario puts it, in Aquinas's thinking satisfaction "is not something God requires of man, or even of Jesus, as a condition for accomplishing his saving plan. Rather it is the means whereby God in very fact accomplishes his plan to bring all men and women into loving union with him."[28] And Aquinas takes the means in question here to accord both with God's mercy and with his justice. Or as he puts it himself:

> The liberation of man through the passion of Christ was consonant
> [conveniens] with both his mercy and his justice. With justice, because
> by his passion Christ made satisfaction for the sin of the human race,
> and man was freed through the justice of Christ. With mercy,
> because since man was by himself unable to satisfy for the sin of all
> human nature.... God gave him his Son to do so, according to Paul:
> "They are justified freely by his grace through the redemption which
> is in Christ Jesus, whom God has set forth as a propitiation by his
> blood, through faith" (Romans 3.24). (ST 3a.46.1 ad 3)

Aquinas thinks that God can always respond to sin with mercy. And he certainly does not think of Christ's death as determined by any natural necessity or by God compelling people to crucify Christ. Yet he recognizes that Christ, in fact, suffered and died, and he sees a great good in this, though he always regards the good *in terms of effect* as tied to people accepting Christ for what he is as God.[29] As should be evident, part of his reason for doing so is that he thinks it possible for one person to satisfy (right the wrong of) another. St. Paul says, "Bear one another's burdens, and in this way you will fulfill the law of Christ" (Galatians 6.2). Aquinas takes Christ in his passion to be bearing the burdens of others and in this sense satisfying for them (cf. Aquinas's *Commentary on the Sentences* 4.20.2).

I said above that Aquinas draws on a number of different notions when talking of the death of Jesus. Two that I have not so far mentioned are "priest" and "sacrifice." Aquinas thinks of Christ as the ultimate priest and the ultimate sacrifice. He takes a priest to be someone mediating between people and God (cf. ST 3a.22.1). And, following Old Testament ways of thinking, he takes a sacrifice to be something pleasing to God, something by which people enter into God's favor (cf. ST 3a.22.2).[30] So he finds plenty of room to wax eloquently about how Christ is given to us by God as a priest and a sacrifice. One needs, though, to stand back from the various concepts on which Aquinas draws when talking about the incarnation and (especially) the death of Jesus. One needs to get a sense of what might be called his big picture concerning Jesus. And this can be briefly summarized thus: for Aquinas, people are alienated from God by sin. God has taken the first step in overcoming this alienation by becoming incarnate, by giving people a human face of God (so to speak), by declaring God's forgiveness to them, by putting himself literally into their hands, by calling them to repentance, by being what the Old Testament sacrificial system was supposed to achieve (union between people and God), and by offering himself up as one willing to take on the sin of humanity so as to restore people (should they want this) to friendship with God in a way that displays both mercy and justice. As I have said, Aquinas does not regard the life and death of Jesus as a magic fix-it. We are not, he thinks, reconciled to God unless we wish to be. But he does think that we can be so reconciled and that our being so derives from God as sharing his Trinitarian life with us, by becoming incarnate (by "slumming it," if you like), and by freely doing for us what we cannot do for ourselves.

This last point, I should add, brings us back again to Aquinas on the topic of grace. He thinks of the life and death of Christ as a matter of God calling us to union with him in an especially fitting (though not necessary) way. He thinks of it as showing God's love for people (as willing great good to them), and doing so with both mercy and justice. But he also thinks of it as leading to the bestowal of grace. The theological virtues of faith, hope, and charity are, Aquinas holds, given to people as those who embrace what he takes to be the purpose of the incarnation. By faith, he thinks, people believe in what Jesus teaches about God the Father. By hope, they stand firm to his promises of eternal life. And by charity they conform themselves to the image of God the Son made flesh. And faith, hope, and charity (so Aquinas always insists) are God's work in us. To be sure, he says, we arrive at them because we want to (they are not forced on us and are not the result of celestial hypnotism). But they are, he thinks, God's work in us nonetheless.

What is the worst thing that could befall a human being? Obvious answers might be loss of all material goods, loss of all one's friends and family, and death. And Aquinas agrees that all of these things are bad and to be prevented by us as far as possible (and by proper means).[31] Yet he also considers that worse than all of them is the failure to arrive at the union with God that he calls beatitude, and he holds that, though philosophy cannot show that this is so, God has offered us beatitude through the life and teachings of Jesus. He goes on to maintain that this offer is continually re-presented through the sacraments of the Christian church, which Aquinas takes to unite us with the saving work of Christ in a tangible and day-to-day manner. But this, I think, is not the place to engage in a discussion of Aquinas's sacramental theology.[32] Instead, let me simply now say that, for Aquinas, the worst that could befall a human being (the loss of beatitude) is something that God has shown himself to have taken steps to prevent us from—given our willingness to accept what he shows himself to be in the life and death of Jesus.

Aquinas certainly believes that not everyone arrives at beatitude. So one might wonder whether something might not be badly askew in his account of the life and death of Jesus and his approach to grace. These seem to imply that God wills all to be saved, as 1 Timothy 2.4 might be taken as saying. So how can Aquinas also countenance the notion that not all are saved and attain beatitude?

Aquinas does so by distinguishing between what he calls God's "antecedent" and "consequent" will. Judges might want everyone who comes into their courts to be declared innocent, because they might want it to be the case that all who appear before them *are* innocent (because they do not want anyone to be guilty of crimes). Yet they might still condemn people to prison who are clearly guilty. Thinking with this kind of model in mind, Aquinas argues that, being goodness itself and freely willing goodness for people, God, of course, wills all people to be saved. But what if they do not want to be? What if they turn their backs on God? What if they do not give a fig about faith, hope, and charity? What if they do not even want to be what someone like Aristotle would have regarded as a virtuous human being? Then, says Aquinas, God leaves them to their lot and, in this sense, wills it:

God wills everything insofar as it is good. Now, a thing may be good or bad at first sight, and looked at in isolation, only to turn out to the reverse when conjoined in its context with another element. For example, it is good, absolutely speaking, for people to live, and bad for them to die. But if we are dealing with people who are murderers or public dangers, then it is good that they should be killed and bad that they should remain at large. Accordingly, we can speak of a justice that *antecedently* wishes every human being to live, but *consequently* pronounces the capital sentence. By analogy, therefore, God antecedently wills all people to be saved, yet consequently wills some to be damned as his justice requires. (ST 1a.19.6 ad 1 [Davies and Leftow: 2006 229])

The union of people with God, thinks Aquinas, depends on them wanting to be united with God. Such union is not, as I have said, something that Aquinas takes God to lay on without respect to the freedom of people. His view is that the saved are those who love Christ and follow his example. What of those who lived before Christ? Aquinas thinks that the best of these, the greatest of Old Testament figures, for example, benefit from Christ's achievement since they were tuned in to what he was about and are therefore as much a part of him as those of his explicit followers. As he writes, while thinking (along the lines of Ephesians 1.23) of the church of Christ as being Christ's body: "The difference between the natural body of a man and the mystical body of the church is that the members of a natural body all exist together, whereas members of the mystical body do not. They are not together in their natural existence, because the body of the church is made up of people from the beginning to the end of the world" (ST 3a.8.3).

So Aquinas's thinking on the work of Christ has, one might say, a universalist element to it. He writes at length about the importance of particular practices (chiefly the celebration of the sacraments of the church) as leading to the salvation of individuals. For him, these amount to the work of grace in the lives of those with faith, hope, and charity. But he is clearly prepared also to speak of people who know nothing specifically of Christ as also being united to him, and to the work of God as leading human beings to beatitude. This, also, is an important element when it comes to the way in which Aquinas thinks of God's goodness. Moses knew nothing of Christ, and he never went to a Christian church. Yet Aquinas thinks of Moses as someone saved by the work of God incarnate. Why so? Because he thinks of Moses as implicitly believing in what Christ taught about himself and his Father. Aquinas clearly does not mean that Moses would have at any time in his life said, "God is three persons in one substance, and the Son of God has become incarnate." Obviously not. But Moses, thinks Aquinas, was very much tuned into what Aquinas takes the incarnation of Christ to be essentially about and, because of this, benefits from the life and work of Christ. In this sense, Aquinas can be taken as supporting something like the notion of anonymous Christianity proposed by Karl Rahner (1904–84). Rahner claimed that salvation is not confined to those who explicitly declare a belief in God as found in the declarations of councils such as those of Chalcedon and Nicea.[33] Aquinas seems to agree with him.

10

Aquinas, God, and Evil

I began this book by noting some significant ways in which people have reacted to the claim that God exists and that evil does so as well. Some have suggested that the reality of evil is reason, on moral grounds, to say that God either certainly or probably does not exist. Others have maintained that God's existence can be defended in the light of evil since God is morally justified in allowing the evils that occur. As we have now seen, however, Aquinas sides with neither of these positions.[1] He affirms that God exists and that God is good, but he does not try to defend God's goodness on moral grounds. So, though he thoroughly disagrees with those who reject belief in God, he is not a theodicist. If we take the problem of evil to be expressed by the question, "How can God justify himself morally for the evil that exists?," Aquinas would dismiss it as a pseudo-problem comparable to questions like "Why is humility shorter than the Eiffel Tower?" or "Why are daisies not as imaginative as buttercups?"
A pseudo-problem is one posed about something while not paying attention to the nature or natures of that with respect to which the problem is supposed to arise. With that understanding in mind, Aquinas would clearly take the problem of evil, as just construed, to be a bogus one. He would regard it as not engaging with what has to be said of God's nature. To ask why humility is shorter than the Eiffel Tower is not to ask a question to be taken seriously since humility is not something that can sensibly be thought of as being shorter or taller than anything. To ask why daisies are not as imaginative as

buttercups is also silly since imagination cannot intelligibly be ascribed either to daisies or to buttercups. And, for Aquinas, to ask whether God can be morally justified when it comes to the evils that occur is to ask a question that should never have been raised in the first place. For him, God is not to be thought of as a moral agent behaving either well or badly. I think it no exaggeration to say that, in Aquinas's view, talk of God's "morally sufficient reasons" should be placed on a level with talk about the morally sufficient reasons of my cat. It is not, of course, that Aquinas thinks of God as being seriously comparable to my cat. Far from it. His point is that God is just not the sort of thing to be evaluated as we evaluate people morally, albeit that he is perfectly happy to say that God is good and just and merciful.

Aquinas on God and Evil: The Big Picture

So God, for Aquinas, is indeed good. Good as what? Not as something within the intelligible world. So Aquinas does not think of God as a good such-and-such. Given what I reported in chapters 2–4, you will now, I hope, realize that Aquinas thinks of God's goodness (not to be thought of as an accident in God) as what accounts for the existence of all substances and accidents—whatever can be thought of as *having* (as opposed to *being*) *esse* (as actually existing without being the source of its being actual). Aquinas does not think that God's being good depends on him creating such things. He takes God to be essentially good. He does, however, think that the goodness involved in the being of creatures derives from God and, therefore, reflects what he is (i.e., good). Aquinas tends to talk about God's perfection before he turns to God's goodness. And, as I have noted, he takes God to be perfect as not being able to be thought of as something able to be better than what it essentially is (this, of course, being a conclusion noting what God is *not*). Aquinas's philosophical discussions of God's perfection tend to proceed without reference to the things that he thinks God has made to be (albeit that they depend on what Aquinas takes himself to have shown when arguing that *Deus est* is true, a position he always defends philosophically by means of causal argumentation). His discussions of God's goodness, however, start from what he takes us to be able to infer on the basis of what God has brought about. We might, Aquinas thinks, abstractly ruminate on God's perfection without thinking of anything made to be by him. Our reasons for speaking of God as good, though, Aquinas holds, need to be (and can in fact be) grounded in what we can know of God on the basis of what he has created, a knowledge, Aquinas thinks, that allows us to proclaim that God is essentially good, regardless of him having created.

Yet what of the evils we encounter? How does Aquinas think that we should think of them when reflecting on God's goodness? I have tried at some length to explain how he does so. But let me now (and drawing on terminology of Aquinas explained above) try to summarize what I have been reporting in order to provide a simple account of Aquinas on God and evil, his big picture on this, so to speak. Thus, for Aquinas:

(1) Evil or badness in the world exists insofar as naturally occurring substances (*entia per se*) lack goodness that is proper to them. It can also, though in a secondary sense, be thought to exist insofar as *entia per accidens* lack some attribute we might want or expect them to have.

(2) Evil or badness is not an illusion. We can truly speak of it as existing or as having occurred. Unlike naturally occurring substances, though, and even unlike accidents, evil or badness (*malum*) lacks *esse*. Considered as such, it cannot be thought of as creatively caused to exist by God.

(3) Yet goodness in the world cannot be thought of in this way. Something is good in that it succeeds in being in some way (as displaying *esse* in some form, whether substantial or accidental). Some things may be deficient or lacking in goodness. Some may be less than perfect. Yet all things are good in that, as displaying *esse*, they succeed somehow in being. The goodness of everything, since it amounts to the possession of *esse* is (unlike badness) creatively caused to exist by God.

(4) Goodness and badness are objective (not just in the eye of the beholder). Things are good insofar as they have *esse* (substantially or accidentally). *Esse* is God's "characteristic" effect. It is what God produces as Creator, as making things to be as against nothing at all. We have reason, even without reference to divine revelation, to suppose that God, as Creator, truly exists.

(5) Insofar as goodness exists in creatures, it is made to be by God, who is the creative source of all creaturely goodness without exception. This "making to be" is not just a matter of making something good to begin to be (as if it could continue on its own steam once God had set things going). It is a matter of making what is good to be for as long as it has *esse* (exists as actual).

(6) If God is what makes everything having *esse* to be, if God is the Creator of what *has* but *is* not *esse*, then God is no substance in the world and no accident either. As the cause of all creaturely (substantial) being, and of all coming to be (of all *accidents*), God is no member of a natural kind and is no passing feature had by any such member. So God is neither material nor changeable. Rather, he is the cause of the existence of *all* that is material and mutable.

(7) We can distinguish between knowing what something is and knowing that something is. Given that our knowledge of objects derives from sensory experience, for us to know what something is requires that we are able to pick

it out as a part of the physical world and to arrive at a definition of it. Since God is not part of the physical world, we cannot, in this sense, know what God is. So we do well to take note of what God is *not*. And, with this thought in mind, we can, at least, note that God the Creator is not changeable, not a member of a kind (not an individual X, Y, or Z), not something the essence of which can be distinguished from what it is, and not something the existence of which is derived from anything other than itself. In short, we can say that God is simple. But accepting this conclusion does not commit us to denying that we can be justified in framing genuine subject-predicate statements about God, ones that are true (albeit that they inevitably distort the reality they are talking about). One of these is "God is good."

(8) To call God good is to try to say what he is by nature. So "God is good" does not, for example, simply mean that God creates things that are good, for God creates freely and has no need of creatures in order to be what he essentially is. Yet we can defend the claim that God is good with reference to creatures. Their goodness derives from God and amounts to his creative action in them. So it tells us something about him. In particular, it tells us that God, in his divine simplicity, must somehow contain in himself the goodness had by all creatures. Since the goodness of creatures is God's action in them, it shows us what God is. It does not show us this as, say, pictures of people show us what they are. It does so on the formal principle that what an agent cause produces reflects what it is. Created goodness comes in many different forms and is possessed by things that fall very short of (and are very different from) what God is by nature. But, as amounting to the possession of *esse*, all created goodness points to God as subsisting being itself (*ipsum esse subsistens*), whose goodness exists before that of creatures and is what makes them to be what creatures are insofar as they are good. To say this is not to attempt a description of God. It is to make a remark about what has to be true about what continually eludes our comprehension (i.e., God).

(9) "Good" is not an adjective singling out a discrete property had by some things and not others. In this sense it differs from adjectives like "rectangular" or "marble." In general, one cannot understand what "X is good" means unless one knows what X is. And, in general, therefore, to call something good is to identify it as a member of some class in the world while evaluating it accordingly. But God is not a member of some class in the world. So we should not think of God as being a good member of any genus or species.

(10) One might be tempted to say that God is a morally good individual—a moral saint, as it were. To give into the temptation would be wrong, however. Our talk of moral goodness has its home in talk about morally worthy human beings, who are good insofar as they display human virtues (as discussed by

Aristotle) or insofar as they act in ways that they are obliged to do. But we cannot think of God as possessing human virtues, which, as Aristotle notes, are dispositions needed by people in order to flourish as people (albeit that our possession of virtue might bring us to our graves). Nor can we think of God as being obliged in any intelligible sense. In this sense, it would be wrong to think of God's goodness as a matter of conforming to some standard to which he is subject. To do so would be to forget about the difference there must be between creatures and God. One can, of course, say that God is truly (and not metaphorically) just. But God's justice cannot amount to him paying what he owes to anything, for God is the debtor of nothing created. Rather, it amounts to him giving creatures what is owed to them given the natures that they have as his creatures (natures of his making and design).

(11) Evil (*malum*) can be thought of as of two kinds: evil suffered (*malum poenae*) and evil done (*malum culpae*). But God cannot be thought of as creatively producing evil in either of these senses. Evil suffered occurs as God makes something to be good while bringing about badness or deficiency in something else. Its explanation lies not in God's willing evil for its own sake but in his willing the goodness of something the goodness of which (as time goes on) involves a lack of being (goodness) in something else. With evil suffered there is always a lack of being and a concomitant good accounting for this (check with the scientists). Not so, however, with evil done. There is no concomitant good here. There is nothing but a failure to choose what is good. But a failure such as this cannot be thought of as created by God. It is, so we might say, brought about by God insofar as he brings about a world in which freely choosing individuals freely choose badly.

(12) To say so, however, is not to suppose that human free choices are not caused to be by God. Human freedom does not, and cannot, consist in people acting independently of God. Indeed, God, if he is indeed the Creator and not a celestial observer (Top Person), must creatively cause all that is real when people freely choose to act as they do. Yet this does not mean that when people act freely they are being determined by God when it comes to what they do. Their freedom remains intact. That is because, as creatively causing them to act as they do, God is making them to be themselves. God causes some created processes to come about as determined by individuals or collections of individuals in the world. Thus, for example, he brings it about that people automatically and inevitably fall asleep when an anesthetic is administered to them. But God also makes to be things that are not proceeding as they do because they are causally determined by something else. For God to create something is not for God to interfere with its way of being (whatever it happens to be). It is for God to make the thing to exist as what it is. And, so we

must add, for God to do this is for God to love the thing in question. Insofar as love is taken to be an emotion, it cannot be ascribed to God (since emotions are, strictly speaking, what physical human beings undergo and since they are the result of something affecting or bringing about a change while God is the unchangeable source of the being and activity of everything other than himself). Yet "to love" can also mean "to will goodness to something." In this sense it can be fittingly ascribed to God since he freely does this insofar as he brings about the existence of anything. All creaturely being and goodness is brought about by God freely (not because his nature constrains him to bring it about and not because he is forced to bring it about by some agent other than himself). In this sense, God loves all creatures (insofar as they reflect the goodness that he is).

(13) Everything noted in items 1–12 above can be defended without recourse to divine revelation. It is philosophical property, so to speak. And it shows that (a) there is no contradiction involved in asserting that God and evil both exist and (b) that we have reason to assert both that God exists and that evil does so as well (allowing for different understandings of "exist" in "God exists" and "evil exists"). On the basis of divine revelation, however, there is more to be said of God's goodness than items 1–12 state.

(14) Important to remember is that, though God creates what is good, though God governs the world so that goodness has its part in the way history develops, and though God gives us many good things in this life, he has also made us to be united with him after death. Human beatitude, the vision of God, is the ultimate good for people, and God brings some people to this (though not those who do not genuinely want it, not those who do not love the goodness that God is). In this life also, God shares his knowledge and nature with people by virtue of the theological virtues of faith, hope, and charity. That the beatific vision is a reality, and that faith, hope, and charity are genuine and important virtues that unite us to God, cannot be established philosophically. Through Jesus Christ, however, God has taught us about our highest end and about himself. And he brings us to himself through grace, which is the outpouring of God's goodness as leading us to him.

(15) God is not essentially the Creator of the universe. There might never have been a universe since the universe and its inhabitants do not exist by nature and since God was not compelled to make them to exist. God, however, is essentially Father, Son, and Spirit (the blessed Trinity)—a life of love transcending the created order. And it is the will of the Trinity (one God, not three gods) that people should share in its joy.

(16) Fittingly to bring this about, God the Son became incarnate so as to teach us about his Father and so as to express God's love for us in concrete

terms—by embracing us in our weakness and humanity, by acting toward us in friendship, and by dying for us.

(17) The Bible frequently says that God became incarnate so as to free us from the consequences of sin. Sin distances us from God. It is, indeed, the state of being distant from or estranged from God. Can it be overcome? Can we sinners be reunited to God? We can in that God can simply forgive our sins (which amount to refusals to act well and in harmony with God's goodness, which is the source of all creaturely goodness). The life and death of Christ, though, show us another (and particularly good) way in which God has chosen to unite us to him. In Christ, God identifies with humanity in an absolute sense—by taking on human nature, by being one of us, by giving us an example of how to behave, and by affirming us (if we embrace what he stands for). Christ, as a matter of fact, died a cruel death. Since this was inflicted on him by the choices of people, it was not inevitable (not causally determined). But Christ, indeed, died a cruel death. How can we think of this death? We can think of it as a way in which God (without having to) provides satisfaction for our sins and for those of anyone at any time. As sinners we owe God in that we have offended against the goodness that he is. As dying on the cross, God cancels this debt on our behalf and as one of us. God's death is of no effect on someone who does not want (explicitly or implicitly) what Jesus shows us God to be about. But it is a very good way to bring us to him.

Concluding Reflections

So there you have Aquinas's basic position on the topic of God and evil, one that depends on both philosophical and theological arguments. But is it to be taken seriously? As I said in my preface and in chapter 1, this book does not aim to evaluate Aquinas's teachings on God and evil (and goodness). It is intended to give readers an overall account of his thinking on this matter. But I cannot resist ending the present volume without briefly saying something about critical questions that might be thought to arise with respect to what I have been reporting in previous chapters. The observations I make will, indeed, be brief. Yet I hope they might help readers when it comes to thinking for themselves about Aquinas on God and evil (and goodness).

Grasping and Understanding God

Some critics of Aquinas on God and evil have tended to dispute what he says for exactly opposite reasons. On the one hand, so some have argued, Aquinas's general approach to God distinguishes between God and things in the world in an unacceptable way. On the other hand, so others have maintained, it does not distinguish between God and things in the world sufficiently.

Defenders of the first thesis are generally arguing that Aquinas is wrong to say that we do not know what God is, wrong to suppose him unchangeable, and wrong to regard him as simple. Favoring a serious comparison between God and human beings, such thinkers often go on to argue that Aquinas's whole approach to God is just not compatible with the biblical portrait of God as person-like.[2] Yet defenders of the second thesis maintain exactly the opposite line while arguing that Aquinas wrongly supposes that he can, so to speak, get his mind around God and reify him somewhat. They take Aquinas mistakenly to be taking God to be, as it were, the biggest thing around, a great being but still one that is only quantitatively different from what can be found in the universe. Sometimes these critics object to Aquinas as thinking of God as an ultimate explanation of things.[3]

The obvious point to note in favor of the first approach is that God is frequently depicted in the Bible (though chiefly in the Old Testament) in anthropomorphic terms, as being very like a human being. He gets into discussions with people, he changes his mind, and he displays emotions. He even goes walking. It is not hard to see why people fond of the formula "God is a person" see themselves as reflecting scriptural ways of talking about God. On the other hand, however, biblical authors often insist on the difference between God and everything else, on his otherness, on his majesty, on the mystery and hiddenness of divinity, and on God being the maker of heaven and earth. Talk emphasizing what we might call God's transcendence is as much in evidence in the Bible as is talk that strongly compares God to people. And Aquinas certainly takes it very seriously. Is he right to do so on biblical grounds? There seems to be no way of answering this question since the Bible does not interpret itself. Instead, it offers us, without comment, different ways of speaking of God, some of them anthropomorphic and some of them decidedly not.[4] Is there some criterion to which we might appeal when trying to decide which of these ways to favor? None is offered by biblical authors. There is, for example, no biblical text that tells us that biblical passages speaking of God anthropomorphically should be privileged over ones that do not, or vice versa. So we clearly need some non-biblical grounds for determining how to read what the Bible says about God (and if we seriously take the Bible as teaching us about God).

Aquinas thinks that we have such grounds. These lie in his reasons for saying that rational reflection can inform us about God to some extent (at least to the extent of being able to say that God exists and that certain things cannot be literally affirmed of him).[5] In this sense, what we might call his philosophy of religion influences the way in which he reads the Bible. Should it? One might say that it should not since, like authors such as Barth, whom I mentioned above, one might take natural theology to be something incompatible with biblical thinking (since one might think that there is nothing to be known of God apart from Christian revelation and since one might take this to be the biblical view). But does the Bible support this conclusion? I doubt so, and mostly for the reasons presented in James Barr's excellent book *Biblical Faith and Natural Theology*.[6] As Barr correctly observes, the Bible does not present systematic arguments concerning God's existence and nature of the kind found in the writings of Aquinas. But neither does it say that God cannot be known to exist apart from Christian revelation. Quite the contrary. Obvious biblical passages to note here are Acts 17 and Romans 1. Having analyzed the first of these texts Barr rightly concludes that it "cannot be fully expounded without opening the gate to some sort of natural theology."[7] Having analyzed the second of these texts he concludes, rightly again, that it appears "to imply that there is something 'known of God' which is revealed through his created works, which is accessible to all human beings through their being human."[8] Aquinas's philosophy of God, so we might say, is prompted by this biblical way of thinking. One might resist it on the ground that the Bible does nothing to endorse the notion of natural theology. But it does. And, as Barr observes, "If you thoroughly reject natural theology, and if natural theology underlies the Bible in any significant degree, then you must judge that the Bible is inadequate as a theological guide."[9]

One might try to fault Aquinas's philosophy of God on philosophical grounds. And one may, of course, think that Aquinas gives us no good philosophical reason to believe in God, or to believe that God is simple and everything else Aquinas takes him to be as I have reported him. Philosophical critics of Aquinas's philosophical reasons for believing in God, and philosophical critics of his philosophical account of God's nature, are legion (as are philosophical defenders of Aquinas's thinking on these matters). In this book I have tried to explain what he thinks about the existence of God and the nature of God. At this point I would simply like to suggest that Aquinas is right to ask why there is something rather than nothing (which I take to be a causal question). This seems to me to be a natural question to ask. And I think that Aquinas is right to conclude that the answer to this question cannot lie in the existence of something that is part of the world, something mutable, something to be thought of as one member of a kind, and something to be thought of as deriving its existence from something else. It has been said that the true atheist is someone who is not struck by the question, "Why is there something rather than nothing?" And I think that this verdict is correct. Self-proclaimed atheists commonly proceed

by declaring that we have no need to invoke God as we go about our way of noting how the world is and what (in the world) brought it to be as it is now. Such
atheists, though, seem clearly to be thinking of "God exists" as a scientific hypothesis. But how can it be this? It certainly is not if we take "God exists" to mean
what generations of Jewish, Muslim, and Christian thinkers have taken it to be.
These have typically taken God to account for the existence of the universe as a
whole and not to be something in it inferred to exist on the basis of data available
to us. And Aquinas is entirely with them on this thought.

Yet, as I noted above, some would take Aquinas to err by dragging God
down to the level of creatures. And, perhaps, one can see why they might wish
to do so. For does not Aquinas approach God by reasoning from effect to cause?
And does his doing so not render God one object of inquiry among others, a
being among beings, effectively part of the universe? Yet, and as I have tried to
make clear, Aquinas has a very strong notion of God's transcendence. He does
not take God to be one cause among a multitude of other causes. He speaks of
God as a cause, and he says that there is but one God. As applied to God,
though, "cause" for Aquinas designates something unique: not a transforming
agent but a creative one, and one (unlike anything in the created order) that is
entirely simple (unchangeable, not an individual, not created).

Some of Aquinas's commentators, anxious to distinguish him from people thinking of God anthropomorphically and anxious to insist that he empha-
sizes God's otherness, have seemed to suggest that Aquinas takes us to have
no knowledge of God at all. And they have a point since, when talking of God's
nature, Aquinas often says that he is considering ways in which God does not
exist. They also have a case to make because Aquinas insists that God is incomprehensible. But, as I have said, Aquinas thinks that we can truly affirm certain
things of God without equivocation and that we can know that what we say
when doing so is true. Aquinas can properly be called an apophatic thinker,
and it is notable that one of the authors he most favorably cites is the so-called
Pseudo-Dionysius, whose emphasis on the transcendence and unknowability
of God is extreme.[10] Yet Aquinas often backs off from some of the ways in
which Dionysius denies that we have knowledge of God. On the other hand,
though, Aquinas clearly does, as I have tried to show, want radically to distinguish between God and creatures, does not regard God as "just another thing
alongside others" (so to speak), and does not take God to be *a* supreme being
among things comparable to him. He does not even take God to be an ultimate explanation of anything. I take an explanation to be something we understand better than what we invoke it to explain (as I said above). Yet Aquinas
never even comes close to suggesting that we understand God better than
anything else.

The Suffering of God

Critics of Aquinas on God and evil have sometimes argued that there can be no room, as Aquinas seems to think there can be, for the claim that God does not suffer. As we have seen, Aquinas does in fact think that God can be thought of as suffering since Jesus (God incarnate) suffered, died, and was buried. As we have also seen, however, Aquinas does not believe that the second person of the Trinity suffered in his divine nature (as God), only in his human one (as a man). For some theologians, however, such a way of thinking is inadequate—and especially inadequate as we think about the evil in the world.

Perhaps the best known contemporary exponent of this view is Jürgen Moltmann. He argues that human suffering requires us to think of God in his whole being as also suffering. Moltmann's view is that all thinking about God should start from Christ being crucified. Someone like Aquinas might say that we can think about God, and even know something about him, even without respect to Christ's crucifixion. Moltmann, though, thinks otherwise. Our reflections on God, he says, must begin from the image of the crucified God. So, Moltmann claims, theologians should not have any time for the notions of divine impassibility and immutability. He also believes that, by insisting that God is essentially one who suffers, we have a message of hope to give to those who suffer. The good news according to Moltmann is that God is essentially one who sides with those who suffer and is in solidarity with them. For Moltmann, God is no immutable individual who cannot be seriously involved with us.[11]

One might, perhaps, validly distinguish between suffering that is voluntarily accepted and suffering that is not. Even so, though, one might also wonder what message of hope there is to give to people while telling them that God is essentially vulnerable and that he has, in fact, been adversely affected by something distinct from himself. Should we feel comforted by God (no matter how well meaning) being essentially in as much of a mess as we are? But it is not hard to see how Moltmann arrives at his basic conclusion (so much at odds with ways in which Aquinas thinks). Start by being horrified by human suffering; then ask, "What has Christianity to say about this?" while discarding purely philosophical reflection on God's existence and nature and also discarding (a) classical Christian texts that insist that the incarnation involves the existence of one subject with two distinct natures, and (b) any Trinitarian thinking that does not involve reference to the crucifixion of Christ. Yet should one set aside philosophical reflection on God's existence and nature a priori even in a context of talk about the cross? And, of course, remembering that the notion of Christ's distinct natures is fundamental to what many would regard as Christian orthodoxy (as represented by the Council of Chalcedon, for example), one might ask why it should be set aside and, if it is set aside, what sense can be made of the claim that Christ is God without it. New Testament talk about God presupposes Old Testament talk, which says nothing of the crucifixion. And, as commonly construed, the doctrine of the Trinity supposes that the Trinity existed prior to the crucifixion (that God, so to speak, did not have to wait until the crucifixion in order to become triune).[12] With thoughts like these in mind we can at least regard Aquinas as offering an interestingly different and more traditional approach to God, goodness, and evil from that offered by Moltmann.

In fact, so one might argue, the fundamental goal of Moltmann and his supporters is one that Aquinas himself actually tries to pursue as he proceeds. What is it that Moltmann and his supporters are most concerned to stress? It seems to be that, so they believe, God exists as thoroughly involved with human beings, even in their suffering. Focusing on the cross of Christ, and insisting that God (by nature, or *as* God) suffers, seems to them to draw attention to this fact in the best possible way. If we take Aquinas's thoughts on God and evil as a whole, however, we can see him as also wanting to stress God's involvement. For him, God is more involved with all of us than any of us can be with each other.

That, he thinks, is because God is present to everything that is real in us as creatively making it to be and, in this sense, is never outside or apart from us. I might "feel with" you, but in doing so I am always an observer and something outside you. For Aquinas, though, God is in us and in all that we are and do, which means that God is wholly involved with us. The point is well made by Herbert McCabe when commenting on Moltmann with an eye on Aquinas:

> Our only way of being present to another's suffering is by being affected by it, because we are outside the other person. We speak of "sympathy" or "*compassion*" just because we want to say that it is *almost* as though we were not outside the other but living her or his life, experiencing her or his suffering. A component of pity is frustration at having, in the end, to remain outside. Now, the creator cannot in this way ever be outside his creature; a person's act of being as well as every action done has to be an act of the creator. If the creator is the reason for everything that is, there can be no actual being which does not have the creator as its centre holding it in being. In our compassion we, in our feeble way, are seeking to be what God is all the time: united with and within the life of our friend. We can say in the psalm "The Lord is compassion" but a sign that this is metaphorical language is that we can also say that the Lord has

no need of compassion; he has something more wonderful, he has his creative act in which he is "closer to the sufferer than she is to herself."[13]

There can, I think, be little doubt that Aquinas's approach to God as Creator is one in which God is indeed involved with us, and more so than writers like Moltmann conceive of him as being. For them, God has what McCabe calls "compassion." For Aquinas, God is involved with us as making us to be ourselves. Critics of Aquinas coming from Moltmann's perspective regularly attack him for saying that God is not changeable and not passive to the actions of anything other than himself. This, they have said, has to mean that God is static (like a stone) or indifferent or even callous, which are surely things that those who believe in God cannot take him to be. Yet, and as I noted above, Aquinas does not take God to be static, indifferent, or callous. His "one cannot ascribe change to God" and "God is not passive to the actions of what is not God" merely tell us what God is *not* and do not imply that God is positively thus-and-so (e.g., static, indifferent, or callous). One might suggest that static, indifferent, and callous are how Aquinas positively describes God as being. But this suggestion seems somewhat implausible given what we have now seen Aquinas to be saying. Far from being static as is a stone, the God of Aquinas is actively present and freely at work throughout the created order. The range and extent of his activity is unsurpassed. And far from being indifferent and callous, the God of Aquinas freely gives creatures the goodness they possess, is drawn to (or positively wills) goodness in its various forms and as it exists perfectly in him, and sends us his Son to live and die so as to bring us to beatitude (assuming that what we want is what the Son of God incarnate wants). How less than static, indifferent, or callous could the God of Aquinas possibly be?[14]

The Person God Is

One might reply, as Moltmann, I think, would not, but as many philosophers of religion writing today certainly would, that Aquinas's whole approach to God and evil fails since it does not allow for God being a person (since, indeed, it contradicts that fact). And, if we take a person to be a changing center of consciousness that learns and is acted on, one can easily see the force of this reply.

Aquinas, to be sure, is not trying to contradict the proposition "God is a person" since that is not a proposition with which he was familiar (except in the contexts of discussions about the Trinity). And none of his contemporaries were out either to defend or to attack it (considered as a proposition telling us what God is essentially). In retrospect, though, we can certainly read Aquinas as, by implication, not buying into the suggestion that God (in the above sense) is a person (indeed, he would positively disparage this suggestion). For, as we have seen, he maintains that God is entirely simple (immutable, not distinct from his nature, and not created). As we have also seen, he denies that God, unlike persons of our acquaintance (people), is subject to moral obligations or is rightly to be evaluated with an eye on human virtues and vices. It has been said that God is a person since he is an other to whom people can relate. And Aquinas does not deny this, as I have noted. He thinks of God as one to whom we can pray and as one whom we can think of as caring and providing for us. But he does not think of God as an invisible Cartesian consciousness existing in time alongside us while viewing our behavior and trying to respond to it.

Aquinas's approach to God and evil is very different from those who approach the topic while assuming that God is a person. Some philosophers would not worry about this fact since they would challenge the idea that our talk of (human) persons can be employed so as to intelligibly to talk about something nonmaterial (as God is supposed to be).[15] Many philosophers (perhaps most analytical ones writing today) think of people as nothing but collections of physical processes whose behavior can be exhaustively explained and described by physics.[16] Others, without going that far, maintain that we cannot make sense of what people (persons) are without taking them to be ineluctably parts of a physical world—yielding the conclusion that "incorporeal person" is a non-sensical expression.[17] Most of these thinkers, however, are not in the business of defending belief in God, as was Aquinas. So should he not be expected to insist that persons are essentially incorporeal and to defend belief in God on that basis?

As a matter of fact, Aquinas did not believe that human persons are essentially incorporeal. He took people to be essentially corporeal and, therefore, looked forward to the resurrection of the dead and not to the immortality of the soul.[18] So he is not at all inclined to say that God is what human persons are. Instead, he stresses the differences between God and people so as to insist on the difference between God and created things. That, I presume, is why he would not have wanted to insist that God is a person, in the above sense of "person," should someone have asked him to determine on the matter. Yet might he have been wrong here?

He might be wrong if God is rightly to be thought of as an inhabitant of the universe, something having a nature and existing alongside other things. But why think of God as being this? Biblical texts do not generally seem to do so, in spite of their often speaking of God in anthropomorphic ways. And the claim that God is the Creator of all things (a claim made by all Jews, Muslims, and

Christians) seems strongly to suggest that God is anything but an inhabitant of the universe. One might say that God, while being the Creator of the world, is still something existing alongside it (as I can coexist with my cake as I am baking it). But what about the traditional idea that for God to create is for God to make all things to be from nothing (*ex nihilo*)? If that idea makes sense, it seems to imply that all existing things have their being from God, who cannot seriously be thought of as being part of the spatiotemporal world or as an inhabitant of the universe in any sense at all. And if God is that from which all existing things have their being, talk of him existing alongside objects in the universe seems out of place and needs to be replaced by talk that insists on how nothing can be compared to God as one thing in the world can be compared with another. It is, perhaps, no accident that the Bible does not press any clear image or picture of God.[19]

Against Aquinas it might be replied that the Bible certainly presents God as being a dutiful or virtuous character, as someone well behaved, as someone always acting from morally sufficient reasons. But it really does not do so. Actually, it most emphatically does not do so. The Bible certainly insists that God is holy, righteous, gracious (to some, anyway), faithful to his promises, merciful (again, to some), and so on. But it never commends God on moral grounds or suggests that God acts (or ought to act) in accordance with moral requirements binding on him or as able to provide his morally sufficient reasons for creating as he does. Old Testament talk of God's righteousness is emphasizing that God can be expected to act as he has said he will with respect to the people of Israel. It is bound up with the concept of covenant.[20] Biblical talk of God's graciousness and mercy never comes with the suggestion that these are owed by him. A classic passage that indicates this is Romans 9. Here St. Paul notes that not all of the "chosen" people have turned to Christ (whom Paul takes to be the Jewish Messiah). How come? Paul goes on to speak of God electing as he sees fit. But does God electing as he does ("loving" Jacob but "hating" Esau, as Paul puts it) imply that God is not just? Paul's answer is "no," but not because he thinks that God has read and learned from what Aristotle says of justice. God, he thinks, is just insofar as he acts as God, not insofar as he conforms to a binding standard of justice with which he is presented. One may think that God is morally bound to act in certain ways toward certain individuals. Paul does not seem to agree, however. If anything, he appears to side with Immanuel Kant (a great exponent of the notion of duty) when he says that God "is the only being to whom the concept of duty is inapplicable."[21] Many philosophers of religion will reply that it is part and parcel of traditional theism that God always does what he ought to do, that his goodness is that of a morally good agent acting with an eye on moral truths. If "traditional" here means "biblical," however, then such philosophers of religion are clearly wrong. Might "traditional" here mean what we can find in the writings of theologians from, say, Augustine of Hippo to Thomas Aquinas? But Christian authors from Augustine to Aquinas never assume that God acts on the basis of a moral claim on him.

That God is a moral agent obeying (or refusing to obey) moral demands made on him seems to me to be an invention of twentieth- or twenty-first-century philosophers who, perhaps influenced by David Hume, appear to think that God (if he exists) is, given what we know of people with whom we live, the best-behaved person around. As we have seen, though, Aquinas does not think along these lines. He does not think of God as being *possibly* morally good or *possibly* morally bad. He thinks of God as making to be a world in which we are able to distinguish between good moral individuals and bad ones. R. F. Holland writes:

> It makes sense for *us* to have or fail to have moral reasons for our doings and refrainings because as human beings we are members of a moral community.... But God is not a member of a moral community or of any community. To be sure there are small "g" gods who have been conceived in that way, like those of the ancient Greeks: such gods are like fairies. To credit the one true God with having a moral reason for doing anything is to conceive Him in the matter of Greek popular religion as a being among beings instead of the absolute being who is the Creator of the world.[22]

Holland is not here writing in defense of Aquinas, but his position succinctly captures what Aquinas thinks about God as having (or lacking) moral grounds. And the position of both of them certainly seems to cohere with biblical accounts of God. Aquinas would say that it is also something forced on us by philosophical reflection on God as Creator. Is he right to think like this? You will realize that I think that he is, and, if he is, then he has a viable and important approach to the topic of God and evil—one that is very different from that adopted by many philosophers and theologians. If Aquinas is right, then the problem of evil is not a serious problem at all but rather the result of a confused way of thinking of God. And, if that is the case, it is well for us to realize it when talking about God, goodness, and evil. Doing so, of course, does not mean that we are not left with sensible questions to ask such as "Does God exist?" "Can God be called good?" "How is God causally related to evil of various kinds"? and "How should we think of God and evil in the light of divine revelation?" As we have seen, though, Aquinas both raises and tries to give answers to these questions. His ensuing discussions take us to the heart of his thinking on God and evil.

Do they do so in a trite or condescending way? I mean, does Aquinas think that he has resolved the problem of evil, and is he writing as someone magisterially claiming to have figured out what has perplexed so many people reflecting on the topic of God and evil? N. T. Wright says, "There is a noble Christian tradition which takes evil so seriously that it warns us against the temptation to 'solve' it in any obvious way. If you offer an analysis of evil which leaves us saying, 'Well, that's all right then, we now see how it happens and what to do about it', you have belittled the problem."[23] And what Wright observes seems to me sound. So one might be naturally suspicious of someone who regards himself as having gotten his or her mind around both God and evil. Is Aquinas such a person, however? Some people seem to assume that he is, that he takes himself as having neatly tidied up anything that we might think of as the mystery of God and evil. Yet such a view of him is deeply misguided, for, in a serious sense, Aquinas has no solution to the problem of evil and does not think of himself as being able to explain the occurrence of evil in the world.

For one thing, and as I have stressed, what goes by the name "the problem of evil" since the time of Hume (or, indeed, Epicurus) is not a problem for Aquinas. Without denying God's omnipotence, omniscience, or goodness, he does not think that God has any moral case to answer.

Then again, though Aquinas in one sense thinks that he can account for why evil occurs, he does not claim anything but a general understanding of what is going on when *malum poenae* and *malum culpae* come to pass. With respect to *malum poenae* his position is nothing other than that of someone who holds that evil suffered must always have a natural or scientific explanation. With respect to *malum culpae* he argues that it always comes about as a freely acting agent turns away from certain goods. But Aquinas never claims to understand why God has made a world containing evil. He thinks that God might have made a world with no evil in it and that even the world as it is reflects God's nature as good. But he does not claim to fathom God's motives in bringing things about as they exactly are. He talks of God as willing the goodness of creatures insofar as he wills the goodness that he is (and as containing the goodness of creatures in a higher way). But he certainly does not think that he has thereby provided what we might call a rationale for God's creating (or not creating) as he does. I might explain why people voted for a certain politician by noting their desires, their circumstances, and their knowledge of the world (or their lack of it). You might then say, "Ah, of course, I see. Now I understand why those votes were cast." But Aquinas does not write as though he has a comparable understanding of God and evil. On his account, there being a world with evil when there might have been no evil at all is thoroughly mysterious (as is God).

Aquinas is convinced that sober reflection ought to lead us to see that "God exists" and "evil exists" are not logically incompatible statements. So he is convinced that we have reasons for asserting that God exists and that evil exists (and, in this sense, takes himself to have an answer to the charge that evil is evidence against God's existence).[24] But he does not take himself to have searched the mind of God so as to be able to come up with an intellectually satisfying ("Ah, now I see") answer to why there is evil at all or why there are the particular evils that have occurred and do occur. And, indeed, one would not expect him to, given his fundamental conviction that we are seriously in the dark when thinking of God.

Yes, he maintains, we can know that *Deus est* is true. And yes, he also maintains, we can speak truly of God both on the basis of philosophical reflection and on the basis of revelation. But, so he also thinks, we have no comprehensive knowledge of God, we do not know what God is (*quid est*), and we cannot produce a neat explanation of particular instances of evil with a view to God's intentions. Instead, so he clearly thinks, when thinking of evil and God we need (so to speak) to balance several balls simultaneously in the air.

We have to remember that God exists and is the Creator of all that is real. We also have to remember that (even apart from what we learn from divine revelation) God can be thought of as good. And we need to remember the goodness that God has brought about (and will bring about) both in the created order as a whole and by virtue of the life and death of Christ. That Aquinas thinks along these lines is reason enough for us to say that he does not claim to have dissolved the mystery of evil. Instead, his basic approach when it comes to talking about evil and God is to try to remind us of ways in which God can be thought of in relation to evil without trying to explain how God might account for himself to us in a discussion over dinner.

One might say that what Aquinas says on God and evil is insensitive in that it does not acknowledge the horrendous evils that have occurred, that it does not speak to victims who have suffered hugely or dreadfully.[25] Yet it would be wrong to say that Aquinas does not acknowledge horrendous evils (of which he must have been aware). It would be more accurate to say that, with the possible exception of his discussions of Christ's crucifixion, he does not spend time dwelling in graphic detail on forms that horrendous evil can take. And, one might ask, why should he? He is concerned to reflect on God's causal relation to evil of any kind, and so he does. And in doing so he offers an account that bears, by implication at any rate, on horrendous evil as well as any other kind. One might think that horrendous evil calls for special comment since it represents a challenge to belief in God of a kind not raised by other evil. But why suppose that? Perhaps because horrendous evil is a lot of evil while other kinds of evil are less in magnitude. But if there is a case to be made against God's existence based on evil, then I (agreeing here with William Rowe) do not see why even any one case of evil, regardless of magnitude, does not make it. As we have seen, Aquinas thinks that there is no evil whose existence counts against God's existence. If he is right, then he might, perhaps, be excused from having spared himself the job of singling out horrendous evil for special attention.

So is Aquinas's approach to God and evil a correct one? Given that God is the Creator of the universe (and not one of its inhabitants), given that God makes the difference between there being something rather than nothing, I would suggest that it is. For what is the alternative? One might say that God should be able so to account for himself (or that his friends should be able to do so on his behalf) since we rightly have expectations of God that the existence of evil seems to show him as not living up to. This is the position of those who start by thinking that there has to be some conflict between God being good and evil being real, a position that assumes that there being both evil and God is prima facie impossible or unlikely. Yet it is not unlikely given what generations of those who have believed in God have thought for centuries. Christians take God to be the Father of Jesus, who died unjustly on a cross. So it seems manifestly absurd to suggest that there being evil conflicts with what Christians think of God. That there is evil is positively *part and parcel* of belief in God as Christians subscribe to it. As for Jewish authors (by which I mean Old Testament ones), it seems clear that they do not take evil as a reason for disbelieving in God. Rather, their view of God takes him to be present in all that we might think of as bad. My point here is that Old Testament thinking incorporates evil into its talk about God while also finding him present in occurring evil. As the psalmist says:

> Where can I go from your spirit?
> Or where can I flee from your presence?
> If I ascend to heaven, you are there;
> if I make my bed in Sheol, you are there. (Psalm 139.7–8)

Old Testament authors do not regard evil as something unlikely should God exist. They take it to be something to be reckoned with in the world that God has made (because he has made a world in which there is evil). They are obviously not thinking along the lines of those who take "God exists" and "evil exists" to be prima facie impossible or unlikely. Yet those who do so typically tell us that they are only reacting to what is believed by those who believe in God. I do not, however, think that they are, and (by implication) neither does Aquinas. The assumption that "God exists" and "evil exists" evidently conflict with each other is not one based on the biblical accounts of God nor on what many Christian and Jewish theologians have taken to be obvious when it comes to what belief in God amounts to. If one wishes to make a case against the existence of God, one needs to pay some attention not only to what might be known of God philosophically but also to what belief in God traditionally amounts to. Aquinas does this and might, therefore, be thought of as someone more in tune than some others with what those who believe in God along traditional lines might actually think about God and evil.

Notes

ꝗ

PREFACE

1. Herbert McCabe's *God and Evil in the Theology of St. Thomas Aquinas*, ed. Brian Davies (London/New York: Continuum, 2010), may be regarded as an exception here. But the text is a short one and, in spite of its title, has nothing to say about what Aquinas would have called "the articles of faith." McCabe's text focuses on Aquinas's philosophy of religion with an eye on explaining how (in McCabe's view) this serves to rebut the charge that God cannot exist given that evil exists. That said, however, I strongly recommend McCabe's book to readers.

CHAPTER I

1. For a nonphilosopher (or, perhaps better, someone who did not earn his living as a professional philosopher) expressing such a view, see what the late George Carlin has to say in his *Napalm and Silly Putty* (New York: Hyperion, 2001), 28.

2. David Hume, *Dialogues concerning Natural Religion*, ed. Stanley Tweyman (London/New York: Routledge, 1991), 57. Epicurus lived from 342/341 to 270 B.C. The quotation from him to which Hume (I presume) refers can be found in Patrologia Latina 7.121, here translated by M. B. Ahern in his much-to-be-recommended book *The Problem of Evil* (London: Routledge & Kegan Paul, 1971), 2: "God either wishes to take away evils, and is unable; or he is able, and is unwilling; or he is neither willing nor able; or he is both willing and able. If he is willing and able, he is feeble, which is not in accordance with character of God; if he is able and unwilling, he is malicious, which is equally at variance with God; if he is neither willing nor

able, he is both malicious and feeble and therefore not God; if he is both willing and able, which is alone suitable to God, from what source then are evils? Or why does he not remove them?"

3. J. L. Mackie, "Evil and Omnipotence," *Mind* 64 (1955).

4. In chap. 9 of *The Miracle of Theism* (Oxford: Clarendon, 1982) Mackie moves from defending the position that evil *disproves* God's existence to endorsing the suggestion that it renders God's existence *unlikely*.

5. For more on Hume and Mackie on God and evil, see my *The Reality of God and the Problem of Evil* (London/New York: Continuum, 2006), chap. 1.

6. Perhaps I should here comment on my use of the word "evil" since it is a strong one that we use fairly infrequently. I am using it as the equivalent of what medieval authors (including Aquinas) had in mind when they employed the term *malum*. For them, *malum* signified anything we might think of as bad, regardless of degree. I sometimes get mild headaches, but would not describe them as evil. People sometimes treat me impolitely, but I would not, therefore, describe them as evil. Yet what word shall we use in order to describe painful terminal cancer, serial killing, genocide, and major natural disasters? Here we might well foreswear the word "bad" and resort to the term "evil." Anyway, take it that when I use the term "evil" henceforth I mean *malum* as medieval writers employed it (evil including everything from a headache to genocide and major natural disasters).

7. William Rowe, "The Problem of Evil and Some Varieties of Atheism," *American Philosophical Quarterly* 16 (1979).

8. I instance Rowe as someone defending an argument of a certain kind. There are others who might be mentioned as doing so. See, for example, Paul Draper, "Pain and Pleasure: An Evidential Problem for Theists," *Nous* 23 (June 1989), who disagrees with Rowe in various ways, but the thrust of his thinking is the same: that available evidence counts against God's existence. For discussions of this view see Daniel Howard-Snyder (ed.), *The Evidential Argument from Evil* (Bloomington/Indianapolis: Indiana University Press, 1996), in which the papers by Rowe and Draper that I mention are reprinted.

9. There have been many people recently trying to resist the conclusions of authors such as Mackie and Rowe. Here I am simply drawing attention to some of the best known, and best published, among them.

10. Some people have suggested that there is no serious distinction to be made between a theodicy and a defense. Such people clearly do not grasp the important distinction that Plantinga is reasonably making and defends perfectly adequately. As he shows, there is a difference between proving that such-and-such an utterance is true and proving that it is not logically impossible.

11. See Alvin Plantinga, *The Nature of Necessity* (Oxford: Clarendon, 1974). By "possible world" Plantinga means a way the world might have been; so Plantinga will say that there are many possible worlds—meaning many different ways the world might have been. Our world is what it is and is, on Plantinga's reckoning, a possible world, but also an actual one.

12. I should note that there have recently been what we might call philosophical "friends of God" who do not turn to theodicy when trying to talk about God and evil. Two examples would be Marilyn McCord Adams, *Christ and Horrors* (Cambridge:

Cambridge University Press, 2006); and D. Z. Phillips, *The Problem of Evil and the Problem of God* (London: SCM, 2004). Adams and Phillips are unusual, though. Most contemporary philosophers think that the existence of God stands or falls on the availability of a good theodicy (understanding "theodicy" as I do in this chapter).

13. Cf. Richard Swinburne, *The Existence of God* (2nd ed.; Oxford: Clarendon, 2004). See also Swinburne, *Providence and the Problem of Evil* (Oxford: Clarendon, 1998).

14. John Hick, *Evil and the God of Love* (2nd ed.; Basingstoke/London: Macmillan, 1985).

15. Alvin Plantinga, "God, Evil, and the Metaphysics of Freedom," quoted from the conveniently reprinted version of this article in *The Problem of Evil*, ed. Marilyn McCord Adams and Robert Merrihew Adams (Oxford: Oxford University Press, 1990), 106.

16. Richard Swinburne, *Is There a God?* (Oxford: Oxford University Press, 1996), 98.

17. It is often said that the free-will defense was invented by St. Augustine of Hippo, who certainly insists on the reality of human freedom. But did he support the free-will defense as philosophers of religion tend to today? Arguably not. See Jesse Couenhoven, "Augustine's Rejection of the Free Will Defence: An Overview of the Late Augustine's Theodicy," *Religious Studies* 43 (2007).

18. It is sometimes said that there were no atheists in medieval Europe. I have always been skeptical of this assertion and have yet to see serious evidence to back it up. Proving a negative, of course, is always difficult.

19. The phrase "the problem of evil" is commonly used to refer to a series of questions to do with the topic of God and evil. For example: Does evil prove God's nonexistence? Can God's existence be defended given the reality of evil? And so on. This is the sense in which I am now using it.

20. Paul Helm notes this in his *John Calvin's Ideas* (Oxford: Oxford University Press, 2004), 33. As Helm also observes, Aquinas's position can be compared with that of Calvin. Helm's excellent book draws attention to parallels between Aquinas and Calvin on a number of issues.

21. They might, of course, try to cobble together texts of Aquinas coming from different works of his. But they would not, I think, be able to produce something giving us an accurate understanding of Aquinas on God and evil without making their texts to be very long ones, and ones with some serious commentary on what Aquinas is saying on a number of different topics (some not obviously to do with God and evil, or the problem of evil). Readers largely unfamiliar with Aquinas's writings might expect his *De Malo* (On Evil) to amount to a sustained essay on God and evil. But it does not. The *De Malo* certainly deals with questions such as "What is evil?" but its focus is on sin and various kinds of vices. It is not an essay on God and evil. It is an essay in moral theology.

22. Aquinas distinguishes between what we can know of God by reason and what we can truly believe about God based on divine revelation. More on this below. It is an essay in moral theology.

CHAPTER 2

1. I use the word "typically" here since there evidently have been people taken to be theologians who seem to have denied that God exists as "God exists" is understood by what we might think of as mainstream theistic thinkers. Here I am thinking of

authors such as Paul Van Buren and Thomas Altizer (prominent exponents of what is called "death of God" theology). See Paul Van Buren, *The Secular Meaning of the Gospel* (New York: Macmillan, 1963); and Thomas Altizer, *The Gospel of Christian Atheism* (Philadelphia: Westminster, 1996).

2. Bertrand Russell, *A History of Western Philosophy* (New York: Simon & Schuster, 1945), 463.

3. Cf. Anthony Kenny, *Aquinas: A Collection of Critical Essays* (Notre Dame: University of Notre Dame Press, 1976); Norman Kretzmann and Eleonore Stump (eds.), *The Cambridge Companion to Aquinas* (Cambridge: Cambridge University Press, 1993); and Brian Davies (ed.), *Thomas Aquinas: Contemporary Philosophical Perspectives* (Oxford/New York: Oxford University Press, 2002).

4. Kenny, *Aquinas*, 1. Kenny has an eminently quotable response to the passage from Russell quoted above. With an eye on Russell's *Principia Mathematica* (2nd ed., 1927), he says that Russell's observations come "oddly from a philosopher who took three hundred and sixty dense pages to prove that $1 + 1 = 2$" (Kenny, *Aquinas*, 2).

5. At its inception, the Order of Preachers was much concerned to rebut the claims of people (exponents of Catharism) strongly insisting that evil is a real force with which God is in combat. It is, perhaps, no accident that the attempt to refute this thesis forms quite a significant part of Aquinas's approach to God and evil.

6. In Aquinas's day, it was standard for teachers of theology to lecture on Lombard's *Sentences*. For an introduction to Lombard, see Philipp W. Rosemann, *Peter Lombard* (Oxford/New York: Oxford University Press, 2004). For a guide to Aquinas as a biblical commentator, see Thomas G. Weinandy, Daniel A. Keating, and John P. Yocum (eds.), *Aquinas on Scripture* (London/New York: Clark, 2005).

7. Mark D. Jordan, *Rewritten Theology: Aquinas After His Readers* (Blackwell: Oxford, 2006), 154.

8. See Leonard Boyle, "The Setting of the *Summa Theologiae*," reprinted in Brian Davies (ed.), *Aquinas's Summa Theologiae: Critical Essays* (London/New York: Roman & Littlefield, 2006). Boyle's essay was originally published by the Pontifical Institute of Medieval Studies (Toronto, 1982).

9. Cf. M.-D. Chenu, "Les 'Philosophes' dans la philosophie chrétienne médiévale," *Revue des sciences philosophiques et théologiques*, (1937), 26. Chenu draws attention to ways in which thirteenth-century authors, especially St. Albert the Great (d. 1280), distinguish between the *philosophi* and the *sancti* (to the detriment of the former).

10. This fact is emphasized in Jordan's *Rewritten Theology*. For Latin texts documenting Aquinas's life written shortly after he died, see A. Ferrura (ed.), *Thomae Aquinatis vitae fontes praecipuae* (Alba: Dominicane, 1968). For comparable English translations of Aquinas's life, see Kenelm Foster, *The Life of Saint Thomas Aquinas: Biographical Documents* (London: Longmans, Green/Baltimore: Halicon, 1959).

11. For an excellent elaboration on this point, see Per Erik Persson, *Sacra Doctrina: Reason and Revelation in Aquinas* (Philadelphia: Fortress, 1970).

12. Actually, Aquinas never completed the *Summa Theologiae*. He died while at work on its third part.

13. *Prologus* (foreword) to the *Summa Theologiae*. Here Aquinas also says that his purpose in writing the *Summa Theologiae* is to set forth Christian teachings in a way that might help those starting their theological studies.

14. Quoted from *Compendium of Theology by Thomas Aquinas*, trans. Richard J. Regan (Oxford/New York: Oxford University Press, 2009).

15. For a translation of Aquinas's 1256 lecture see Simon Tugwell (ed.), *Albert and Thomas: Selected Writings* (New York/Mahwah: Paulist Press, 1988). This volume provides a very scholarly chronology of Aquinas's life and an excellent account of ways in which he changed his mind on at least one topic.

16. As John F. Wippel observes: "Throughout his [Aquinas's] literary corpus, both in his philosophical and theological writings, various elements of his philosophy, and especially of his metaphysics, are to be found." See John F. Wippel, *Metaphysical Themes in Thomas Aquinas II* (Washington, DC: Catholic University of America Press, 2007), 23.

17. Here, I am not saying that philosophical reflection on God should happily proceed without noting what people believe about God on the basis of revelation. Quite the contrary. In my view, philosophical discussions of belief in God should pay serious attention to what people who believe in God believe as a whole. And that might well involve, or be grounded on, belief in divine revelation.

18. Paradigm examples are the best indication of what I mean by "philosophy" since the word admits of no clear or uncontroversial definition. What I am basically trying to do at this point is to use the word "philosophy" to signify what people engage in when not starting from the assumption that any religious beliefs are true (even though they might wish to argue that certain religious beliefs actually are true).

19. Jordan, *Rewritten Theology*, 155.

20. The influence of Aristotle on Aquinas is well documented. The influence of Avicenna (980–1037) on Aquinas is less well documented. For a superb introduction to Avicenna, see Jon McGinnis, *Avicenna* (Oxford/New York: Oxford University Press, 2010).

21. Cf. A. Dondaine (ed.), *Historia Ecclesiastica Nova* 22.24, in "Les 'opuscula fratris Thomae chez Ptolomée de Lucques,'" *Archivum Fratrum Praedicatorum* 31 (1961). In 1265 Aquinas was appointed by his religious superiors to establish a house of studies for Dominicans in Rome.

22. See Jean-Pierre Torrell, *Saint Thomas Aquinas: The Person and His Work* (Washington, DC: Catholic University of America Press, 1996), chaps. 8 and 12.

23. Why did Aquinas comment on Aristotle? Most likely because by his day, and in no small measure due to the influence of St. Albert the Great, the study of Aristotle was something encouraged in Dominican houses (or "convents" as they were called). See M.-D. Chenu, *Toward Understanding Saint Thomas* (Chicago: Regnery, 1964), chap. 6. For Albert and Aristotle, see pp. 42–46.

24. Quoted from Anton C. Pegis's translation (Notre Dame/London: University of Notre Dame Press, 1975), 1.66.

25. This point is correctly emphasized by Norman Kretzmann in *The Metaphysics of Theism* (Oxford: Clarendon, 1997), chap. 1.

26. When it comes to someone offering a philosophical attack on natural theology (on principle, so to speak) an obvious example (though not a recent one) is A. J. Ayer

(1910–89). Writing as representing a movement commonly referred to as "Logical Positivism," Ayer famously argued that all statements with God as subject are meaningless and, therefore, cannot be defended philosophically. See A. J. Ayer, *Language, Truth, and Logic* (2nd ed.; London: Gollancz, 1946). Ayer basically defended this conclusion on the ground that God is not an object of sensory experience or something the existence of which is derivable from what our senses reveal to us—that the existence of God is not an empirical hypothesis (as, indeed, it is not and as Aquinas never supposed it to be).

27. Søren Kierkegaard, *Philosophical Fragments* (Princeton: Princeton University Press, 1962), 49.

28. Karl Barth, "No!" in Emil Brunner and Karl Barth, *Natural Theology* (Eugene, OR: Wipf & Stock, 2002), 75. The essay from which this quotation comes was originally published in 1934.

29. I offer a discussion of Kierkegaard and Barth on natural theology in "Is God beyond Reason?" *Philosophical Investigations* 32 (Oct. 2009).

30. Rude Te Velde, *Aquinas on God* (Aldershot UK/Burlington: Ashgate, 2006), 5.

CHAPTER 3

1. Brian Davies, *Aquinas* (London/New York: Continuum, 2002), chap. 3.

2. ST 1a,12,12. Here I am speaking of knowledge as what Aquinas thinks we can achieve by human reflection and investigation (he calls it "knowledge that is natural to us"), not knowledge of revealed truth. As we shall later see, however, Aquinas is prepared to speak of knowledge of revealed truth, which he thinks of as a sharing in God's knowledge. For more on Aquinas's view of what is presupposed by certain statements, see Herbert McCabe, "Categories," *Dominican Studies*, Volume VII (1954).

3. We might, of course, make an identity statement such as "Mark Twain is Samuel Clemens." Yet Aquinas does not deny this. He allows for what he calls *predicatio per identitatem*. He would, however, argue that to say what is true of Mark Twain (e.g., that he was also known as Samuel Clemens) presupposes the individual existence of Mark Twain.

4. For a clear account of Aquinas on substance, one that stresses that Aquinas does not take a substance to be an "unknowable substratum" lying behind appearances, see F. C. Copleston, *Aquinas* (Harmondsworth: Penguin, 1955), chap. 2. Based on what he says in *An Essay concerning Human Understanding* 2.23, the notion of substance as an unknowable substratum lying behind appearances is commonly associated with John Locke (1632–1704).

5. Quoted from Timothy McDermott (ed.), *Thomas Aquinas: Selected Philosophical Writings* (Oxford/New York: Oxford University Press, 1998), 104.

6. The Latin text reads: *Si non sit aliqua res cuius essentiam definitio significet nihil differt definitio a ratione exponente significationem alicuius nominis.*

7. Cf. Alvin Plantinga, *The Nature of Necessity* (Oxford: Clarendon, 1974).

8. A sober warning, perhaps, to all would-be presidents.

9. In various places (e.g., SCG 1.15) Aquinas speaks of God as a substance. He does so because he thinks of God as an independently existing individual (albeit a unique one). For the moment, though, I am not concerned with what Aquinas says about the substance that God is. I am concerned with what he thinks about substances without presupposing belief in God. Note, however, that in ST 1a.3.5 Aquinas denies that God belongs to the genus of substance on the ground that God belongs to no genus and on the ground that the existence of substances can be distinguished from their essence while this is not so when it comes to the existence of God. I return to this distinction below.

10. For a recent philosophical defense of a notion of substance strongly like that of Aquinas, see P. M. S. Hacker, *Human Nature: The Categorical Framework* (Oxford: Blackwell, 2007), chap. 2.

11. *Esse*, as it occurs in Aquinas (and though it is an infinitive) can often be translated into English as "existence" or "being." So when Aquinas speaks of something as having *esse* what he means is that it actually exists or is actually a being (an existing substance).

12. For more on this see my *The Thought of Thomas Aquinas* (Oxford: Clarendon, 1992), chap. 11.

13. C. J. F. Williams, *What Is Existence?* (Oxford: Clarendon, 1981). Williams provides a more popular version of his position on existence in *Being, Identity, and Truth* (Oxford: Clarendon, 1992), chap. 1. For Williams defending his view of existence in a direct attack on Aquinas, see his "Being," in *A Companion to the Philosophy of Religion*, ed. Philip L. Quinn and Charles Taliaferro (Oxford: Blackwell, 1997), chap. 27.

14. Peter Geach, *God and the Soul* (London: Routledge & Kegan Paul, 1969), chap. 4.

15. Kenny, *Aquinas on Being*, 43.

16. My only reservation in saying this derives from the fact that, though Aquinas takes God to be a *causa*, he does not, in a serious sense, take God to be an explanation (on the understanding that an explanation is something we understand better than that with respect to which we invoke it as an explanation). I return to this point below.

17. I say "several things" since it is often quite wrong to suppose that there is something that is *the* cause of something that happens. Is there, for example, a single cause when it comes to a car crash? We might reasonably ask, for example, "Who shot Fred?" while looking for a particular and nameable individual. When it comes to things like car crashes, however, we are surely looking for an explanation that refers us to a number of things and their ways of working (or maybe not working).

18. Cf. Ludwig Wittgenstein, *Philosophical Occasions*, ed. James C. Klagge and Alfred Nordmann (Indianapolis/Cambridge: Hackett, 1993), 373.

19. David Hume, *A Treatise of Human Nature*, ed. L. A. Selby-Bigge (2nd ed.; Oxford: Clarendon, 1978), 79.

20. Quoted from McDermott, *Thomas Aquinas: Selected Philosophical Writings*, 84.

CHAPTER 4

1. Here Aquinas is explicitly drawing on Aristotle. Cf. Aristotle's *Ethics* 1.1.1094a3.

2. J. L. Mackie, *Hume's Moral Theory* (London/Boston: Routledge & Kegan Paul, 1980), 1.

3. Ibid., 2.

4. P. T. Geach, "Good and Evil," *Analysis* 17 (Dec. 1956).

5. Ibid., 33.

6. Ibid.

7. As Herbert McCabe neatly observes, for Aquinas, "what is common to good things is not that they share a characteristic but that they share a Creator." See *God and Evil in the Theology of St. Thomas Aquinas*, ed. Brian Davies (London/New York: Continuum, 2010), 59.

8. When Aquinas writes about goodness in general he is normally thinking in terms of the goodness of naturally occurring substances that have essences. But he says enough to show that he would extend his general thinking on goodness to *entia per accidens*. He would, I think, take an *ens per accidens* to be good insofar as it meets conventional requirements for calling it good considered as what it is. In other words, I think he would say that even though a telephone, for example, is somehow faulty, it can be thought of as good insofar as it manages to function as a telephone in some serious sense.

9. Cf. ST 1a.5.1 ad 1: "Although 'good' and 'being' signify a single reality, we do not in the same way say that something is a being without qualification and good without qualification. For 'good' and 'being' have different meanings" (Davies and Leftow 2006: 52).

10. Some philosophers have said that we should sharply distinguish between "statements of fact" and "statements of value." For these thinkers, no description of anything entails that the thing in question is good. Aquinas obviously does not subscribe to this view. For him, justifying the claim that something in the world is good positively has to involve a description of the thing.

11. Aquinas distinguishes between what we might call "real" existence and "existence in the sense of the true." We might say of a particular cat that it really exists (is a substance), and this, for Aquinas, would be to ascribe real existence to the cat. But, he also thinks, statements like "blindness exists" or "sickness exists" do not ascribe real existence to any substance even though they are perfectly true. Cf. *Sententia Super Metaphysicam* (Commentary on Aristotle's "Metaphysics") 50.5.9. For a detailed account of this distinction as Aquinas develops it, see C. F. J. Martin, *Thomas Aquinas: God and Explanations* (Edinburgh: Edinburgh University Press, 1997), chap. 5.

12. For St. Augustine on this matter see his *Enchiridion* 11.

13. For some other texts of Aquinas taking the same line, see, for example, QDM 1.2, CT 114, and SCG 3.3.6–7.

14. McCabe, *God and Evil in the Theology of St. Thomas Aquinas*, 65.

15. Aquinas distinguishes between being good *simpliciter* (simply) and being good *secundum quid* (in a certain respect). Like many medieval thinkers, therefore, he can

allow for something being good considered as thus-and-so but not good considered in a different way. Cf. ST 1a.5.1 ad 1; 1a.11.2 ad 1; 1a2ae.27.1 ad 1; *Quaestiones Disputatae de Veritate* (Disputed Questions on Truth) 21.5 ad 2; QDM 11.1.

16. Herbert McCabe, *God Matters* (London: Chapman, 1987), 29.

CHAPTER 5

1. Strictly speaking, Aquinas does not think of those who believe that God exists (with or without reasons for doing so) as believing in God's existence. As we shall see, in Aquinas's view God's existence (*esse*) is not to be distinguished from God's nature, which Aquinas takes to be seriously unknown to everyone in this life, a point well made by Lubor Velecky in his book *Aquinas' Five Arguments in the Summa Theologiae 1a,2,3* (Kampen: Kok Pharos, 1994). Whereas most people today would naturally speak of someone as believing (or not believing) in the existence of God, Aquinas would speak of people believing (or not believing) that *Deus est* (God exists) is a true proposition. With this point made, however, I shall sometimes (as in the sentence to which this note is attached) use the familiar phrase "belief in God's existence," though always on the understanding that I take it to mean "belief that 'God exists' is true."

2. For which see ST 2a2ae.4. I return to Aquinas on faith in chapter 8.

3. For Aquinas, "knowing," in "knowing that God exists," means having *scientia* when it comes to "God exists" (*Deus est*). By *scientia* Aquinas means knowledge arrived at by means of demonstrative argument employing premises that are somehow naturally evident to us. Sometimes he uses the term *scientia* when referring to reasoning that does not depend on premises the truth of which are evident to us. This is so when he talks about *sacra doctrina* being *scientia* since it borrows its premises from what is revealed by God. For the moment, though, I am focusing on Aquinas's use of *scientia* where he takes it to involve no reliance on divine revelation.

4. I shall later be qualifying this remark somewhat.

5. Aquinas thinks that "God exists" *is* self-evident in the sense that, *were* we to be able to understand God as God understands himself, we would see, straight off, that God cannot but exist. But Aquinas does not think that we understand God as God understands himself. For him, therefore, "God exists" is not self-evident to us.

6. For what I am alluding to in this paragraph see, for example, ST 1a.2.1 and SCG 1.10–11.

7. Cf. Francisco Suarez, *Disputationes Metaphysicae* 28. For an English translation of this text see Francisco Suarez, *The Metaphysical Demonstration of the Existence of God*, trans./ed. John P. Doyle (South Bend IN: St. Augustine's Press, 2004). Here I cite a classical author, but the notion that the big distinction between God and creatures is that God is necessary while all creatures are contingent is commonly found in contemporary writings on philosophy of religion.

8. For Aquinas on angels, see ST 1a.50–64.

9. This is what Aquinas argues in his *De Aeternitate Mundi*, in which he maintains that one does not contradict oneself by asserting that something that has always existed is created by God.

10. *De Ente et Essentia* 4, quoted from Timothy McDermott (ed.), *Thomas Aquinas: Selected Philosophical Writings* (Oxford/New York: Oxford University Press, 1998), 104.

11. Cf. Anthony Kenny, *Aquinas on Being* (Oxford: Clarendon, 2002), 35.

12. I develop this point in "Kenny on Aquinas on Being," *Modern Schoolman* 82.2 (Jan. 2005). As Jon McGinnis explains, Aquinas is here thinking along the lines of the Muslim philosopher Avicenna (980–1037). See Jon McGinnis, "The Avicennan Sources for Aquinas on Being," *Modern Schoolman* 82.2 (Jan. 2005); and *Avicenna* (Oxford/New York: Oxford University Press, 2010).

13. Aquinas makes exactly the same point in, for example, his Commentary on the *Sentences* of Peter Lombard 2.1.1.1. See also SCG 1.22 and 2.52 and ST 1a.65.1.

14. For texts by Aquinas on God as Creator, and for a fine introduction to and commentary on these, see Steven R. Baldner and William E. Carroll, *Aquinas on Creation* (Toronto: Pontifical Institute of Medieval Studies, 1997). Baldner and Carroll go into details on the topic of Aquinas and creation in a way that space prevents me from doing in the present volume.

15. Aquinas develops a philosophical case for knowledge being ascribable to God in, for example, ST 1a.14. Aquinas takes knowing to occur as form exists nonmaterially (as understood). Taking God to be wholly nonmaterial, he argues that knowledge belongs to God by nature. For an account of Aquinas on God's knowledge see my *The Thought of Thomas Aquinas* (Oxford: Clarendon, 1992), chap. 7.

16. Aquinas's thinking here might strike some readers as suggesting that God is narcissistic. That, I should stress, is not Aquinas's meaning. His point is that, knowing the perfect good (himself), God is at rest in it and does not aim/desire/will (nor could aim/desire/will) for any other good than the perfect good that he is.

17. I use the word "real" in this sentence in order to flag a distinction, which Aquinas acknowledges, between what we might call "real" change and "notional" change. If I gain weight, I undergo a genuine modification. But what if I come to be loved by someone? We might report this occurrence by saying, "Davies has come to be loved by X," which looks like a proposition ascribing a change to me. Of course, though, someone can come to love me without my even knowing so or being affected by the love of the one who loves me. In this sense, "Davies has come to be loved by X" does not ascribe a *real* change to me. Rather, it reports a real change in X (X's coming to love me). For Aquinas's recognition of this point, see ST 1a.13.7, where he talks about how it can be that X can be related to Y where the truth that Y is related to X is not due to anything real in Y. See also P. T. Geach, who usefully distinguishes between what he calls "real" and "merely Cambridge" changes; *God and the Soul* (London: Routledge & Kegan Paul, 1969), 71ff.

18. "'Who did you pass on the road?' the King went on, holding out his hand to the messenger for some more hay. 'Nobody,' said the Messenger. 'Quite right,' said the King: 'this young lady saw him too. So of course nobody walks slower than you.' 'I do my best,' the Messenger said in a sullen tone. 'I'm sure nobody walks much faster than I do!' 'He can't do that,' said the King, 'or else he'd have been here first.'"

19. I offer more detailed accounts in the following places: Brian Davies (ed.), *Language, Meaning, and God* (London: Chapman, 1987), chap. 3; *The Thought of Thomas*

Aquinas (Oxford: Clarendon, 1992), chap. 3; Charles Taliaferro and Chad Meister (ed.), *The Cambridge Companion to Christian Philosophical Theology* (Cambridge: Cambridge University Press, 2010), chap. 3. For a splendid account and discussion of Aquinas and God's simplicity, see Peter Weigel, *Aquinas on Simplicity: An Investigation into the Foundations of his Philosophical Theology* (Bern: Peter Lang, 2008).

20. Familiar as Aquinas was with Scripture, he must have been aware that there is no biblical verse that reads "God is simple." Yet he does hold that we can reflect on what Scripture says so as to bring out its implications, just as he thinks that we can reflect on Scripture so as to distinguish (though biblical authors do not) between what in it should be read as literally true when it comes to God and what is only metaphorically true. When it comes to divine simplicity, Aquinas's view is that this is something implied by what biblical authors say about God as Creator.

21. Note, though, that he argues for this conclusion philosophically. In ST 1a.3.1, for example, he argues for it as follows: (1) bodies causing change are always themselves changed by other material things; but God accounts for all bodily changes; (2) in what accounts for the *esse* of things the essence of which is not equivalent to their existence there can be no potentiality and, therefore, no change (on the understanding that real change involves something that is potentially thus-and-so coming to be actually this). With respect to the Bible and the nonmateriality of God I take it to be evident that biblical authors do not take God to be some kind of material individual (that they take God to be, in Aquinas's language, "essentially nonmaterial"). New Testament authors (some of them, anyway) clearly take Jesus to be divine. Does this mean that they take God to be essentially material? Aquinas thinks not, but more on this later.

22. Aquinas's various discussions of matter and individuation are, I should note, complex and not obviously consistent. Here I have tried merely to give an outline of what he seems to think overall. For a detailed discussion of Aquinas on matter and individuation see John F. Wippel, *The Metaphysical Thought of Thomas Aquinas* (Washington, DC: Catholic University of America Press, 2000), chap. 9.

23. For a solid development of this point see David B. Burrell, *Aquinas, God, and Action* (London/Henley: Routledge & Kegan Paul, 1979), chap. 2.

CHAPTER 6

1. Richard Swinburne, *The Coherence of Theism* (rev. ed.; Oxford: Clarendon, 1993), chap. 5. Swinburne is alluding to John Duns Scotus (c. 1266–1308). For a distinguished account of Scotus's thinking see Richard Cross, *Duns Scotus* (Oxford/New York: Oxford University Press, 1999).

2. Swinburne seems to write as though Scotus is critical of Aquinas on talk about God. Actually, though, Scotus's target (in what he says about univocity) is Henry of Ghent (who died in 1293 and who was critical of Aquinas on many counts). See Stephen Dummont, "Henry of Ghent and Duns Scotus," in *Medieval Philosophy*, ed. John Marenbon (London/New York: Routledge, 1998). What I am presently reporting Aquinas to be saying does not, I think, conflict with what Scotus thought. Both held that we can speak of God using words we also use of creatures while also speaking

literally. And both thought that our doing so should not lead us to forget about the difference between God and creatures.

3. Quoted from Anton C. Pegis's translation (Notre Dame/London: University of Notre Dame Press, 1975), 146–47. Swinburne cites this passage on *Coherence of Theism*, 77. The word "name" (*nomen*) in the quotation does not mean what we would call a proper name. It refers to any term we might try to use when saying what God is.

4. Comparable examples would be "bat" as in "tennis bat" and "bats are furry mammals with wings," or "pen" as in "I keep my pigs in a pen" and "I keep my pen in my pocket."

5. How does Aquinas take us to be able to distinguish between what is true of God metaphorically and what is true of him literally? His view seems to be that one can always intelligibly deny what is said of God metaphorically while one cannot intelligibly deny what is said of God literally. Take "God is a mighty fortress." Is that intelligibly deniable? Aquinas thinks that it is since, regardless of the truth we might find in it, God is not made of stone, or whatever mighty fortresses are made of. Yet what of "God is good"? Is that intelligibly deniable? Aquinas thinks not. So he takes "God is good" to be literally or unequivocally true.

6. "Names" in "divine names" does not here signify what we would think of as proper names (e.g., Mary or Bill). By *nomen* here Aquinas is thinking of any term we might use when trying to say what can be truly asserted of God.

7. For a fine and detailed development of this point see Gregory P. Rocca, *Speaking the Incomprehensible God* (Washington, DC: Catholic University of America Press, 2004), chap. 11.

8. Cf. Ralph McInerny, *Aquinas and Analogy* (Washington, DC: Catholic University of America Press, 1996).

9. Here one needs to bear in mind Aquinas's account of *ens* as I tried to present it in chapter 3. One might think of a kind (or a class) so as to allow anything mentionable as belonging to one. Thus, for example, one might think of all hopes had by people as constituting a kind, or of all things left behind on trains as doing so. But Aquinas does not. So when denying that God belongs to a kind his meaning is that God is not an *ens per se* that belongs to a genus or species. Cf. ST 1a.3.4.

10. Here Aquinas is thinking in terms of the Latin word *perficere*, meaning "thoroughly made" or "well made" (Davies and Leftow 2006: 44).

11. Gregory is Pope St. Gregory the Great (d. 604). The reference is to his *Magna Moralia* 5.36.

12. In Oscar Wilde's *The Importance of Being Earnest*, Jack says to Gwendolen "You're quite perfect, Miss Fairfax." She replies "Oh! I hope I am not that. It would leave no room for developments." Aquinas thinks that God has no room for developments.

13. Aquinas's claim that God's essence and nature are indistinguishable from God is not, I think, best read as an identity statement in the sense in which, say, "the creator of Poirot is identical with Agatha Christie" ("Agatha Christie is the creator of Poirot") is. Such a statement has a common noun lurking in the background. It is telling us that "the creator of Poirot" and "Agatha Christie" refer to one and the same human being. This is not the case with what Aquinas says about God and his essence

and nature (or God's nature and God's existence). He does not mean that God and his essence and nature (or God's nature and God's existence) are one and the same X. Rather, and as is the case with all that he says when it comes to God's simplicity, his point is a negative one: that, whatever God is, he is *not* something to be thought of as being really distinct from his essence or nature. That this is so ought to be clear from Aquinas prefacing in the *Summa Contra Gentiles* what has to say about God's nature by observing that, when it comes to this, we have to "especially make use of the method of remotion [i.e., negation]" since "the divine substance surpasses every form that our intellect reaches." We are, Aquinas continues, "unable to apprehend it by knowing what it is. Yet we are able to have some knowledge of it by knowing what it is not" (SCG 1.14, quoted from Pegis's translation, 96). Aquinas strikes exactly the same note in the introduction to ST 1a.3.

14. Cf. G. E. Moore, *Principia Ethica*, published in 1903 and variously reprinted.

15. All quotations from this article come from Davies and Leftow 2006: 63–64.

16. For what seems to be the same argument, see SCG 1.37.

17. For *omne agens agat sibi simile* in Aquinas, also see (among other places) SCG 1.49; *Quaestiones Disputatae de Potentia* (Disputed Questions on the Power of God) 3.6; 3.17.

18. Herbert McCabe, *Faith within Reason* (London/New York: Continuum, 2007), 118.

19. Here I am going to have to deal with this topic in a very brief manner. For a substantial treatment, see Stephen J. Pope (ed.), *The Ethics of Aquinas* (Washington, DC: Georgetown University Press, 2002). For a lively appropriation of Aquinas's take on moral goodness, see Herbert McCabe, *The Good Life* (London/New York: Continuum, 2005).

20. I say "generally" since Aquinas does not assert that acting virtuously will always contribute to our happiness or well-being. Indeed, one can easily imagine it leading us to our death in certain circumstances.

21. Swinburne, *Coherence of Theism*, 187.

22. Ibid., 184.

23. Ibid., 185.

24. All quotations from this article come from Davies and Leftow 2006: 251–53.

25. "All things being equal" since, of course, circumstances can change in ways that might be thought to remit debts. For example, having bought a car from you and before paying you for it, I might have an accident and, while brain dead, be on a life-support system. Arguably, in these circumstances I have no obligation to pay you anything even though I owe you (not, at any rate, if "ought" implies "can").

26. Romans 11.35 as Aquinas read it in the translation available to him.

27. I would advise readers to connect this quotation with what I said above about the issue of God's moral status.

28. For a discussion in which Aquinas makes similar points to those found in ST 1a.21.1, see SCG 2.29.

CHAPTER 7

1. Quoted with slight modification from Anton C. Pegis's translation (Notre Dame/London: University of Notre Dame Press, 1975), 270.

2. Norman Kretzmann has suggested that some remarks of Aquinas indicate that he really thought that God has to create since he is good. See *The Metaphysics of Theism* (Oxford: Clarendon, 1997), 223ff. It seems to me, though, that Kretzmann is wrong here. Aquinas strongly and several times over insists (a) that there is no absolute necessity about there being creatures (even "necessary" ones), (b) that God's goodness would by no means be modified or eroded by his not having created, and (c) that there is no natural or external compulsion causing God to create. The passages from Aquinas to which Kretzmann refers in defense of his suggestion all seem to me to be compatible with these theses. For a critique of Kretzmann on God and creation, see John F. Wippel, "Norman Kretzmann on Aquinas's Attribution of Will and of Freedom to Create to God," *Religious Studies* 39 (2003).

3. The notion of God's omnipotence has always been an issue in discussions of God and evil. I have not touched on it directly so far, but it is appropriate for me to say something about it at this stage.

4. Peter Geach has argued that one should distinguish between "God is almighty" and "God is omnipotent" in favor of the claim that God is almighty. See P. T. Geach, *Providence and Evil* (Cambridge: Cambridge University Press, 1977), chap. 1. In the senses in which Geach takes exception to the formula "God is omnipotent," Aquinas does not believe that God is omnipotent, though he does speak of God as being omnipotent—as in ST 1a.25.3, for example.

5. His view is that contradictions just cannot be true because of what is meant by the terms used in stating them.

6. "Do" here clearly has the sense of "make to be," not "perform any logically possible feat." For the same thinking as is found in this passage, see ST 1a.25.3.

7. Aquinas actually thought that there was once such a world made by God. See his account of Adam and Eve in paradise as presented in texts such as ST 1a.94–97.

8. Aquinas regards all *malum poenae* as the consequence of the sin of Adam. And he takes Adam to have been a historical individual (as all Christians did in his day). So he never seeks to challenge what we read in Genesis 3 (read literally), which says that, Adam having sinned, God's verdict on him and (presumably) his descendants was that they should live in a world inhospitable to them in various ways, one in which they would die. In this book I do not offer an account of Aquinas on the sin of Adam, though I do so in *On Evil* (Oxford: Oxford University Press, 2003), 43–49.

9. I derive the phrase from Herbert McCabe, who, helpfully (I think) uses it in several places as a rendering of Aquinas's *malum poenae*. See, for example, *God Matters* (London: Chapman, 1987), chap. 3.

10. People often think that the only badness worth noting is that which affects people. Aquinas does not. Today, perhaps, this might lead some people to consider him as being very politically correct.

11. Cf. ST 1a.22.2 ad 2, where Aquinas speaks of loss to one thing arising from gain in another.

12. Cf. ST 1a.49.1–2: "Evil has an efficient [agent] cause, but it is one which acts indirectly, not directly.... That evil which consists in a decay of some things is traced back to God as its cause.... Insofar as from its strength it produces a form which expels another form, an agent of its power causes loss [in natural

things]. God's principle purpose in created things is clearly that form or good which consists in the order of the universe. This requires...that there should be some things that can, and sometimes do, fall away. So then, in causing the common good of the ordered universe, God causes loss in particular things as a consequence and, as it were, indirectly" (Blackfriars edition, 8.135, 139 with some modifications).

13. For a comparable text, cf. ST 1a2ae.79.1.

14. For a comparable text, cf. ST 1a2ae.79.2.

15. Aquinas allows for evil done as chosen by angels and not just human beings. But his account of it, and its causal relation to God, is essentially the same as what we find in his account of human wrongdoing.

16. It is important to recognize that, for Aquinas (and forgetting about heavenly bodies, which he does not think of as able to undergo substantial change), evil suffered is built into the notion of a material world, one composed of things having form and matter, one composed of things able to undergo accidental and substantial change. Something material, thinks Aquinas, is always undergoing evil suffered (a lack of form) since it is continually undergoing change in which accidental forms get replaced by other accidental forms insofar as it interacts with other material things. And material things are always potentially able to undergo substantial change. We tend to think selectively of evil suffered as consisting only in certain changes we deem undesirable. But Aquinas thinks of it in a universal way: as occurring whenever one form is extinguished by the natural power of something in the world.

17. Quoted with some modification from Vernon J. Bourke's translation (Notre Dame/London: University of Notre Dame Press, 1975), 220–21.

18. Quoted from Timothy McDermott (ed.), *Thomas Aquinas: Selected Philosophical Writings* (Oxford/New York: Oxford University Press, 1998), 277ff. For a complete translation of the commentary, see *Aristotle: On Interpretation*, trans. Jean T. Oesterle (Milwaukee: Marquette University Press, 1962).

19. Quoted from McDermott, *Thomas Aquinas: Selected Philosophical Writings*, 282–83. For a comparable passage see *Quaestiones Disputatae de Veritate* (*Disputed Questions on Truth*) 24.1 ad 3.

20. See, for example, QDM 6.1, where Aquinas says that "if nothing is within our power, and we are necessarily moved to will things, deliberation, exhortation, precept, punishment, and praise and blame, of which moral philosophy consists, are destroyed" (Regan 2001: 257). Aquinas then goes on to explain what he takes human freedom to involve. He takes it to lie in our ability to make choices that our intellect does not present to us as absolutely necessary. For a helpful and clear account of Aquinas on human choice, see Herbert McCabe, *On Aquinas* (London/New York: Continuum, 2008), chaps. 9–10. For a contemporary philosopher defending belief in human freedom with an eye on moral praise and blame, see Peter Van Inwagen, *An Essay on Free Will* (Oxford: Clarendon, 1983), 16.

21. Alvin Plantinga, *The Nature of Necessity* (Oxford: Clarendon, 1974), 166.

22. James F. Ross, "Creation II," in *The Existence and Nature of God*, ed. Alfred J. Freddoso (Notre Dame/London: University of Notre Dame Press, 1983), 128–34. For another text of Aquinas defending this position, see QDM 6.3 ad 3: "The impulse of a

higher cause moves irrational animals to definite things by way of particular forms, and the perception of these forms activates animals' sense appetite. And God indeed inevitably moves the will because of the efficacy of his causal power, which cannot fail. But because the nature of the will so moved is indifferently disposed to different things, no necessity results, and freedom abides. Just so, God's providence works infallibly in every kind of thing, although effects result contingently from contingent causes, insofar as God moves every kind of thing proportionally, each in his own way" (Regan 2001: 261). Cf. also *Quaestiones Disputatae de Veritate* (Disputed Questions on Truth) 24.1 ad 3.

23. Cf. McCabe, *God Matters*, 6.

24. That Aquinas thinks this is well explained by Herbert McCabe in *God and Evil in the Theology of St. Thomas Aquinas* (London/New York: Continuum, 2010).

CHAPTER 8

1. Quoted from the New Revised Standard Version, which does not differ in sense from what Aquinas read in Latin: "God is light and in him is no darkness at all." Cf. SCG 1.39.

2. Cf. SCG 1.39, where we find Aquinas arguing: "God is goodness and not simply good. There cannot, therefore, be any non-goodness in him." He goes on to argue that since God is essentially good he cannot be what is opposed to what he is essentially, and is therefore such that there cannot be badness in him (as in "if I am essentially human then I cannot be what excludes my being human"). He also argues that if God is perfect, it is absurd to suppose that he is somehow bad since badness is real only in the sense that something lacks a good appropriate to what it essentially is, which cannot, thinks Aquinas, be the case with God.

3. All of Aquinas's discussions of prayer are helpfully assembled and translated by Simon Tugwell in *Albert and Thomas: Selected Writings* (New York/Mahwah: Paulist Press, 1988).

4. René Descartes, *Meditations on First Philosophy*, Second Meditation. For this in translation, see *The Philosophical Writings of Descartes*, trans. John Cottingham, Robert Stoothoff, and Dugald Murdoch (Cambridge: Cambridge University Press, 1984), vol. 2.

5. A good example of such an author is Richard Swinburne, *The Coherence of Theism* (rev. ed.; Oxford: Clarendon, 1993), introduction and chaps. 7–8. Swinburne clearly takes God to be a person considered as a nonmaterial thinking and choosing agent existing in time.

6. Hence we find Aquinas arguing that God knows things other than himself only insofar as he knows himself as being their Creator and as containing perfections that reflect him. Cf. ST 1a.14.5: "We must say that God sees himself in himself, because he sees himself through his essence. He sees things other than himself not in themselves but in himself, because his essence contains the likeness of things other than himself" (Davies and Leftow 2006: 176).

7. For more on this formula see my *The Reality of God and the Problem of Evil* (London/New York: Continuum, 2006), chap. 3.

8. For Aquinas on emotions in us (and in nonhuman animals), see ST 1a2ae.22–30.

9. For a comparable, though more complicated, discussion of God's love, see SCG 1.91.

10. In addition to what I have already quoted from Aquinas, a classic text here is ST 1a.12.12: "The knowledge that is natural to us has its source in the senses and therefore extends just so far as it can be led by sensible things. But our understanding cannot reach to a vision of God's essence from these, for sensible creatures are effects of God which are unequal to the power of their cause. So, knowing them does not lead us to understand the whole power of God, and we do not thereby see his essence. Yet they are effects which are causally dependent, so we can at least be led from them to know of God that he exists and that he has whatever must belong to him as the first cause of all things, a cause that surpasses all that he causes" (Davies and Leftow 2006: 135).

11. For a good account of Aquinas on this, see Brian Shanley's commentary on ST 1a.12 in *Thomas Aquinas: The Treatise on the Divine Nature*, trans. Brian J. Shanley (Indianapolis/Cambridge: Hackett, 2006).

12. Aquinas's point here is that, whatever store we might set by happiness derivable in this life, such happiness is not the ultimate happiness of the beatific vision. His thinking comes out well in ST 1a2ae.2, where he works his way through a list of sources of happiness (for example, riches, honors, fame, power, bodily well-being, and sensory pleasures) so as to conclude that none of them are ultimately desirable when set beside the beatific vision. We must, therefore, attribute to him the view that God is the source of human happiness enjoyed in this life and is also the source of happiness that exceeds all of this.

13. In *The Problem of Evil and the Problem of God* (London: SCM, 2004), D. Z. Phillips criticizes the view that God can be morally excused for allowing evil since he lays on for us a very jolly time in the life to come by way of compensation or something like that. Yet Aquinas's talk about the beatific vision is not presented by him as an example of what Phillips is attacking. Aquinas does not take the beatific vision to amount to any kind of moral exoneration of God. He simply takes it to be something good to which God (ultimately inscrutable) brings some people, something that, along with many other things, reflects the good that God is.

14. By "evidence to the contrary" I am thinking of something like my party host coming up to me before the person calling himself John does and saying, "The person about to address you is mentally unbalanced and always lies about his name."

15. G. E. M. Anscombe, "What Is It to Believe Someone?" in *Rationality and Religious Belief*, ed. C. F. Delaney (Notre Dame/London: University of Notre Dame Press, 1979), 143. For a developed statement of what Anscombe is driving at, see Michael Welbourne, *The Community of Knowledge* (Aberdeen: Aberdeen University Press, 1986).

16. Anscombe, "What Is It to Believe Someone?" 143–44.

17. Aquinas's belief in Christian revelation is anything but an afterthought. This should be clear to anyone reading him carefully. He is prepared to talk about God

without relying on explicitly Christian premises and is, therefore, an exponent of natural theology. But "God" for him is evidently the God as proclaimed by the Christian creeds. His *Summa Contra Gentiles* has often and understandably been read as a purely philosophical work and not one concerned to recommend belief in Christianity (as Aquinas understands it). Yet, read in its entirety, it obviously is concerned to do so, as is clear from the foreword to and the contents of SCG 4. In the foreword Aquinas distinguishes between what can be known of God philosophically ("imperfect knowledge" as he calls it) and what is true of God as revealed by him. He then goes on to talk about the doctrine of the Trinity, the doctrine of the incarnation, and other explicitly Christian teachings. Aquinas's *Summa Theologiae* is explicitly Christian from the outset, though some have complained that he turns to the doctrine of the Trinity only having been prepared to talk about God without reference to this. He does so, I think, because he takes to be obvious (as it is, indeed obvious) that one cannot ask what it means for God to be three in one without having asked what it might mean to speak of God in the first place (and on the understanding that belief in God, as Creator of the Universe, is common to Christians, Jews, and Muslims).

18. I should emphasize that in this chapter I am focusing on Aquinas's mature thinking on grace as presented in the *Summa Theologiae*. As is commonly acknowledged by scholars, Aquinas's thinking on grace developed somewhat during his career.

19. Aquinas does not think that all human beings have the same abilities. He recognizes that, for example, some people are blind, brain damaged, or in other ways incapacitated. But the very word "incapacitated" here makes sense only with reference to a norm—this being human nature in an uninhibited or flourishing form. So Aquinas thinks it possible to speak of human nature even though people differ in what he would call their accidental forms.

20. I should, however, note that Aquinas also thinks that as sin-prone creatures we need help from God even to arrive at what is good for us as people living in this world. And he thinks that God, in his goodness, provides this. See ST 1a2ae.109.2.

21. Someone who famously makes use of the image of an elevator when talking of God is St. Thérèse of Lisieux. See *Story of a Soul: The Autobiography of St. Thérèse of Lisieux*, trans. John Clarke (2nd ed.; Washington DC: Institute of Carmelite Studies, 1976), 207.

22. "Better," of course, since Aquinas does not take God strictly to have a "way of being"—should that phrase be taken to suggest that God is a thing of a certain kind, a member of a world containing things of different natural kinds.

23. For an extended discussion of faith by Aquinas, see ST 2a2ae.1–7. I offer a more expanded account of Aquinas on faith in *The Thought of Thomas Aquinas* (Oxford: Clarendon, 1992), chap. 14. Aquinas regards faith as a virtue since he takes it to be a disposition (or *habitus*) that makes us to be good. But he regularly distinguishes between natural and supernatural virtues. Natural virtues (such as temperance) are, for him, ones that we can in principle acquire by effort and with a rational eye on our human well-being. Supernatural virtues are ones that we cannot come to possess simply by being human. They are established in us directly by God and are not

explicable by any account of what we are by nature or by any account of what in the universe is acting on us.

24. I take Aquinas to be here thinking along the lines of Elizabeth Anscombe as noted above. He regards faith as believing what is true without being able personally to demonstrate that what is believed in faith is true. He does not, however, think that those with faith believe without reason, just as my faith in my doctors does not lack reason (albeit that I cannot personally confirm their diagnoses). For this see ST 2a2ae.1.4 ad 2.

25. I should note that Aquinas always proceeds on the assumption that the New Testament gives us a substantially accurate account of the teachings of Jesus, whom Aquinas calls the "first teacher" of the Christian faith. Is he right to do so? New Testament scholars have differed when it comes to the historicity of the Gospels, and this is not the place for me comment on their various findings. For a survey of work on these, see Mark Allan Powell, *Jesus as a Figure in History* (Louisville: Westminster/ John Knox, 1998). I might add that if it can be shown that the Gospels do not provide an account of Jesus that is fundamentally accurate from the historical point of view, then we would have to regard almost all of Aquinas's theology as completely wrongheaded. It surprises me that people defending Aquinas's theology hardly ever pay attention to the possible effect on it of findings by New Testament scholars. I am sure that Aquinas would be keenly concerned with this issue were he alive today.

26. One might naturally think that to have charity is to be willing to help other people in various ways. And Aquinas certainly thinks that those with charity are so willing (cf. ST 2a2ae.25.1). But talking of the virtue of charity his focus is on the notion of loving the good that is God. It is, he thinks, because of our love for this that, by the virtue of charity, we will good to others (and especially will their eternal good).

27. One might, however, argue that they ought to be so interested insofar as they claim to be contributing to a discussion of belief in God, insofar as what Aquinas says about grace is very much part and parcel of his account of what God is, and insofar as Aquinas is clearly a major and traditional exponent of belief in God.

28. Note, though, that Aquinas does not present this claim so as to suggest that God can be somehow defended on moral grounds. As we have seen, he does not take God to have any moral case to answer.

29. I am raising this question with respect to human beings and beatitude. We have already seen how Aquinas accounts for some created things being less good than others in terms of his approach to the topic of *malum poenae*.

30. Aquinas read this text in Latin translations available to him, but I have no reason to think that he did not think them to give a rendition of Romans 8.29–30 as the New Revised Standard Version presents it in modern English.

31. Aquinas makes the distinction between "predestine" and "predetermine" in, for example, ST 1a.23.1 ad 1.

32. Classical examples of people taking this view are Clement of Alexandria (c. 150–c. 215) and Origen (c. 185–c. 254). Condemned by the Council of Constantinople in 543, the view has been recently defended, with an eye on God and evil, by, among others, John Hick, *Evil and the God of Love* (London: Macmillan, 1985

[first published 1966]), and Marilyn McCord Adams, *Horrendous Evils and the Goodness of God* (Ithaca/London: Cornell University Press, 1999).

CHAPTER 9

1. *The Oxford Dictionary of the Christian* Church, 3rd ed., edited by E.A. Livingstone (Oxford University Press: Oxford, 1997), 1105.

2. For one presentation of this charge see Colin Gunton, *Act and Being* (Grand Rapids: Eerdmans, 2002). Cf. also Karl Barth, *The Göttingen Dogmatics: Instruction in the Christian Religion* (Edinburgh: Clark, 1981), vol. 1. Gunton, I assume, takes himself to be writing in the tradition of John Calvin. It is therefore, perhaps, worth noting that Calvin himself distinguishes between *de Deo Uno* and *de Deo Trino* and that he is prepared to discuss the former before turning to the latter. See Paul Helm, *John Calvin's Ideas* (Oxford: Oxford University Press, 2004), 34. Helm goes on to note that Calvin, nevertheless, "does not readily separate the doctrine of God from the doctrine of the Trinity." Exactly the same can be said of Aquinas even if he differs from Calvin when it comes to what can be known of God by reason.

3. Rowan Williams makes this clear in "What Does Love Know? St. Thomas on the Trinity," *New Blackfriars* 82 (June 2001).

4. When Christians began developing their formulations of the doctrine of the Trinity they assumed, as do all New Testament authors, that "God" is a word with meaning apart from anything that might be thought of as Christian revelation. Aquinas works on the same assumption.

5. For a detailed analysis of Aquinas on the Trinity, see Gilles Emery, *The Trinitarian Theology of Saint Thomas Aquinas* (Oxford: Oxford University Press, 2007).

6. Cf. ST 2a2ae.174.6: "At the time of grace, the mystery of the Trinity was revealed by the Son of God himself."

7. Quoted from Armand Maurer, *Faith, Reason, and Theology* (Toronto: Pontifical Institute of Medieval Studies, 1987). Cf. ST 1a.32.1 and CT 36.

8. G. E. M. Anscombe and P. T. Geach, *Three Philosophers* (Oxford: Blackwell, 1973), 118–19. Cf. ST 1a.32.1.

9. Aquinas's use of the verb "proceed" when he talks of the Trinity derives from the Bible. He has in mind texts such as John 8.42 (as he understood them, anyway).

10. This is not an idea peculiar to Aquinas. You can find it, for example, in St. Anselm's *Epistola de Incarnatione Verbi* 13.

11. Lest you should think that Aquinas's language here is regrettably noninclusive, I should note that he does not, of course, think of the Trinity in gender terms. He speaks of Father and Son when talking about the Trinity only because the language is biblical and traditional. He does not take it to imply that the Father or the Son have a gender (though he thinks of God incarnate as having a gender since he thinks of Jesus as being a man). Without doing any violence to Aquinas's Trinitarian theology we could, I assume, replace his talk of God the Father and God the Son with talk about God the Mother and God the Daughter.

12. Some medieval theologians argued that knowing the good that God is does not compel one to love him. Aquinas thinks otherwise since he takes will and intellect

to be inextricably linked and since he thinks that one cannot but will what one knows to be good without reservation. For him, to know what is absolutely good is just to recognize it as desirable and, therefore, to will it (i.e., to love it or be drawn to it).

13. Cf. John Hick (ed.), *The Myth of God Incarnate* (London: SCM, 1977).

14. Aquinas offers various criticisms of people not accepting what he takes to be the teaching of Chalcedon on the incarnation. See, for example, CT 202–11.

15. As I have said, Aquinas denies that, for example, there cannot be people who are also iguanas, or dogs who are also cats. Is Aquinas contradicting himself as he speaks of incarnation? He does not think so. He does not take himself to be saying that a god can be a man. He is saying that God the Son can become human as assuming a human nature without losing his divine nature. In very traditional terms Aquinas always insists that the divine and human natures of Christ are distinct. So he will, for example, say that as man Christ ate food, while denying that Christ, as God, ate anything. Note, though, that Aquinas holds that, since Christ is God, anything ascribable to him can be ascribed to God. So, given his belief in the incarnation, Aquinas is happy to say that, for example, God ate food and that God died.

16. For Aquinas, Christ is the Word of God (as in John 1). So he thinks that believing what Christ says is literally taking God's Word for it.

17. I offer a more detailed account of it in my Aquinas (London/New York: Continuum, 2002), chap. 17. For an excellent sense of Aquinas on the logic of the incarnation, see Herbert McCabe, *God Still Matters* (London/New York: Continuum, 2002), chap. 10.

18. Aquinas's discussion of sin always involves reference, at least implicitly, to what he calls original sin, the sin of Adam. So as to focus on what I take to be the most significant elements in Aquinas's treatment of Jesus and sin, I do not in this book discuss Aquinas on original sin. I do, however, aim to explain how he thinks of this in my introduction to *On Evil* (Oxford/New York: Oxford University Press, 2003), 43–49.

19. The reference to Augustine is to *De Trinitate* 13.17. Note that Aquinas several times stresses that the incarnation does not involve a change in God. "The Word became flesh" (John 1.14) does not, he argues, mean that the divine nature goes through some kind of process. It means that the immutable God brings about a change in the world—the birth of one who is both human and divine. Cf. ST 3a.1.1: "The mystery of the incarnation did not involve any sort of change in the state of God's eternal existence. Instead it took place by his uniting himself in a new fashion to a creature, or, more precisely, by a creature becoming united to him."

20. At this point I am definitely not referring to Jürgen Moltmann, for whom the cross of Christ is crucial when it comes to an account of what God is. I shall be referring to Moltmann in the next chapter. Here I am concerned with a view of Christ's death that is very different from that of Moltmann and the many theologians he has influenced when writing about the crucified God.

21. Quoted (with slight emendations) from Romanus Cessario's translation of Aquinas, *The Godly Image: Christ and Salvation in Catholic Thought* (Petersham MA: St. Bede's Publications, 1990), 30.

22. Herbert McCabe, *God Matters* (London: Chapman, 1987), 99.

23. Cf. F. J. A. de Grijs, "Thomas Aquinas on Ira as a Divine Metaphor," in *Tibi Soli Peccavi: Thomas Aquinas on Guilt and Forgiveness*, ed. Henk J. M. Schoot (Leuven: Peeters, 1996).

24. For a translation of St. Anselm's Cur Deus Homo, see Brian Davies and G. R. Evans (eds.), *Anselm of Canterbury: The Major Works* (Oxford/New York: Oxford University Press, 1998).

25. Quoted from *Compendium of Theology* by Thomas Aquinas, trans. Richard J. Regan (Oxford/New York: Oxford University Press, 2009), 150–51.

26. I find nothing in the writings of Aquinas to suggest that those who killed Christ were forced by God to do so. And his general position on human freedom (and assuming that those bringing about the crucifixion of Christ were acting freely [which Aquinas never denies]) seems flatly incompatible with the idea that the crucifixion was determined by God or determined by anything in the world. So we can presume Aquinas to have thought that Christ might never have been crucified. And we can, therefore, presume, that he would have thought it possible to develop a theology of Christ's life without any mention of the cross. The fact of the cross governs what he says about Christ, but, philosopher as he is, Aquinas is also aware of counterfactuals with respect to which one might reason.

27. As I try to indicate above, I am not taking this to be the view of Moltmann, on whom more, as I have promised, below.

28. Cessario, *Godly Image*, xviii.

29. This point is stressed by Eleonore Stump in "Atonement according to Aquinas," in *Philosophy and the Christian Faith*, ed. Thomas V. Morris (Notre Dame: University of Notre Dame Press, 1988). As Stump says, Aquinas believes the satisfaction of Christ to take effect insofar as sinners turn to him as wanting what he wants. In terms of Aquinas's thinking, "the point of making satisfaction is to return the wrongdoer's will to conformity with the will of the person wronged, rather than to inflict retributive punishment on the wrongdoer or to placate the person wronged.... The aim of any satisfaction (including vicarious satisfaction) is not to cancel a debt incurred by sin but to restore a sinner to harmony with God.... Given the understanding of satisfaction on which Aquinas's theory of the Atonement is based, satisfaction for sin made by a substitute for the sinner effects reconciliation only in case the sinner allies himself with the substitute by willing the restitution the substitute makes. The medicine of Christ's satisfaction is unavailing unless a person applies it to himself by accepting Christ's suffering and death as making satisfaction for his own sins" (pp. 67, 69, 71). Stump's account of Aquinas on the satisfaction achieved by Christ seems to me an accurate one. It also does much to render Aquinas's thinking intelligible by means of concrete examples. For another fine discussion of Aquinas on the satisfaction of Christ, see Rik Van Nieuwenhove, "'Bearing the Marks of Christ's Passion': Aquinas' Soteriology," in *The Theology of Thomas Aquinas*, ed. Rik Van Nieuwenhove and Joseph Wawrykow (Notre Dame: University of Notre Dame Press, 2005).

30. For a helpful account of Aquinas on Christ with respect to Old Testament notions of priesthood and sacrifice, see Matthew Levering, *Christ's Fulfillment of Torah and Temple* (Notre Dame: University of Notre Dame Press, 2002).

31. Aquinas would not, for example, approve of people trying to preserve their material goods by entering into an unjust war leading to the deaths of many innocent civilians. There are, he thinks, just and unjust ways of preserving one's well-being.

32. I talk about this in my *The Thought of Thomas Aquinas* (Oxford: Clarendon, 1992), chap. 17.

33. Speaking of what he calls "anonymous Christianity," Rahner says, "Anonymous Christianity means that a person lives in the grace of God and attains salvation outside of explicitly constituted Christianity—Let us say, a Buddhist monk—who, because he follows his conscience, attains salvation and lives in the grace of God; of him I must say that he is an anonymous Christian; if not, I would have to presuppose that there is a genuine path to salvation that really attains that goal, but that simply has nothing to do with Jesus Christ. But I cannot do that. And so, if I hold if everyone depends upon Jesus Christ for salvation, and if at the same time I hold that many live in the world who have not expressly recognized Jesus Christ, then there remains in my opinion nothing else but to take up this postulate of an anonymous Christianity"; Karl Rahner, Paul Imhof, and Hubert Biallowons, *Karl Rahner in Dialogue: Conversations and Interviews, 1965–1982*, ed. Paul Imhof, Hubert Biallowons, and Harvey D. Egan (New York: Crossroad, 1986), 207.

CHAPTER 10

1. Aquinas often says that pain and suffering can be good for people in that it can be thought of as medicinal and as leading them to union with God if they accept it willingly and with a love for God (and what else would you expect him to say?). But he does not say this as trying to explain what God's "morally sufficient reasons are." That, of course, is because Aquinas does not take God to have or to lack morally sufficient reasons. We have or lack these, but God, Aquinas thinks, does not.

2. One can find this approach in a lot of contemporary pro-theistic philosophical literature. See, for example, R. E. Creel, *Divine Impassibility* (Cambridge: Cambridge University Press, 1986); Richard Swinburne, *The Coherence of Theism* (rev. ed.; Oxford: Clarendon, 1993); and Alvin Plantinga, *Does God Have a Nature?* (Milwaukee: Marquette University Press, 1980). I have elsewhere referred to the approach I have in mind here as "theistic personalism." See my *An Introduction to the Philosophy of Religion* (3rd ed.; Oxford: Oxford University Press, 2004), chap. 1.

3. Here I have in mind authors who attack Aquinas for being a representative of ontotheology. Writings on ontotheology offer a number of (sometimes none too clear) accounts of what it amounts to. Here I am simply working with the understanding of it to be found in Kevin L. Hughes, "Remember Bonaventure? (Onto)theology and Ecstasy," *Modern Theology* 19 (Oct. 2003). Hughes discusses ontotheology with special reference to two authors commenting on it, these being Richard Kearney, "The God Who May Be: A Phenomenological Study," *Modern Theology* 18 (2002); and Merold Westphal, *Overcoming Ontotheology: Toward a Postmodern Christian Faith* (New York: Fordham University Press, 2001). In "Aquinas and Onto-theology," *American Catholic Philosophical Quarterly* 80.2 (2006), Westphal offers what seems

to me a thoroughly cogent refutation of the claim that Aquinas is an ontotheologian (on a certain understanding of ontotheology).

4. By "without comment" I mean "without an explicit indication of how various biblical passages are to be understood." On the other hand, there are places in the Bible where an anthropomorphic way of speaking of God seems to be quickly countered or corrected by a passage pulling in a different direction. One example comes in Exodus 33.11, where we read that God spoke to Moses "face to face, as one speaks to a friend," and are then told that God said to Moses, "You cannot see my face; for no one shall see me and live" (33.23). Moses is then described as seeing God's glory by seeing his back. Again, note 1 Samuel 15.11, where God regrets having made Saul the king of Israel. But a few verses later the prophet Samuel says, "The Glory of Israel will not recant or change his mind; for he is not a mortal, that he should change his mind" (15.29).

5. Aquinas, in fact, believes that the Bible itself provides warrant for the idea that people can come to know something of God without special divine revelation. He has in mind texts like Acts 17 and Romans 1.

6. James Barr, *Biblical Faith and Natural Theology* (Oxford: Clarendon, 1993).

7. Ibid., 26.

8. Romans 1 has often been taken as stating that there can be a knowledge of God apart from that provided by Christian revelation. See, for example, the "Dogmatic Constitution on the Catholic Faith" (*Dei Filius*) of the First Vatican Council.

9. Barr, Biblical Faith and Natural Theology, 104.

10. I take an apophatic thinker to be one strongly stressing the unknowability and transcendence of God. And thinkers do not get much more apophatic than Pseudo-Dionysius, sometimes called Dionysius the Areopagite (an unknown author whose works can be dated to the fifth or sixth century). For the Dionysian corpus, see *Pseudo-Dionysius: The Complete Works*, trans. Colm Luibheid (New York/Mahwah: Paulist Press, 1987). For a modern commentary on Dionysius's texts, see Paul Rorem, *Pseudo-Dionysius* (New York/Oxford: Oxford University Press, 1993). For a study of Aquinas and Dionysius, see Fran O'Rourke, *Pseudo-Dionysius and the Metaphysics of Aquinas* (Leiden/New York/Köln: Brill, 1992).

11. For all of this, see Jürgen Moltmann, *The Crucified God* (London: SCM, 1974).

12. For reference to questions such as these, and for some guide to critical literature on Moltmann's general way of thinking about God as suffering, see Daniel Castelo, *The Apathetic God* (Milton Keynes/Colorado Springs: Paternoster, 2009).

13. Herbert McCabe, *God Matters* (London: Chapman, 1987), 44–45.

14. That Aquinas's way of developing his account of divine immutability points away from the suggestion that God does not govern the world by a caring providence is well documented by Michael J. Dodds in *The Unchanging God of Love* (2nd ed.; Washington, DC: Catholic University of America Press, 2008).

15. Cf. Paul Draper, "Seeking But Not Believing," in *Divine Hiddenness*, ed. Daniel Howard Snyder and Paul K. Moser (Cambridge: Cambridge University Press, 2002), 202–3: "Nothing mental (and human) happens unless something physical happens . . . [which] is very strong evidence for the position that human consciousness

and personality are properties of brains or nervous systems or bodies rather than properties of immaterial substances.... This supports naturalism over theism because the non-existence of immaterial human minds is much more likely on naturalism than theism."

16. An example of a philosopher thinking along these lines would be Daniel Dennett. See his *Content and Consciousness* (London: Routledge & Kegan Paul, 1969).

17. An example here would be Wittgenstein, with respect to whom an excellent introduction is Marie McGinn, *Wittgenstein and the Philosophical Investigations* (London/New York: Routledge, 1997).

18. For more on this, see Robert Pasnau, *Thomas Aquinas on Human Nature* (Cambridge: Cambridge University Press, 2002), chap. 12.

19. With respect to God, the Bible, indeed, often commends to its readers a variety of (sometimes incompatible) images (even nonhuman ones). Cf. Genesis 3.8; Deuteronomy 32.11; Psalms 24.8; 44.4; Isaiah 40.28; 42.14; Hosea 5.12. And from time to time it reminds us that God is incomparable—as in Isaiah 40.18–26: "To whom then will you liken God, what likeness compare with him?...To whom then will you compare me, or who is my equal? Says the Holy One. Lift up your eyes on high and see: Who created these?"

20. Cf. Walter Eichrodt, *Theology of the Old Testament* (Philadelphia: Westminster, 1961), 1.339ff. Cf. also P. J. Achtemeier's article "Righteousness in the NT," in *The Interpreter's Dictionary of the Bible*, ed. G. A. Buttrick et al. (New York/Nashville: Abingdon, 1962), 4.98–99: "If, as has been stated, righteousness is to be understood basically as a relational term, then it is also true that it cannot mean basically 'conformity to a (moral) norm.'...Aside from the fact that righteousness as meaning conformity to a moral norm would mean that God too conforms to this norm, since he is called 'righteous' (an idea incompatible with NT views of God's sovereignty), such an understanding makes it difficult to see how the term 'righteous' can so often be applied to God's saving act on behalf of those who are supremely unrighteous and thus morally delinquent (Rom. 5:8, among others)....The clear statement of Paul that no man is counted righteous before God on the basis of works should be enough to eliminate moral conformity from consideration (Gal. 3:11 etc.)." Also worth noting is a comment of Jacob Joshua Ross: "Jewish tradition is firmly convinced that God loves His people Israel, and there is an imperative necessity for the Children of Israel, both corporately and individually, to love God. But that God loves every individual person equally and indiscriminately is not an explicit teaching of the Hebrew scriptures or a central theme of rabbinic teaching." See Jacob Joshua Ross, "The Hiddenness of God," in *Divine Hiddenness*, ed. Daniel Howard Snyder and Paul K. Moser (Cambridge: Cambridge University Press, 2002), 182.

21. Immanuel Kant, "Toward Perpetual Peace," in his *Practical Philosophy*, trans./ed. Mary J. Gregor (Cambridge: Cambridge University Press, 1996), 323.

22. R. F. Holland, *Against Empiricism* (Totowa NJ: Barnes & Noble, 1980), 237ff.

23. N. T. Wright, *Evil and the Justice of God* (London: SPCK, 2006), 20.

24. It would be wrong to suggest that Aquinas directly deals with the so-called evidential argument against the existence of God based on evil. For he does not, as do

contemporary authors like William Rowe and Paul Draper, ask whether God's existence is unlikely given the evil that occurs. My point is that from what he says we can ascribe to Aquinas the conclusion that there is no case against the existence of God to be made on the basis of the occurrence of evil as we find it in our world.

25. By "horrendous evil" I mean what Marilyn McCord Adams has in mind in *Horrendous Evils and the Goodness of God* (Ithaca/London: Cornell University Press, 1999).

Bibliography

Adams, Marilyn McCord. *Christ and Horrors*. Cambridge: Cambridge University Press, 2006.

———. *Horrendous Evils and the Goodness of God*. Ithaca/London: Cornell University Press, 1999.

Adams, Marilyn McCord, and Robert Merrihew Adams (eds.). *The Problem of Evil*. Oxford: Oxford University Press, 1990.

Aertsen, Jan. *Nature and Creature: Thomas Aquinas's Way of Thought*. Leiden: Brill, 1988.

Ahern, M. B. *The Problem of Evil*. London: Routledge & Kegan Paul, 1971.

Anscombe, G. E. M. "Faith." In Anscombe's *Collected Philosophical Papers*, vol. 3. Oxford: Blackwell, 1981.

———. "What Is It to Believe Someone?" In *Rationality and Religious Belief*. Edited by C. F. Delaney. Notre Dame/London: University of Notre Dame Press, 1979.

Anscombe, G. E. M., and P. T. Geach. *Three Philosophers*. Oxford: Blackwell, 1961.

Aquinas, Thomas. *On Evil (Quaestiones Disputatae de Malo)*. Translated by Richard Regan. New York/Oxford: Oxford University Press, 2001. [Cited as Regan 2001.]

———. *On the Power of God I (De Potentia Dei)*. Translated by the English Dominican Fathers. London: Burns, Oates & Washbourne, 1932–34.

———. *The Soul (Quaestio Disputata de Anima)*. Translated by J. H. Robb. Milwaukee: Marquette University Press, 1984.

———. *Summa Contra Gentiles*. Translated by Anton Pegis, James F. Anderson, Vernon J. Bourke, and Charles J. O'Neil. Notre Dame: University of Notre Dame Press, 1975.

——. *Summa Theologiae*. 61 vols. Various translators. London: Eyre & Spottiswoode/ New York: McGraw-Hill, 1964–80. [Cited as Blackfriars edition.]

——. *"Summa Theologiae" Questions on God*. Edited by Brian Davies and Brian Leftow. Cambridge: Cambridge University Press, 2006. [Cited as Davies and Leftow 2006.]

——. *Truth (Quaestiones Disputatae de Veritate)*. Translated by Robert W. Mulligan, J. V. McGlynn, and R. W. Schmidt. Chicago: Regnery, 1952–54.

Baldner, Steven E., and William E. Carroll. *Aquinas on Creation*. Toronto: Pontifical Institute of Medieval Studies, 1997.

Ballantine, Samuel. *The Hidden God: The Hiding of the Face of God in the Old Testament*. Oxford: Oxford University Press, 1983.

Barr, James. *Biblical Faith and Natural Theology*. Oxford: Clarendon, 1993.

Bauerschmidt, Frederick Christian. *Holy Teaching: Introducing the "Summa Theologiae" of St. Thomas Aquinas*. Grand Rapids: Brazos, 2005.

Burrell, David B. *Aquinas, God, and Action*. London/Henley: Routledge & Kegan Paul, 1979.

——. *Freedom and Creation in Three Traditions*. Notre Dame: University of Notre Dame Press, 1993.

——. *Knowing the Unknowable God: Ibn-Sina, Maimonides, Aquinas*. Notre Dame: University of Notre Dame Press, 1986.

Cessario, Romanus. *The Godly Image: Christ and Salvation in Catholic Thought from Anselm to Aquinas*. Petersham MA: St. Bede's Publications, 1990.

Chenu, M.-D. *Toward Understanding Saint Thomas*. Chicago: Regnery, 1964.

Copleston, F. C. *Aquinas*. Harmondsworth: Penguin, 1955.

Crenshaw, James L. *Theodicy in the Old Testament*. Philadelphia: Fortress/London: SPCK, 1983.

Dauphinais, Michael, and Matthew Levering. *Knowing the Love of Christ: An Introduction to the Theology of St. Thomas Aquinas*. Notre Dame: University of Notre Dame Press, 2002.

Davies, Brian. "The Action of God." In *Mind, Method, and Morality*. Edited by John Cottingham and Peter Hacker. Oxford: Oxford University Press, 2010.

——. *Aquinas*. London/New York: Continuum, 2002.

——. "Aquinas on What God Is Not." *Revue Internationale de Philosophie* 52.204 (1998).

—— (ed.). *Aquinas's "Summa Theologiae": Critical Essays*. London: Roman & Littlefield, 2006.

——. "Classical Theism and the Doctrine of Divine Simplicity." In *Language, Meaning, and God*. Edited by Brian Davies. London: Chapman, 1987. Reprinted in *Philosophy of Religion: A Guide and Anthology*. Edited by Brian Davies. Oxford: Oxford University Press, 2000.

——. "Kenny on Aquinas on Being." *Modern Schoolman* 82 (2005).

——. *The Reality of God and the Problem of Evil*. London/New York: Continuum, 2006.

——. "Simplicity." In *The Cambridge Companion to Christian Philosophical Theology*. Edited by Charles Taliaferro and Chad Meister. Cambridge: Cambridge University Press, 2010.

——— (ed.). *Thomas Aquinas: Contemporary Philosophical Perspectives*. Oxford/New York: Oxford University Press, 2002.

———. *The Thought of Thomas Aquinas*. Oxford: Clarendon, 1992.

Davies, Brian, and Eleonore Stump (eds.). *The Oxford Handbook of Thomas Aquinas*. Oxford/New York: Oxford University Press, 2011.

Dodds, Michael J. *The Unchanging God of Love: Thomas Aquinas and Contemporary Theology on Divine Immutability*. 2nd edition. Washington, DC: Catholic University of America Press, 2008.

Draper, Paul. "Pain and Pleasure: An Evidential Problem for Theists." *Nous* 23 (June 1989.

Eichrodt, Walter. *Theology of the Old Testament*, vol. 1. Philadelphia: Westminster, 1961.

Emery, Gilles. *The Trinitarian Theology of Saint Thomas Aquinas*. Oxford/New York: Oxford University Press, 2007.

Flew, Antony. *The Presumption of Atheism and Other Essays*. London: Elek/Pemberton, 1976.

Geach, P. T. *God and the Soul*. London: Routledge & Kegan Paul, 1969.

———. "Good and Evil." *Analysis* 17 (1956).

———. *Providence and Evil*. Cambridge: Cambridge University Press, 1977.

Grant, G. M., "Can a Libertarian Hold That Our Free Acts Are Caused by God?" *Faith and Philosophy* 27 (2010): 22–24.

———. "Aquinas on How God Causes the Act of Sin without Causing the Sin Itself," *The Thomist* 72 (2009): 455–96.

Helm, Paul. *The Providence of God*. Leicester: Inter-Varsity, 1993.

Hick, John. *Evil and the God of Love*. 2nd edition. London: Macmillan, 1977.

Holland, Roy. *Against Empiricism*. Totowa NJ: Barnes & Noble, 1980.

Howard-Snyder, Daniel. *The Evidential Argument from Evil*. Bloomington/Indianapolis: Indiana University Press, 1996.

Hume, David. *Dialogues concerning Natural Religion*. Edited by Stanley Tweyman. London/New York: Routledge, 1991.

———. *An Inquiry concerning Human Understanding*. Edited by Tom L. Beauchamp. Oxford: Clarendon, 2000.

Jordan, Mark D. *Rewritten Theology: Aquinas after His Readers*. Oxford: Blackwell, 2006.

Kant, Immanuel. *Critique of Pure Reason*. Edited by Paul Guyer and Allen W. Wood. Cambridge: Cambridge University Press, 1997.

———. "Toward Perpetual Peace." In Kant's *Practical Philosophy*. Edited by Mary J. Gregor. Cambridge: Cambridge University Press, 1996.

Kenny, Anthony. *Aquinas on Being*. Oxford: Clarendon, 2002.

Kerr, Fergus (ed.). *Contemplating Aquinas: On the Varieties of Interpretation*. London: SCM, 2003.

Kretzmann, Norman. *The Metaphysics of Creation: Aquinas's Natural Theology in "Summa Contra Gentiles" II*. Oxford: Clarendon, 1999.

———. *The Metaphysics of Theism: Aquinas's Natural Theology in "Summa Contra Gentiles" I*. Oxford: Clarendon, 1997.

Kretzmann, Norman, and Eleonore Stump (eds.). *The Cambridge Companion to Aquinas.* Cambridge: Cambridge University Press, 1993.

Levering, Matthew. *Christ's Fulfillment of Torah and Temple: Salvation according to Thomas Aquinas.* Notre Dame: University of Notre Dame Press, 2002.

Mackie, John. *The Miracle of Theism.* Oxford: Clarendon, 1982.

Martin, C. F. J. *Thomas Aquinas: God and Explanations.* Edinburgh: Edinburgh University Press, 1997.

McCabe, Herbert. *Faith within Reason.* London/New York: Continuum, 2007.

———. *God and Evil in the Theology of St. Thomas Aquinas.* London/New York: Continuum, 2010.

———. *God Matters.* London: Chapman, 1987.

———. *The Good Life.* London/New York: Continuum, 2005.

———. *On Aquinas.* London/New York: Continuum, 2008.

McDermott, Timothy. *Aquinas.* London: Granta, 2007.

———. *"Summa Theologiae": A Concise Translation.* London: Eyre & Spottiswoode, 1989.

———. *Thomas Aquinas: Selected Philosophical Writings.* Oxford/New York: Oxford University Press, 1998.

McGinn, Marie. *Wittgenstein and the Philosophical Investigations.* London/New York: Routledge, 1997.

Moltmann, Jürgen. *The Crucified God.* London: SCM, 1974.

O'Rourke, Fran. *Pseudo-Dionysius and the Metaphysics of Aquinas.* Leiden: Brill, 1992.

Pasnau, Robert. *Thomas Aquinas on Human Nature.* Cambridge: Cambridge University Press, 2002.

Persson, Per Erik. *Sacra Doctrina: Reason and Revelation in Aquinas.* Translated by Ross Mackenzie. Oxford: Blackwell, 1970.

Phillips, D. Z. *The Problem of Evil and the Problem of God.* London: SCM, 2004.

——— (ed.). *Whose God? Which Tradition?* Aldershot/Burlington VT: Ashgate, 2008.

Plantinga, Alvin. *God, Freedom, and Evil.* London: Allen & Unwin, 1975.

———. *The Nature of Necessity.* Oxford: Clarendon, 1974.

Reichenbach, Bruce R. *Evil and a Good God.* New York: Fordham University Press, 1982.

Rocca, Gregory P. *Speaking the Incomprehensible God.* Washington, DC: Catholic University of America Press, 2001.

Ross, James F. "Creation II." In *The Existence and Nature of God.* Edited by Alfred J. Freddoso. Notre Dame/London: University of Notre Dame Press, 1983.

Rundle, Bede, *Why There Is Something Rather than Nothing.* Oxford: Clarendon, 2004.

Sertillanges, A. D. *Foundations of Thomistic Philosophy.* London: Sands/St. Louis: Herder, 1931.

Shanley, Brian J. *The Treatise on the Divine Nature: Summa Theologiae I 1–13,* Indianapolis/Cambridge: Hackett, 2006.

Stump, Eleonore. *Aquinas.* London/New York: Routledge, 2003.

———. "Aquinas on the Sufferings of Job." In *Reasoned Faith.* Edited by Eleonore Stump. Ithaca/London: Cornell University Press, 1993.

———. "Atonement according to Aquinas." In *Philosophy and the Christian Faith.* Edited by Thomas V. Morris. Notre Dame: University of Notre Dame Press, 1988.

————.*ith and the Problem of Evil*. Grand Rapids: Calvin College, 1999.

Surin, Keneth. *Theology and the Problem of Evil*. Oxford: Blackwell, 1986.

Swinburn, Richard. *The Coherence of Theism*. Revised edition. Oxford: Clarendon, 1993.

————. *T Existence of God*. 2nd edition. Oxford: Clarendon, 2004.

————. *Pidence and the Problem of Evil*. Oxford: Clarendon, 1998.

Tanner, Karyn. *God and Creation in Christian Theology*. Oxford: Blackwell, 1988.

Te Velde, Rdi. *Aquinas on God: The "Divine Science" of the "Summa Theologiae."* Aldershot/Burlington VT: Ashgate, 2006.

Tugwell, Simon (ed.). *Albert and Thomas: Selected Writings*. New York/Mahwah: Paulist Press, 188.

Turner, Deni. *Faith, Reason, and the Existence of God*. Cambridge: Cambridge University Press, 2004.

Van Inwagen Peter (ed.). *Christian Faith and the Problem of Evil*. Grand Rapids: Eerdman, 2004.

————. *The Pblem of Evil*. Oxford: Clarendon, 2006.

Van Nieuwenhve, Rik, and Joseph Wawrykow (eds.). *The Theology of Thomas Aquinas*. Notre Dare: University of Notre Dame Press, 2005.

Wawrykow, Joseph P. *The SCM Press A–Z of Thomas Aquinas*. London: SCM, 2005.

Weigel, Peter. *Aquinas on Simplicity: An Investigation into the Foundations of His Philosophicl Theology*. Oxford/New York: Peter Lang, 2008.

Weinandy, Thomas G. *Does God Change?* Still River, MA: St. Bede's Publications, 1985.

Welbourne, Michael. *The Community of Knowledge*. Aberdeen: Aberdeen University Press, 1986

Westphal, Merol. "Aquinas and Onto-theology." *American Catholic Philosophical Quarterly* 80:2 (2006).

Whitney, Barry L. *Theodicy: An Annotated Bibliography on the Problem of Evil, 1960–1991*. Bowling Green, OH: Philosophy Documentation Center, 1998.

Williams, C. J. F. "Being." In *A Companion to the Philosophy of Religion*. Edited by Philip L. Quim and Charles Taliaferro. Oxford: Blackwell, 1997.

————. *What Is Existence?* Oxford: Clarendon, 1981.

Williams, Rowan. "Redeeming Sorrows." In *Religion and Morality*. Edited by D. Z. Phillips. New York: St. Martin's, 1996.

————. "What Does Love Know? St. Thomas on the Trinity." *New Blackfriars* 82 (June 2001).

Wippel, John F. *Metaphysical Themes in Thomas Aquinas*. Washington, DC: Catholic University of America Press, 1984.

————. *Metaphysical Themes in Thomas Aquinas II*. Washington, DC: Catholic University of America Press, 2007.

————. *The Metaphysical Thought of Thomas Aquinas*. Washington, DC: Catholic University of America Press, 2000.

Wissink, J. B. M. (ed.). *The Eternity of the World in the Thought of Thomas Aquinas and his Contemporaries*. Leiden: Brill, 1990.

Wright, N. T. *Evil and the Justice of God*. London: SPCK, 2006.

Index

accidental form, 23, 34, 48, 53
accidents, 21–22
Aeterni Patris (Leo XIII), ix
agent causes, 49, 58
    cause and effect distinction, 26–27
    defining, 25–26
    effects of, 27–28
    evil and, 72, 146n12
    God as first cause to, 73
Ahern, M. B., 133n2
Alice through the Looking Glass
    (Carroll), 47
analogy, 55
angels, 42, 147n15
anonymous Christianity, 111, 155n33
Anscombe, Elizabeth, 87–88, 151n24
Anselm, 105–6
antecedent will, 109–10
apophatic thinkers, 122, 156n10
Aristotle
    Aquinas commentaries on, 14–16,
      21, 27, 74
    Aquinas influenced by, 10, 12, 37,
      137n20
    moral philosophy and, 89
    on teaching, 27
    on types of causes, 25

    on virtues, 60, 62, 109, 117
Athanasian Creed, 97, 98
atheism, 121–22, 135n18
attributive adjectives, 31, 33, 36
Augustine of Hippo (Saint), 11, 35,
    103, 128, 135n17, 153n19
Avicenna, 14, 137n20
Ayer, A. J., 137n26

bad moral choices, 70–72
badness
    as absence of goodness, 35, 37, 115
    Aquinas on, 33–37
    as displacement of good, 35–36
    evil done and, 70–72
    evil suffered and, 68
    Hume on, 30
    as lack of being, 34
    naturally occurring, 68
Barr, James, 121
Barth, Karl, 11, 16, 17, 121
beatific vision, 86, 94, 105, 149n10,
    149n13
beatitude (*beatitudo*), 85–86, 95, 118
    Jesus Christ as offer of, 109
being
    Aquinas on, 22–25

being (*continued*)
  badness as lack of, 34
  God as cause of, 67
  goodness and, 32–33
beings, 19–20
  necessary, 41–42
belief
  faith and, 86, 88
  in God, 88–89
  knowledge and, 87–88
Biblical Faith and Natural Theology (Barr), 121
Boethius, 98
Boyle, Leonard E., 11

Calvin, John, 11, 152n2
cardinal virtues, 60
Carlin, George, 133n1
Carroll, Lewis, 47
Catharism, 136n5
causes, 139n18
  agent, 25–28, 49, 58, 72, 73, 146n12
  created, 93
  evil done and, 70–72
  evil suffered and, 67–70
  final, 25
  formal, 25
  God as, 58, 67, 122, 139n17, 147n22
  God enabling, 73
  human choice and, 72
  Hume on, 26–27
  material, 25
  predestination and, 93–94
  types of, 25
Cessario, Romanus, 103
change
  God accounting for, 143n21
  real *vs.* notional, 142n17
charity, 90–91, 108–9, 151n26
church, as body of Christ, 110
Clemens, Samuel, 54
The Coherence of Theism (Swinburne), 52
Commentarium Super Epistolam I ad Corinthios 15 (Commentary on St. Paul's First Letter to the Corinthians) (Thomas Aquinas), 23

Commentary on the Sentences (Thomas Aquinas), 101, 108
commutative justice, 62
compassion, 125
Compendium Theologiae (Thomas Aquinas), 13
consequent will, 109–10
contingency of creatures, 41–42
Council of Chalcedon, 100, 111, 123
Council of Nicea, 111
created causes, 93
created goodness, 116
crucifixion
  human freedom and, 154n26
  as starting point for thinking about God, 123
  Trinity and, 124
Cur Deus Homo (Anselm), 105

De Anima (Aristotle), 14
"death of God" theology, 135n1
De Ente et Essentia (Thomas Aquinas), 14, 21, 43
definition, 21
De Malo (Thomas Aquinas), 76, 135n21
De Principiis Naturae (Thomas Aquinas), 14, 25
Descartes, René, 10, 14, 80
desire, will and, 82–83
determinism, 72
Dialogues concerning Natural Religion (Hume), 1
Dionysius the Areopagite. *See* Pseudo-Dionysius
dispositions, 59–60
distributive justice, 62–63
divine justice, 62–64
divine names, 53, 144n6
divine nature, 98, 153n15, 153n19
divine simplicity, 47–49, 54, 99, 143n20
Dominic Guzmán (Saint), 11
Draper, Paul, 134n8

efficient cause, 58
ens/entia, 19–20, 144n9

ens per accidens, 20, 21, 23, 140n8
ens per se, 20, 21, 23, 33
Epicurus, 2, 129, 133n2
esse, 22–25, 34, 35, 41. *See also* being
   defining, 139n12
   evil as privation of, 69–70
   evil done and, 71
   God as source of things having, 56,
     80, 115
   God bringing about, 46–47, 51, 65
   as God's effect, 67
   goodness and, 114–16
essence, 20–22
   existence, God, and, 41–44
Ethics (Aristotle), 14
ethics, philosophical and virtue, 60
evidentialist argument, 2, 157n24
evil (*malum*). *See also* badness; problem
   of evil
   agent causes of, 72, 146n12
   Aquinas on God and, 5–8, 16–17
   defenders of theism on, 3–5
   defining, 134n6
   detractors of theism on, 1–3
   as disproof of God, 2, 79, 134n4
   horrendous, 130–31, 158n25
   naturally occurring, 68
   as privation of *esse*, 69–70
   as real, 115
   types of, 117
"Evil and Omnipotence" (Mackie), 2, 6
evil done (*malum culpae*), 129, 147n15
   as failure to choose good, 117
   free will and, 71–72
   God's causation and, 70–72
   as lack of goodness, 70–72
evil suffered (*malum poenae*), 117, 129,
   146n8, 147n16
   badness and, 68
   God's causation and, 67–70
   as good, 69
   as privation of *esse*, 69–70
existence
   Aquinas distinguishing types of,
     140n11

essence, God, and, 41–44
   of God, 79, 141n1
   of God, knowing, 39–41, 141n3, 149n10
   God creating, 43–44
   types of, 140n11
Expositio Super Librum Boethium de
   Trinitate (Thomas Aquinas), 98

failure, 70
faith
   Aquinas defining, 40
   Aquinas on, 88–89, 150n23, 151n24
   beatitude and, 86
   belief and, 86, 88
   defining, 86–87
   God sharing through, 118
   grace and, 90–91
   hope and, 91
   incarnation and, 108–9
   knowledge and, 87–88
felicitas, 84–85
final causes, 25
forgiveness of sin, 104–7, 119
formal causes, 25
free choice
   of God, 65
   human, 73–75, 117, 147n20
freedom, 72, 75, 154n26
free will
   causation of God and, 73
   evil done and, 71–72
   grace and, 93–94
   human choices and, 72–73
free-will defense, 4–5, 72–73, 135n17

Geach, Peter, 24, 31, 98
God
   analogically talking of, 55
   anthropomorphic depictions of, 120,
     126, 156n4
   Aquinas's approach to, 119–22
   Aquinas on evil and, 5–8, 16–17
   being caused by, 67
   belief in, 88–89
   benevolence of, 104

God (*continued*)
biblical depictions of, 120, 126–27
causal constraint on, 67–68
as cause, 58, 67, 122, 139n17, 147n22
causes enabled by, 73
change accounted for by, 143n21
charity and love for, 91
compassion of, 125
creation by, 146n2
as Creator, 45–47
creatures distinguished from, 42
crucifixion as starting point for
thinking about, 123
defenders of theism on, 3–5
detractors of theism on, 1–3
as efficient cause, 58
enjoyment of, 85–86
esse as effect of, 67
esse brought about by, 46–47,
51, 65
essence, existence, and, 41–44
evidentialist argument against, 2,
157n24
evil as disproof of, 2, 79, 134n4
evil done and causation of, 70–72
evil suffered and causation of, 67–70
existence created by, 43–44
existence of, 79, 141n1
free choice of, 65
freedom and, 75
free will and causation of, 73
as good, 57–59, 82, 114, 116, 148n2
human choices and, 72–77, 117
humans brought to perfect happiness
by, 86
human virtues and, 116–17
incarnation of, 100–111, 119, 153n15,
153n19
Jesus Christ as, 102, 107
justice and, 62–64
knowing existence of, 39–41, 141n3,
149n10
knowledge of, 115–16
law and, 63

literal *vs.* metaphorical truths
concerning, 144n5
love and creation by, 118
love and knowledge of, 99–100, 152n12
love of everything by, 83–84
as moral agent, 128
moral goodness of, 59–62, 89, 116–17
as morally good, 4
natural kinds and, 48–49
nature of, 98, 144n13
as not created, 49
omnipotence of, 66–67, 101, 146n3
as perfect, 55–57, 114, 148n2
as person, 80–81, 125–32
properties applied to, 53–54
providence of, 81–84
reason and knowledge of, 98
reconciliation with, 108
righteousness and, 157n20
sharing knowledge and nature, 118
sharing self-knowledge through
grace, 91
simplicity of, 47–49, 54, 99, 143n20
sin preventing union with, 104–5, 108
as source of all goodness, 115
as source of things having *esse*, 56,
80, 115
as substance, 139n10
suffering of, 123–25
supernatural virtues and, 150n23
talking about, 52–55, 120
unchangeability of, 48, 153n19
understanding, 119–22
union with, 88–89, 93, 104–5, 107–10
as unqualified goodness, 32
what is not, 44–47, 116
will and, 44–45, 65, 74, 82, 109–10
good
evil done as failure to choose, 117
God as, 57–59, 82, 114, 116, 148n2
identifying things as, 116
moral, 60
perfect *vs.*, 33
goodness, 29

Aquinas on, 30–33, 140n8
badness as absence of, 35, 37, 115
badness as displacement of, 35–36
beatitude and, 85–86
being and, 32–33
created, 116
esse and, 114–16
evil done as lack of, 70–72
evil suffered as, 69
God as source of all, 115
Hume on, 30
love as, 84
moral, of God, 59–62, 89, 116–17
unqualified, 32
grace
   Aquinas on, 89–92, 151n27
   defining, 89
   faith and, 90–91
   free will and, 93–94
   God sharing self-knowledge through,
      91
   moral philosophy and, 89–90
   predestination and, 93
   work of Christ and, 108–9

habitus, 59–60
happiness, 84–86, 90, 149n12
Henry of Ghent, 143n2
Hick, John, 3–4
Holland, R. F., 128
Holy Spirit, 91
hope, 90–91, 108–9
horrendous evil, 130–31, 158n25
Huckleberry Finn (Twain), 54
human choices, 117. *See also* free choice
   causation and, 72
   free, 73–75, 117, 147n20
   free will and, 72–73
   God and, 72–77, 117
human nature, 89–90, 103, 150n19,
     153n15, 153n19
human virtues, 116–17
Hume, David, 10, 14, 128, 129, 133n2
   on cause and effect, 26–27

on God and evil, 1–2
on goodness and badness, 30

identity statement, 138n3, 144n13
incarnation, 119
   Aquinas on, 100–101
   death of Christ and, 103–6
   faith and, 108–9
   of God, 100–111, 119, 153n15, 153n19
   God not changing in, 153n19
   human and divine natures in, 153n15,
     153n19
   purpose of, 101–2
   significance of, 103
   sin and, 101–2, 103, 119
   value to people of, 104
   work of Christ and, 102–11
In Libros Physicorum (Thomas Aquinas), 27
Irenaeus of Lyon, 4

Jesus Christ
   call to union with God through, 108
   church as body of, 111
   death of, 103–6, 119, 154n26
   as "first teacher," 151n25
   as God, 102, 107
   God suffering through, 123
   grace and work of, 108–9
   human and divine natures of, 153n15
   as man, 106–7
   as offer of beatitude, 109
   as priest, 108
   as sacrifice, 108
   satisfaction of, 154n29
   work of, 102–11
Jordan, Mark D., 11, 14
justice
   commutative, 62
   distributive, 62–63
   divine, 62–64
   law and, 63

Kant, 10
Kenny, Anthony, 10, 24–25

Kierkegaard, Søren, 16, 17
knowledge
    belief and, 87–88
    of existence of God, 39–41, 141n3,
        149n10
    faith and, 87–88
    of God, 115–16
    God sharing, 118
    of God through grace, 91
    of God through love, 99–100,
        152n12
    of God without revelation, 156n5,
        156n8
    of human nature, 90
    of objects, 115
    reason and, of God, 98
    sensory experience and, 20, 115, 138n2,
        149n10
Kretzmann, Norman, 146n2

law, 63
Leibniz, 10
Leo XIII (pope), ix
Locke, 10
logical contradictions, 66
Logical Positivism, 137n26
love
    charity and, 91
    defining, 118
    God creating things and, 118
    of God for everything, 83–84
    knowledge of God through, 99–100,
        152n12
    as willing goodness, 84
Luther, Martin, 11

Mackie, J. L., 2, 6, 30
malum. See evil
malum culpae. See evil done
malum poenae. See evil suffered
material causes, 25
McCabe, Herbert, 36, 37, 59, 104,
    124–25, 133n1
Metaphysics (Aristotle), 14

Milton, John 3
Moltmann, Jürgen, 123–25
monotheism, 97
moral agent, God as, 128
moral good, 60
moral goodness, of God, 59–62, 89, 116–17
moral philosophy, 89–90
moral virtue, 61

naturalism, 156n15
natural kinds, 48–49
naturally occurring evil, 68
natural theology, 98, 121, 137n26
natural virtues, 150n23
necessary beings, 41–42
negative existential statements, 24
notional change, 142n17

Obama, Barack, 20–22
omnipotence, 66–67, 101
"On the Trinity" (Boethius), 98
ontotheology, 155n3
Order of Preachers, 11, 136n5
original sin, 153n18
Oxford Dictionary of the Christian Church, 97

Paradise Lost (Milton), 3
Paul (saint), 62, 92–93, 106, 108
perfect happiness, 86
Peri Hermeneias (Aristotle), 74
Peter Lombard, 11, 136n5
philosophical ethics, 60
philosophy, 137n18
philosophy of religion, 120–21, 133n1
Physics (Aristotle), 27
Plantinga, Alvin, 3, 5, 134n10, 134n11
Plato, 10, 12
predestination, 92–95
predetermination, 93
predicative adjectives, 31
priest, Jesus Christ as, 108
problem of evil, x, 17, 77–78, 135n19
    Aquinas and, 6, 113, 128–30
    as pseudo-problem, 113

providence, 81–84, 93, 147n22
Psalm 19, 1
Pseudo-Dionysius, 122, 156n10

Rahner, Karl, 111, 155n33
real change, 142n17
reason
 knowledge of God through, 98
reconciliation, 108
reprobation, 94
revelation, 89, 118, 130
 Aquinas on, 149n17
 knowledge of God without, 156n5, 156n8
righteousness, 157n20
Ross, James, 76
Rowe, William, 2, 6, 134n8
Russell, Bertrand, 10, 22

sacra doctrina, 12–13, 17, 141n3
sacrifice, 108
satisfaction, 105–7, 154n29
scientia, 40–41, 141n3
Scotus, John Duns, 143n2
sensory experience, knowledge and, 20,
 115, 138n2, 149n10
Sentences (Peter Lombard), 11, 136n6
Sententia Super Posteriora Analytica
 (Thomas Aquinas), 21
simplicity, 47–49, 54, 99, 143n20
sin
 Aquinas on, 102, 105–6, 135n21,
  153n18
 forgiveness of, 104–7, 119
 incarnation and, 101–2, 103, 119
 malum poenae and, 146n8
 original, 153n18
 satisfaction and, 105–7
 union with God prevented by, 104–5,
  108
skepticism, 88
statements of fact, 140n10
statements of value, 140n10
Stump, Eleonore, 154n29
substances, 22, 138n4, 139n10

substantial form, 23, 48
suffering of God, 123–25
Summa Contra Gentiles (Thomas
 Aquinas), 14–15, 16, 67, 97–98,
 149n17
Summa Theologiae (Thomas Aquinas),
 5–6, 11–13, 15, 16, 47, 55, 83, 97–98,
 101, 149n17, 150n18
supernatural virtues, 150n23
Swinburne, Richard, 3–5, 52–53, 61–62,
 143n2

teaching, 27
Te Velde, Rude, 16
theism. See also atheism
 defenders of, 3–5
 detractors of, 1–3
 human choice and, 72
 monotheism, 97
 naturalism vs., 156n15
theodicy, 3, 134n10, 134n12
theological virtues, 118. See also charity;
 faith; hope
Thomas Aquinas, ix–x
 on accidents, 21–22
 on agent causes, 25–28
 on alienation of man from God, 108
 analogy and, 55
 approach to God of, 119–22
 Aristotle commentaries by, 14–16, 21,
  27, 74
 Aristotle influencing, 10, 12, 37, 137n20
 on badness, 33–37
 on being, 22–25
 on beings, 19–20
 on causes, 25–28
 on charity, 151n26
 on Christ as "first teacher," 151n25
 on definition, 21
 on divine justice, 62–64
 on enjoyment of God, 85–86
 on essence, 20–22
 on essence, existence, and God, 41–44
 on evil done, 70–72

Thomas Aquinas (*continued*)
  on evil suffered, 67–70, 147n16
  on existence of God, 79, 141n1
  on existence types, 140n11
  on faith, 88–89, 150n23, 151n24
  faith defined by, 40
  on free choice of God, 65
  on God and evil, 5–8, 16–17
  on God and human choices, 72–77
  on God as Creator, 45–47
  on God as perfect, 55–57, 114, 148n2
  on God creating, 146n2
  on "God is good," 57–59, 114
  on God's love for everything, 83–84
  on goodness, 30–33, 140n8
  on grace, 89–92, 151n27
  on happiness, 84–86, 149n12
  on human free choice, 73–75, 147n20
  on incarnation, 100–101
  on knowing God exists, 39–41
  on moral goodness of God, 59–62
  moral philosophy and, 89–90
  on omnipotence, 66–67
  on personhood of God, 80–81
  as philosopher, 13–16, 88–89
  philosophy of religion of, 120–21,
    133n1
  on predestination, 92–95
  problem of evil and, 6, 113, 128–30
  on providence, 81–84
  on revelation, 149n17
  on satisfaction of Christ, 154n29
  on simplicity of God, 47–49
  on sin, 102, 105–6, 135n21, 153n18
  on substances, 22, 138n4, 139n10
  on talking about God, 52–55
  on teaching, 27
  as theologian, 11–13
  as thinker, 10
  on Trinity, 97–100, 152n11
  on vice, 135n21

  on virtues, 59–61
  on what God is not, 44–47
  on will, 44–45
  on work of Christ, 102–11
Tolomeo of Lucca, 14
Trinity
  Aquinas on, 97–100, 152n11
  crucifixion and, 124
  will of, 118
Twain, Mark, 54

universalism, 110
University of Paris, 11
unqualified goodness, 32

vice, 135n21
virtue, 89–90, 92, 109
  Aquinas on, 59–61
  Aristotle on, 60, 62, 109, 117
  cardinal, 60
  human, 116–17
  moral, 61
  natural, 150n23
  supernatural, 150n23
  theological, 118
virtue ethics, 60

What Is Existence? (Williams), 24
will. *See also* free will
  antecedent, 109–10
  Aquinas on, 44–45
  consequent, 109–10
  in creatures, 65
  desire and, 82–83
  evil done and, 71–72
  God and, 44–45, 65, 74, 82, 109–10
  of Trinity, 118
Williams, C. J. F., 24
Wippel, John F., 137n16
Wittgenstein, 10, 14
Wright, N. T., 129

CPSIA information can be obtained
at www.ICGtesting.com
Printed in the USA
LVHW092338210721
693373LV00014B/406